IMAGES
of America

DESOTO

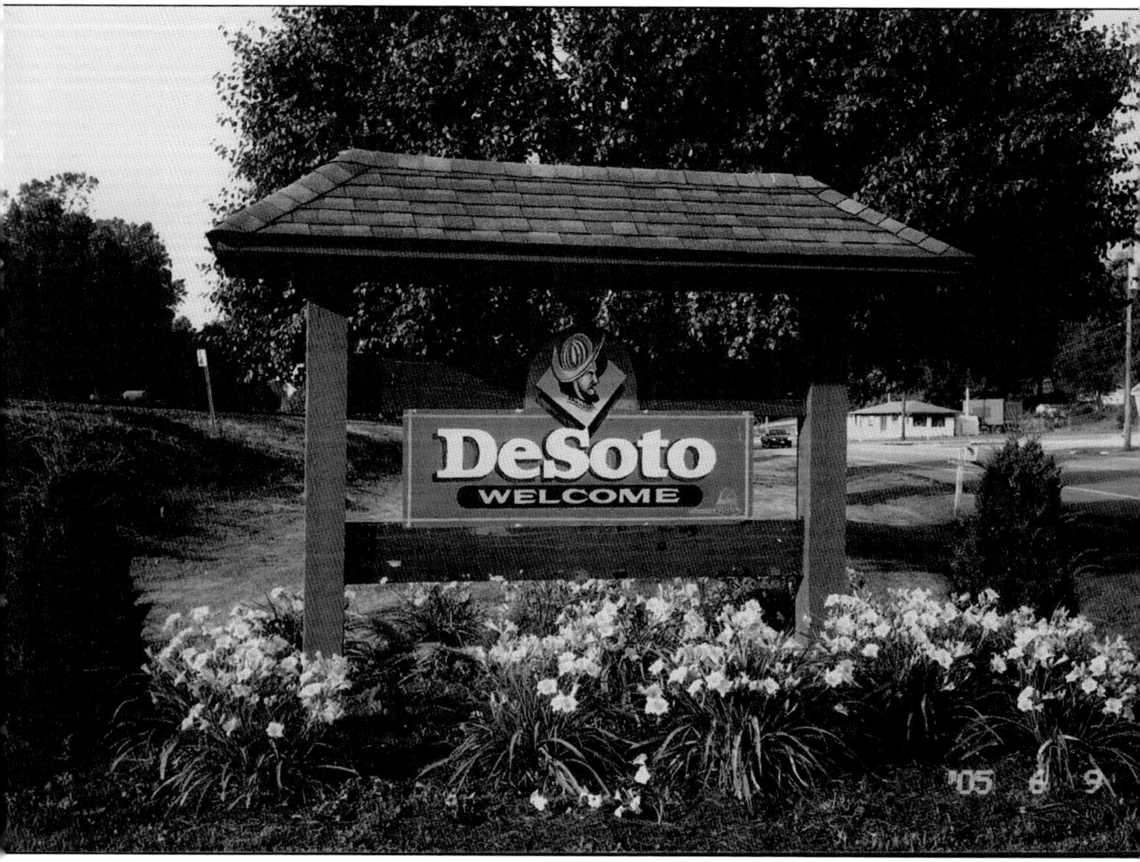

Welcome Sign. This sign welcomes everyone to delightful DeSoto.

IMAGES
of America

DESOTO

DeSoto Historical Society

ARCADIA
PUBLISHING

ISBN 978-0-7385-3993-7

Published by Arcadia Publishing
Charleston, South Carolina

Printed in the United States of America

Library of Congress Catalog Card Number: 2005932363

For all general information contact Arcadia Publishing at:
Telephone 843-853-2070
Fax 843-853-0044
E-mail sales@arcadiapublishing.com
For customer service and orders:
Toll-Free 1-888-313-2665

Visit us on the Internet at www.arcadiapublishing.com

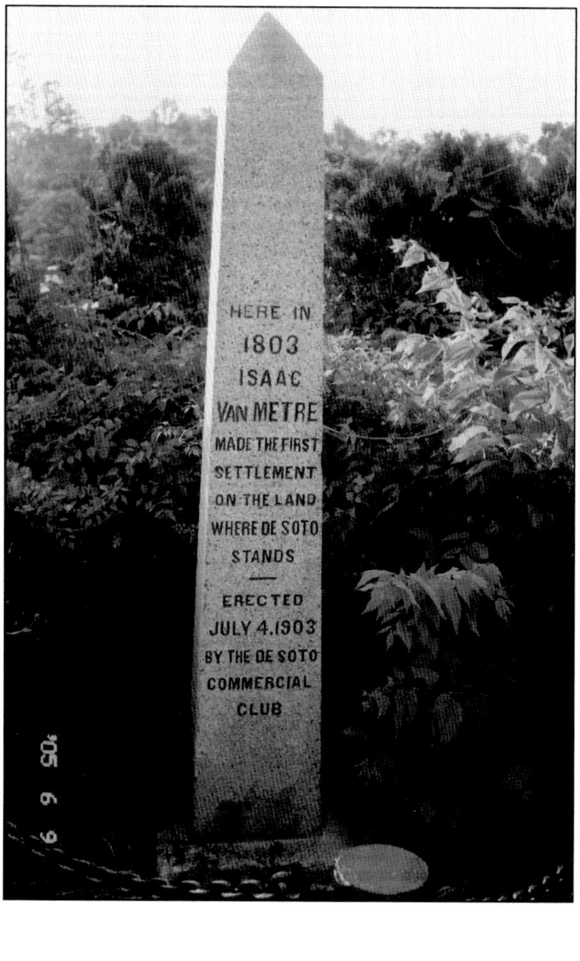

MEMORIAL TO ISAAC VAN METRE. The memorial to Isaac Van Metre, founder of DeSoto in 1808, is erected on South Main Street opposite the DeSoto Public Library

Contents

ACKNOWLEDGMENTS

Many of the photos in this book are from the DeSoto Public Library, Fo-Jo Studio, and the DeSoto Historical Society. Special notes of thanks are due to Betty Olson, librarian at the DeSoto Public Library, and her generous staff, and to Felix Milfeld for the photos from Fo-Jo (Laurella) studio.

Also included are photos from Arlington Bed and Breakfast, Adelaide Camp, Leatha Watt Combs, Kathleen Goff Dietz, Dava Lee England, Loretto Shannon Goehring, Diana Johnson, Stephen Pipitone, Dr. Martha Reed, Cathy Roop, Ursula Sellars, and Dave Williamson.

The members of the DeSoto Historical Society are grateful to all who assisted in making this book a reality. To those individuals who submitted photos, we are especially grateful.

This book is dedicated to Rosemary Meiman, O.S.U.

INTRODUCTION

The earliest person to settle in what is now DeSoto was Isaac Van Metre. He built a cabin in the area on Main and Stone Streets in 1803 and the stone marker on Main Street indicates this fact. After several years, Van Metre departed this area and his property was bought by Walter DeWitt. By 1812, DeWitt had built a double log house for his family on 15 acres of cleared land. In 1818, DeWitt sold his land to Rufus Easton, a lawyer and land speculator. Although Easton never lived in DeSoto, he was identified with the landed interests in the town for a long time. Easton and William Russell were partners in land speculation for some time, but by 1826, Easton was ruined financially. In order to pay his debts he conveyed the DeSoto lands that he owned to his partner William Russell.

For many years, DeSoto remained a small country community, depending almost entirely on mining and agriculture for its economic livelihood. By the year 1850, the population of the town had grown to about 200 people and some businesses were being established. In 1857, a Mr. Kester built a frame structure in the vicinity of Main and Pratt Streets that had a 10-pin alley on the first floor and a public hall on the upper floor. Henry Euler built the first gristmill that was operated by waterpower. George Flint was the first blacksmith, and Col. William W. Fletcher built a steam saw mill. The first auction sale of lots was held May 1, 1858, and from that time the town began to grow.

Thomas Fletcher, who later became Missouri's first native-born governor, suggested that a railroad be established in DeSoto. He and his brother-in-law, Louise James Rankin, had acquired a great deal of property and presented a plan to the railroad to consider DeSoto as a base for some of its future operations. In 1853, construction was begun on the St. Louis and Iron Mountain Railroad, and in September 1857 the first work train arrived in DeSoto, followed a month later by the first passenger service train.

A post office was established in 1857 with Clement B. Fletcher, father of Thomas Fletcher, as postmaster. For a short time the town was called Nopton after Fletcher's good friend, William B. Nopton, judge of the Missouri Supreme Court. But Fletcher and Rankin preferred to call the town DeSoto to honor the Spanish explorer Hernando DeSoto, who claimed the Louisiana Territory for Spain.

The town of DeSoto was incorporated in 1869 after a petition was presented by J. W. Fletcher and J. J. Davis to the Jefferson County Court in Hillsboro. The first board of trustees consisted of James J. Davis, G. G. Ackerson, Reuben Burroughs, Gust Hamel, and John W. Fletcher. An early name for DeSoto was Fountain City, due to the prevalence of large artesian wells in the town. Water from these natural springs was bottled and sent to St. Louis for use during the World's Fair of 1904. Most of these wells have since been capped.

The Iron Mountain Railroad merged with Missouri Pacific in 1917, and a new brick depot was built at Main and Easton Streets. Passenger train service was eliminated some years ago, but Amtrak still passes through DeSoto.

Electricity arrived in DeSoto in 1905 with the Consumer's Electric Light and Power Company. They were bought out by Union Electric in 1917.

The 1907 *City Directory* of DeSoto listed a variety of businesses in town, including an art studio, a broom manufacturer, two colleges, a corn mill, two harness and saddlery shops, four shoemakers, and three tinners. The building of the first shoe factory began in 1907 when 10 businessmen proposed to construct a site and building with access to the railroad. Other businesses in the DeSoto area include Trojan Manufacturing Company, Hamilton Shoe Company, Haake Manufacturing Plant, Mueller Electric, and Fo-Jo Photography. The last three are still in operation today.

During the 1950s, the city won two All America City awards. On receiving the second recognition of this award in 1959, the city was honored by Look Magazine at an awards dinner on March 3, 1960. DeSoto was one of the smallest towns ever to win the award and the first in Missouri to gain this distinction. The award read, "DeSoto is an outstanding example of progress achieved in community betterment as a result of energetic, purposeful, intelligent citizen action."

In the 1960s, beautiful Walther's Park was given to the town by the Theodore Walther family and made ready for public use. The removal of rock bluffs to make way for the DeSoto Plaza Center began in 1965, and the Town of the Year award was presented to DeSoto in 1966. Kathy Goff, a local girl, became Miss Missouri in 1968 and she represented the state in the Miss America Pageant.

A distinctive recognition that was given to DeSoto was the identification of the town as the Center of Population of the United States for the decade 1980–1990. This center is determined by the U.S. Department of Geological Survey after the census is taken every 10 years.

The residents of the DeSoto area are proud of their accomplishments and heritage, and they continue to cherish the history from the past as they embrace the future.

One

Early Scenes

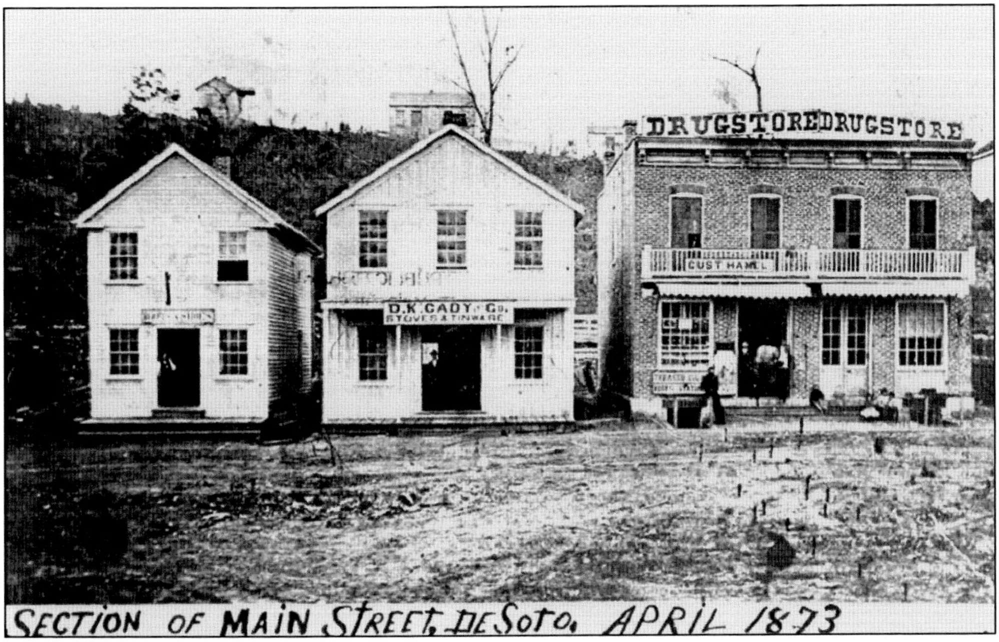

Main Street, 1873. This is one of the earliest photos of Main Street in DeSoto. (Photograph courtesy DeSoto Public Library.)

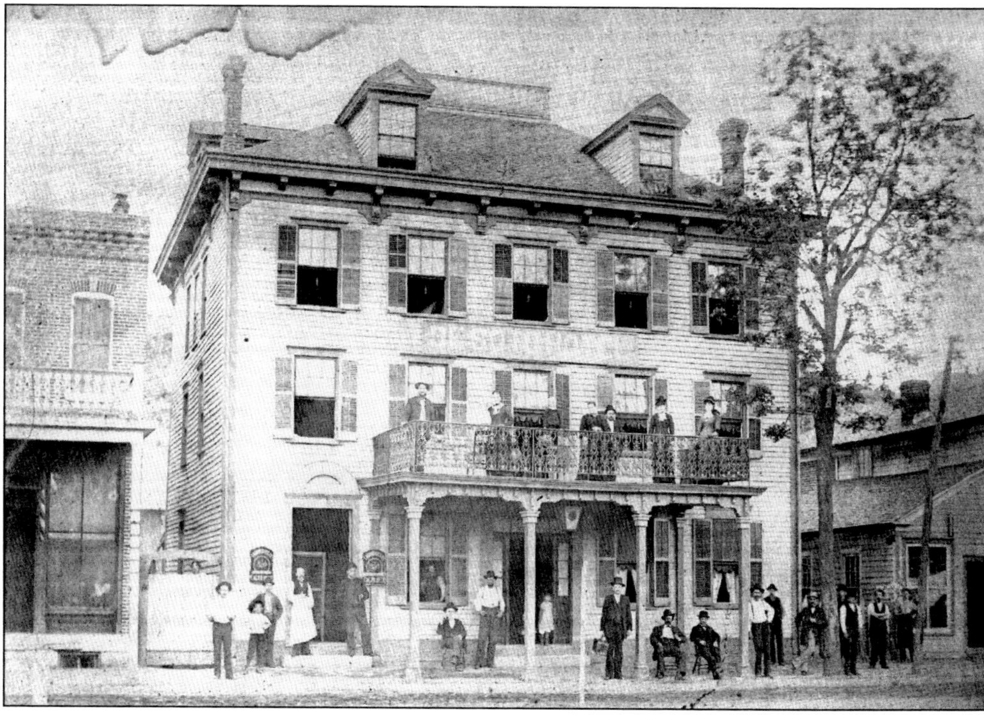

DeSoto Hotel, 200 Block of South Main Street. This hotel was a popular spot in the late 1800s. The sign over the door on the left indicates the "Saloon." This location was a later site for the Commercial Hotel that burned in the 1980s. (Photograph courtesy Dr. Martha Reed.)

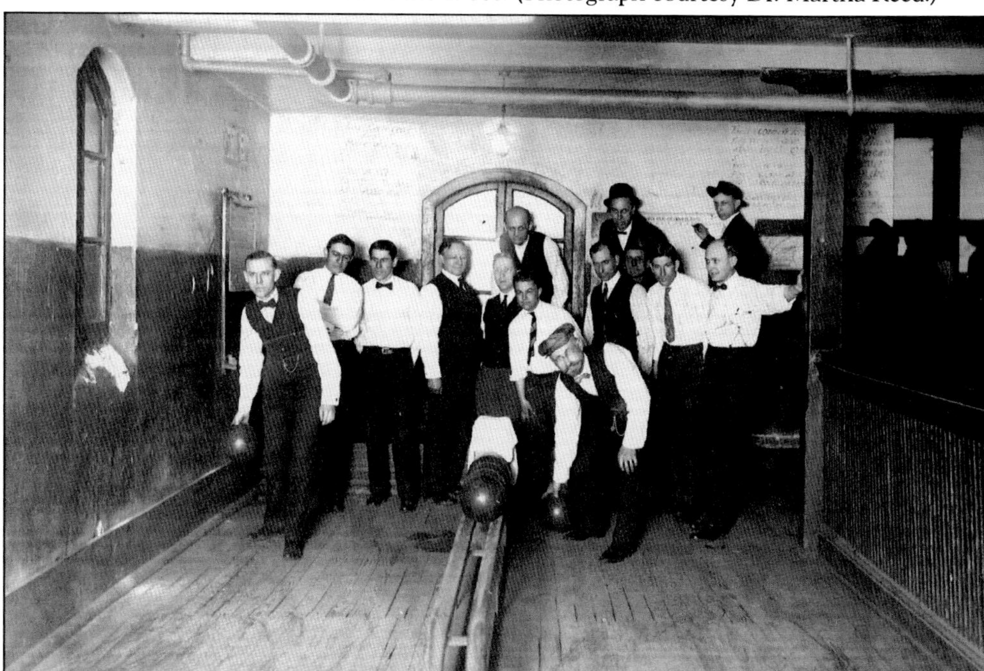

DeSoto Bowling Alley. Among those pictured here, one of the men holding a bowling ball is E. S. Fauth with Kirk Jones, and Bernard Duffner. (Photograph courtesy DeSoto Public Library.)

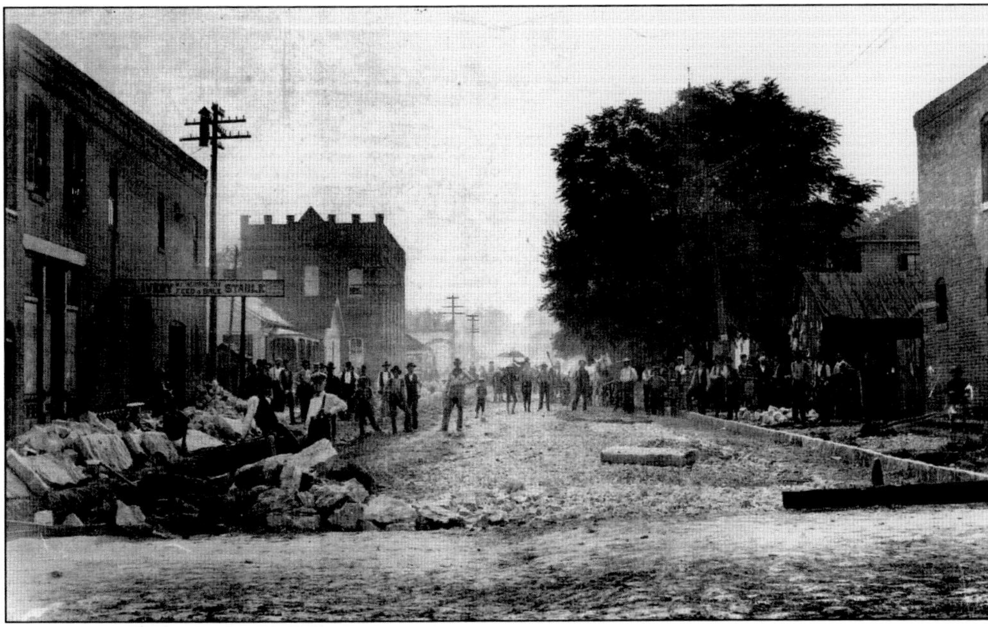

CONSTRUCTION ON BOYD STREET. Boyd Street, currently one of the major streets in DeSoto, was constructed around 1898. (Photograph courtesy DeSoto Public Library.)

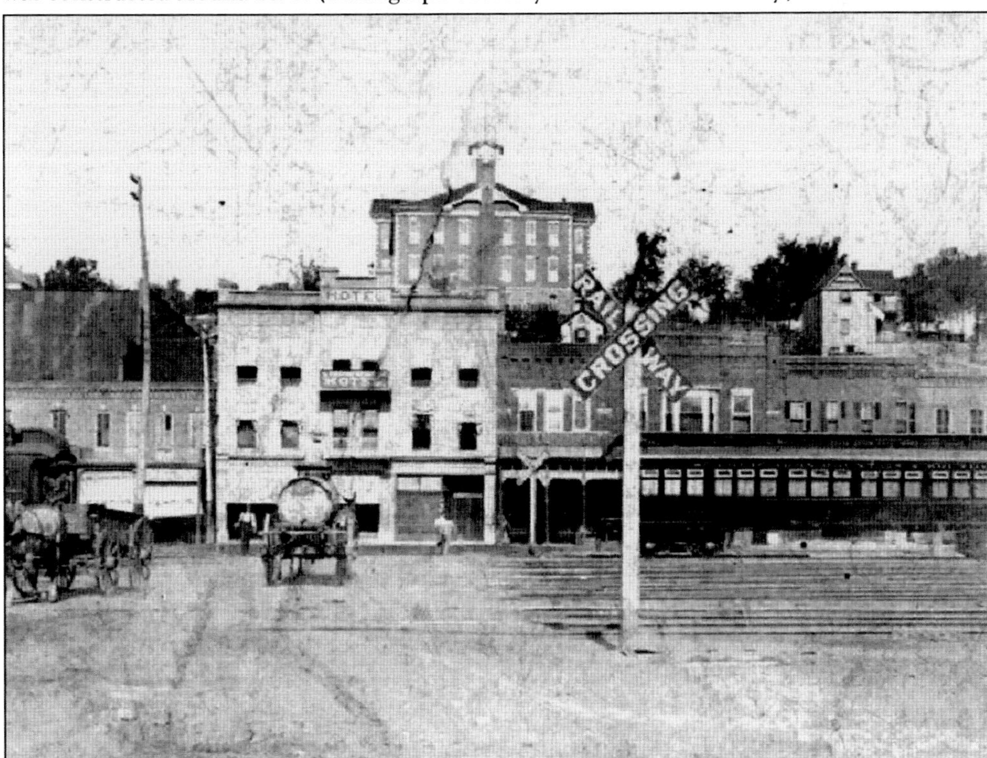

COMMERCIAL CROSSING. This is the Commercial Crossing, as it looked in 1898. Also visible in this photograph are the Iron Mountain Railroad car on the tracks and the DeSoto High School building on the hill above Main Street. (Photograph courtesy DeSoto Public Library.)

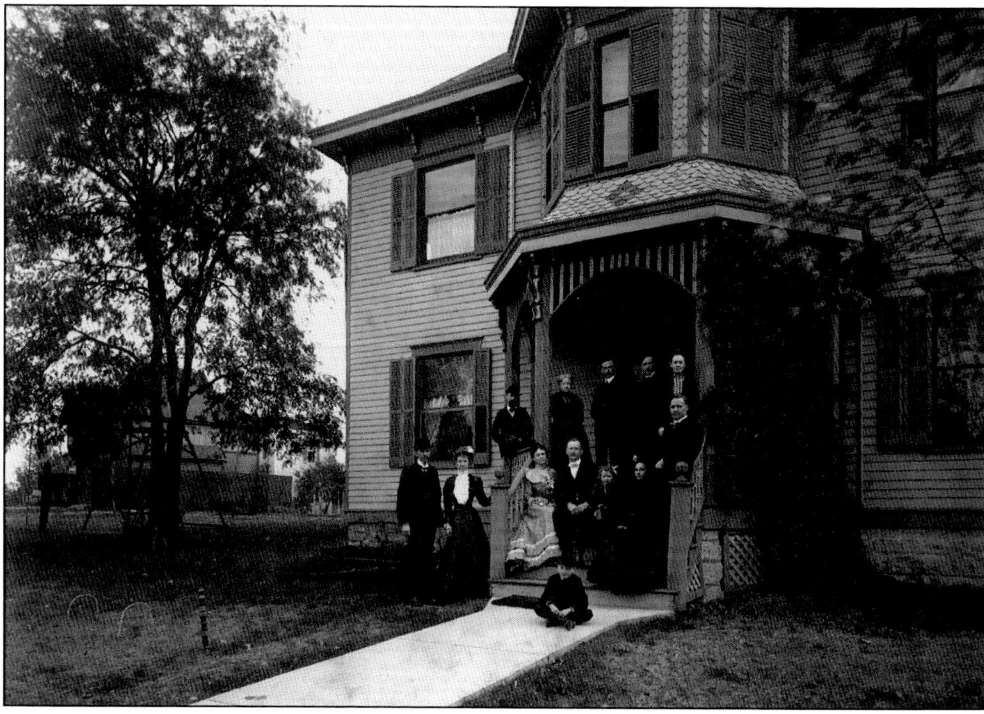

HINCHEY RESIDENCE. This home was located on West Pratt Street in DeSoto. Pictured in this photograph are members of the Hinchey family. (Photograph courtesy DeSoto Public Library.)

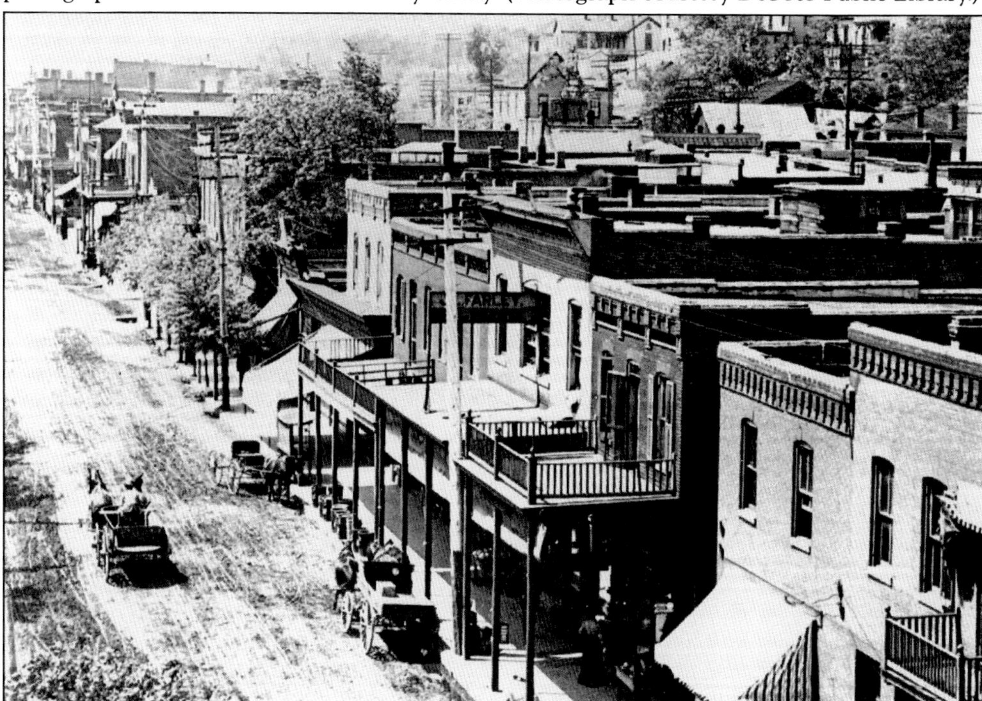

MAIN STREET. This view shows unpaved Main Street, horse-drawn buggies, and houses on the upper hill. (Photograph courtesy DeSoto Public Library.)

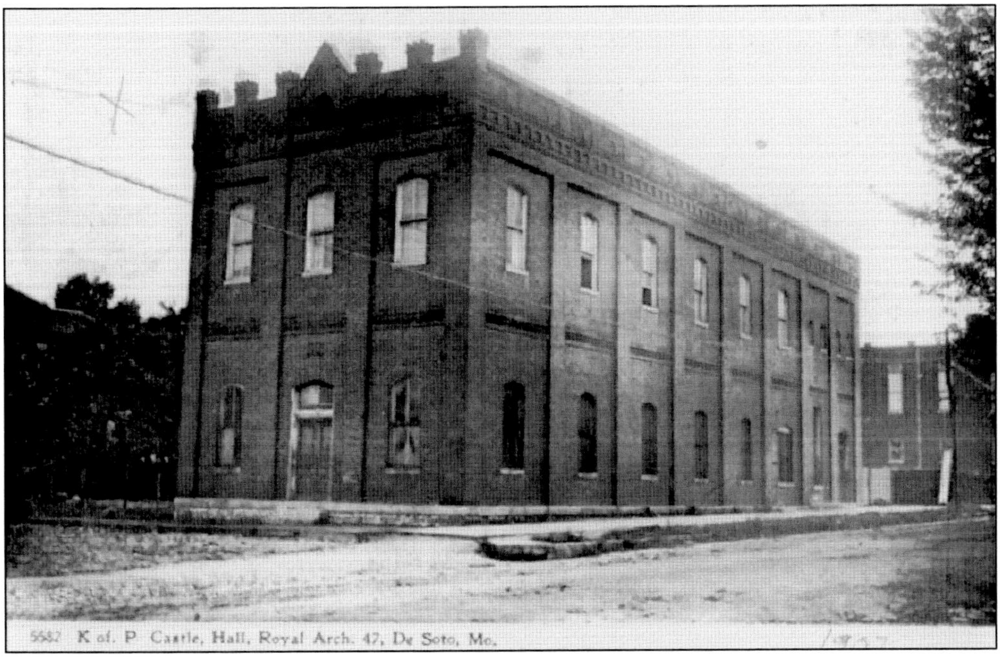

KNIGHTS OF PYTHIAS HALL. The Knights of Pythias Hall, located at Second and Boyd Streets, has served many uses through the years. It is presently a place for several businesses on the lower floor and residences on the upper floor. (Photograph courtesy DeSoto Public Library.)

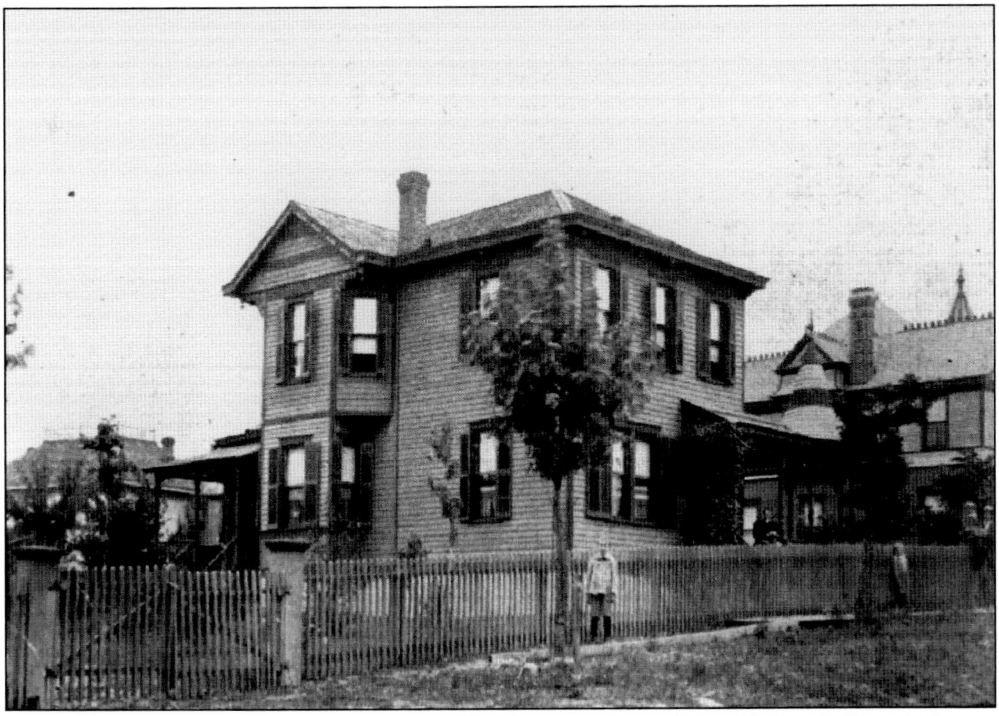

RESIDENCE OF JUDGE JAMES F. GREEN. This home is located at 409 South Fourth Street. According to the DeSoto Directory of 1897, J. F. Green was a judge of the circuit court. (Photograph courtesy DeSoto Public Library.)

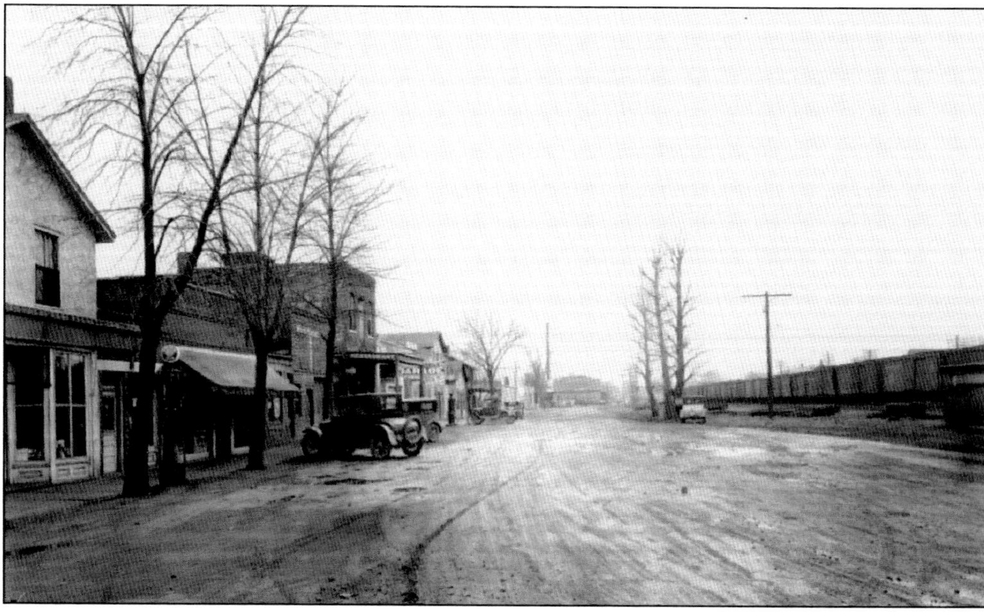

EAST SIDE, DESOTO. This early photo of DeSoto's East Side shows some of the businesses that were established there. (Photograph courtesy DeSoto Public Library.)

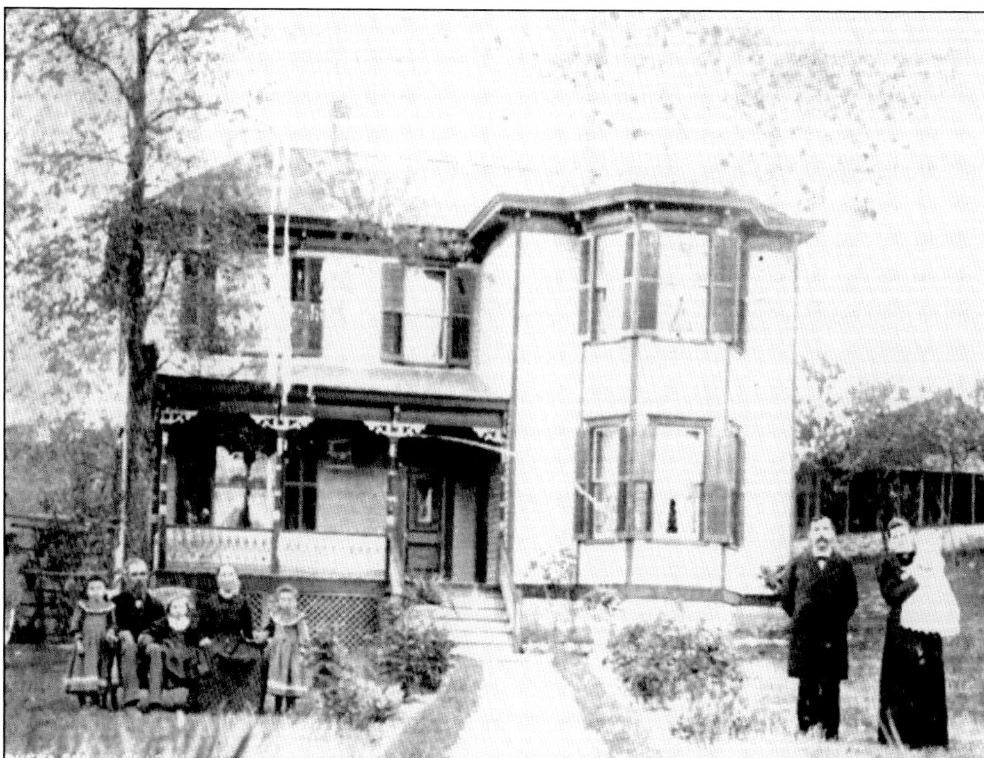

GIERTH RESIDENCE. Charles A. Gierth lived at 203 A South Main Street, and according to the Directory of 1897 he was a shoemaker. (Photograph courtesy DeSoto Public Library.)

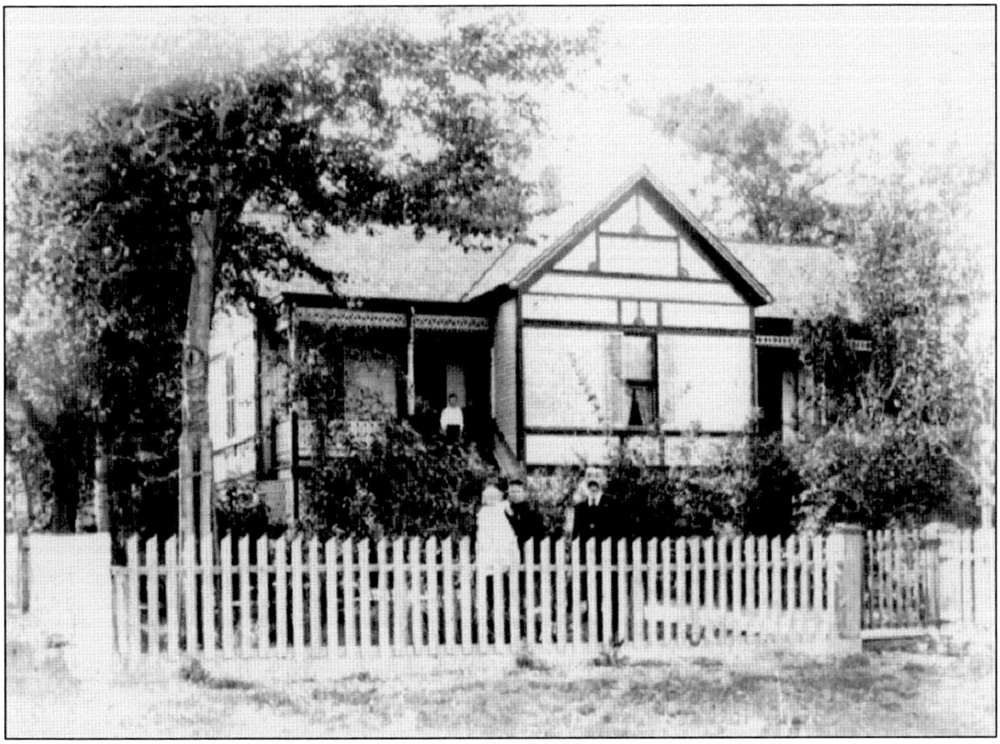

RESIDENCE OF W. T. HUSKEY. According to the 1897 Directory, William T. Huskey was a grocer and lived at 600 Boyd Street. (Photograph courtesy DeSoto Public Library.)

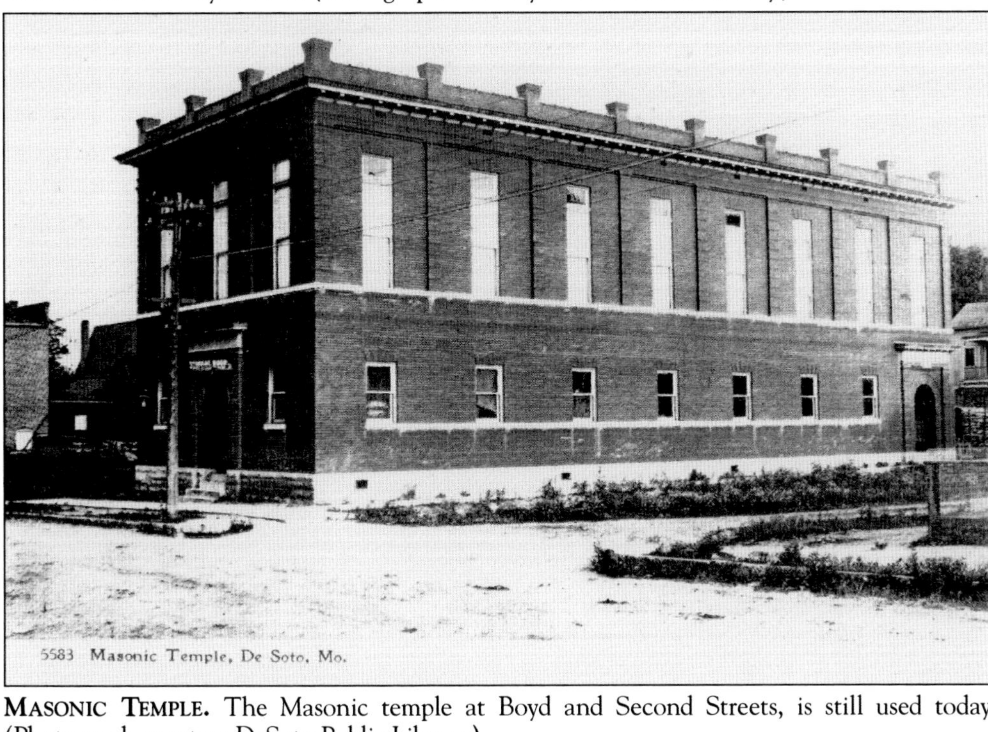

MASONIC TEMPLE. The Masonic temple at Boyd and Second Streets, is still used today. (Photograph courtesy DeSoto Public Library.)

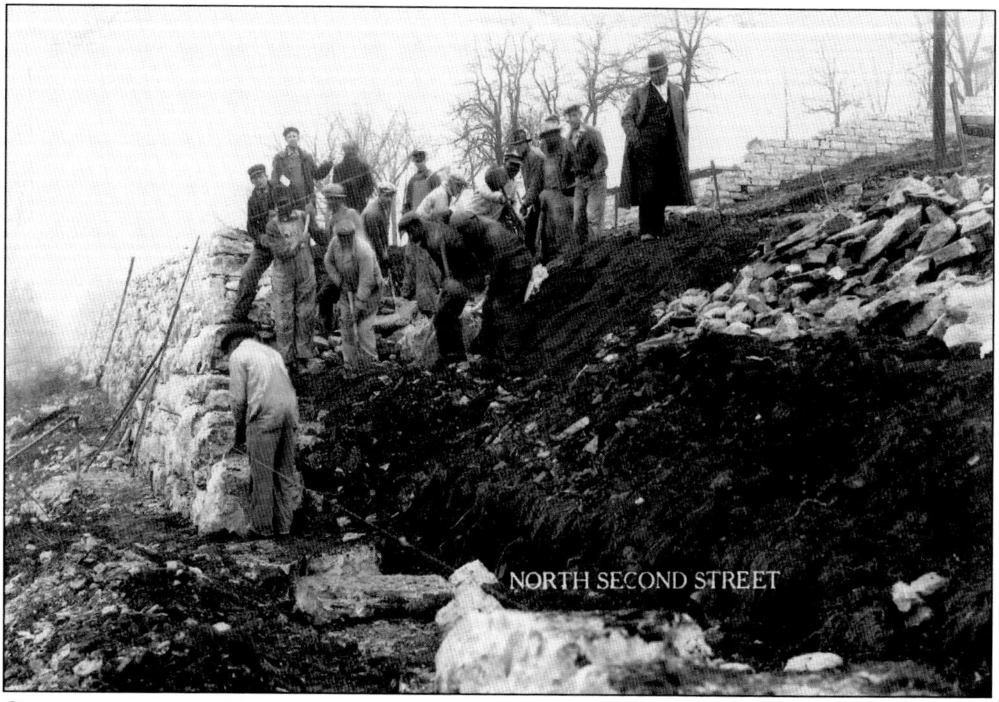

Construction on North Second Street. The street crew worked in the 1930s on the construction of Second Street. This was possibly a WPA project. The man in the suit, far right, is George Rainwater. (Photograph courtesy DeSoto Public Library.)

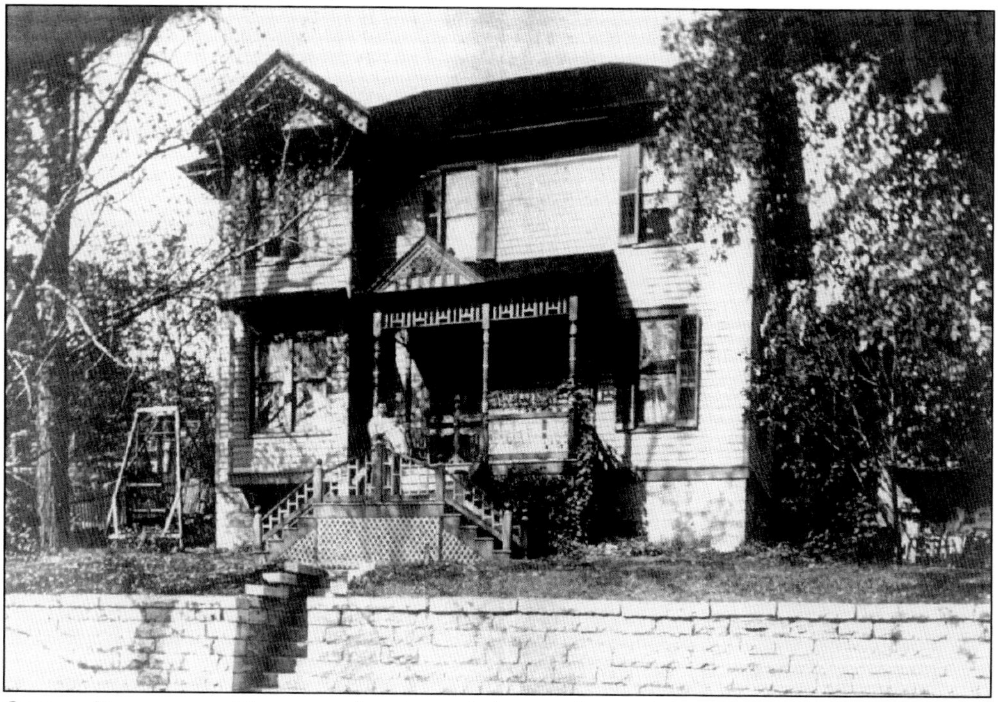

Couch Residence. The exact location of this residence, known as the Couch home, is unknown. (Photograph courtesy DeSoto Public Library.)

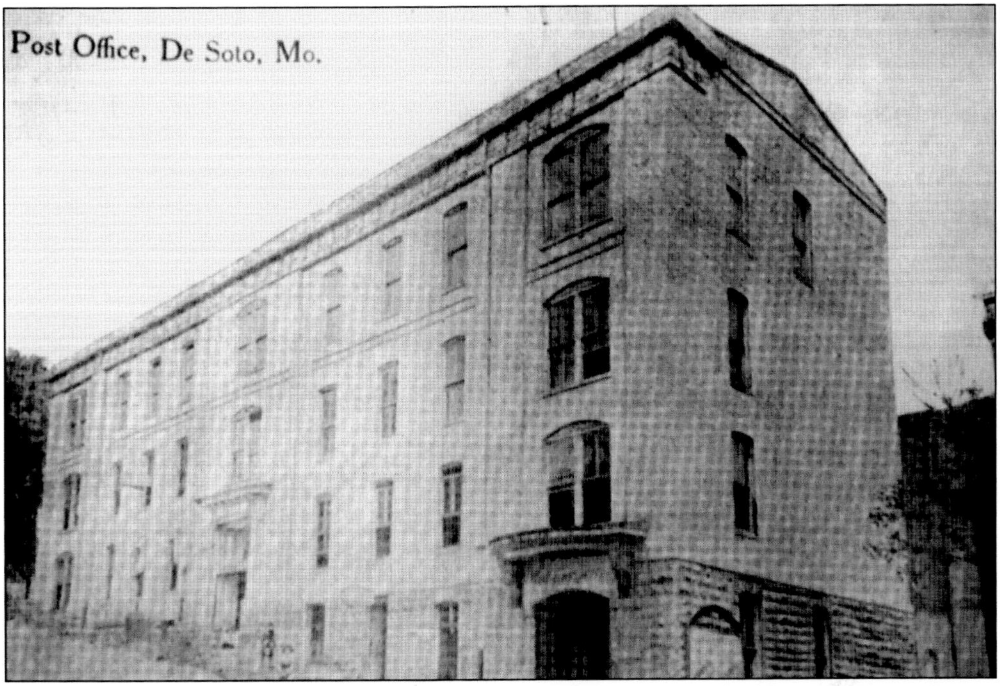

OLD POST OFFICE. The post office was on the ground floor of this building on Easton Street. The opera house was located on the upper floor. (Photograph courtesy DeSoto Public Library.)

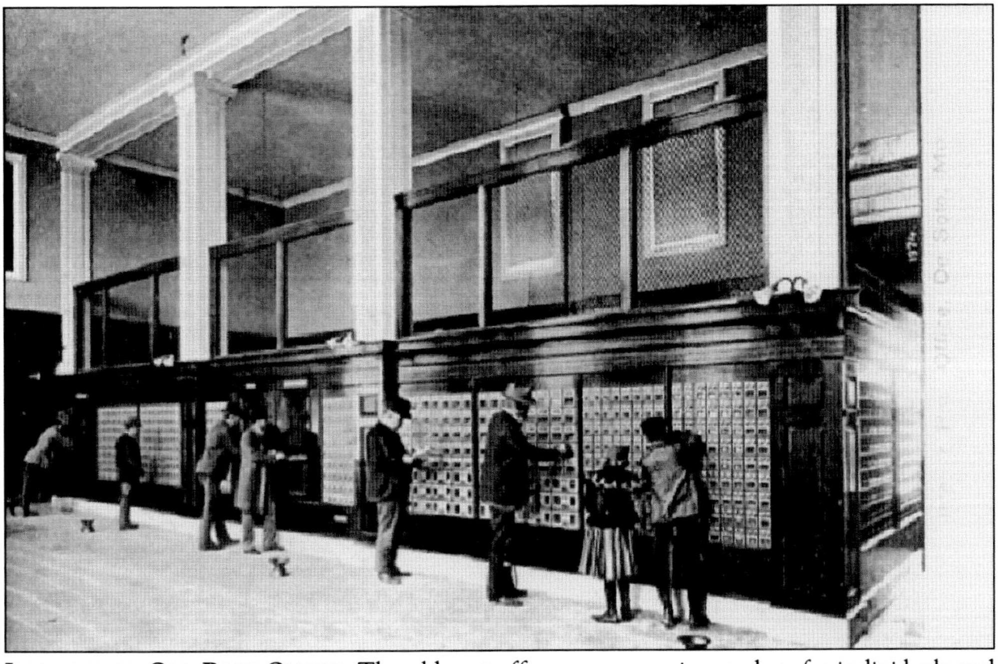

INTERIOR OF OLD POST OFFICE. The old post office was a prominent place for individuals and businesses. (Photograph courtesy DeSoto Public Library.)

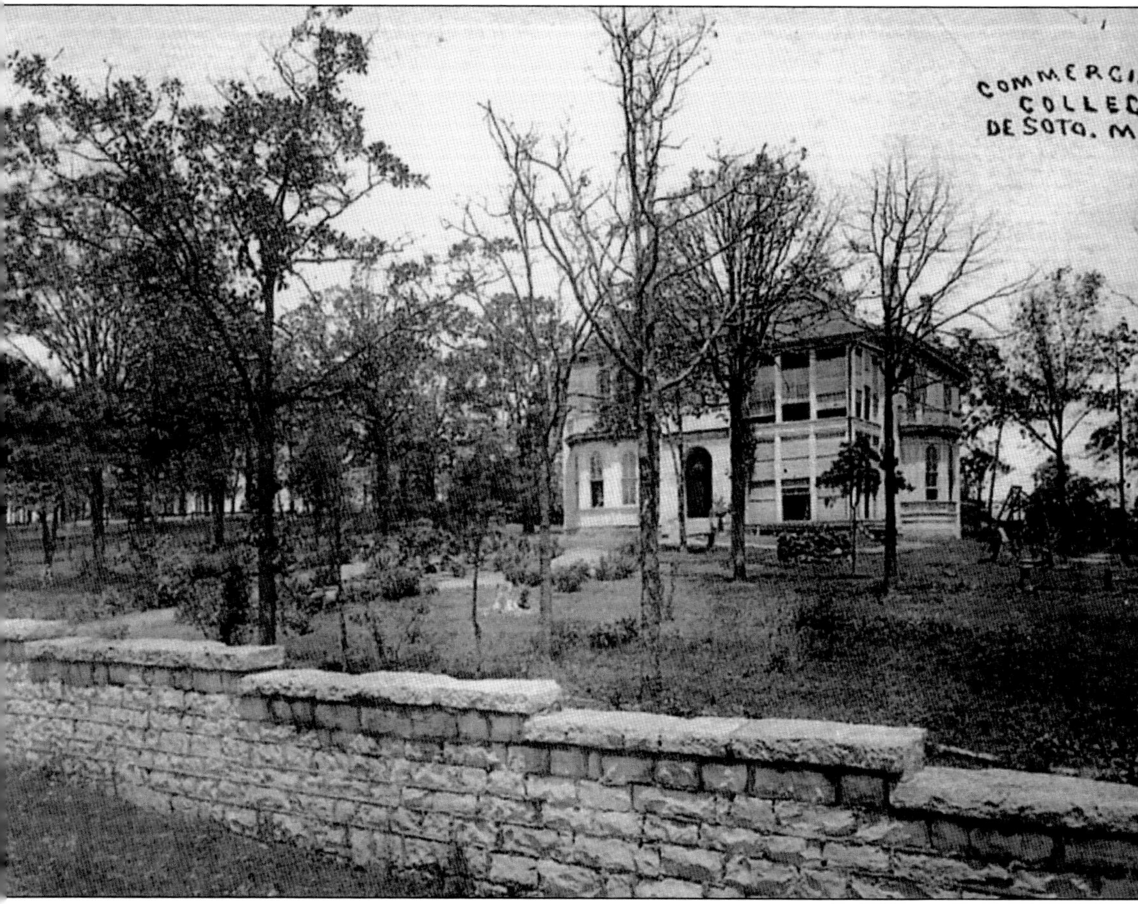

"ALTA VISTA." This home of Louis Rankin, located on North Second Street, later became the Commercial College. The house no longer exists but the rock wall and the gate to the estate still remain. (Photograph courtesy DeSoto Public Library.)

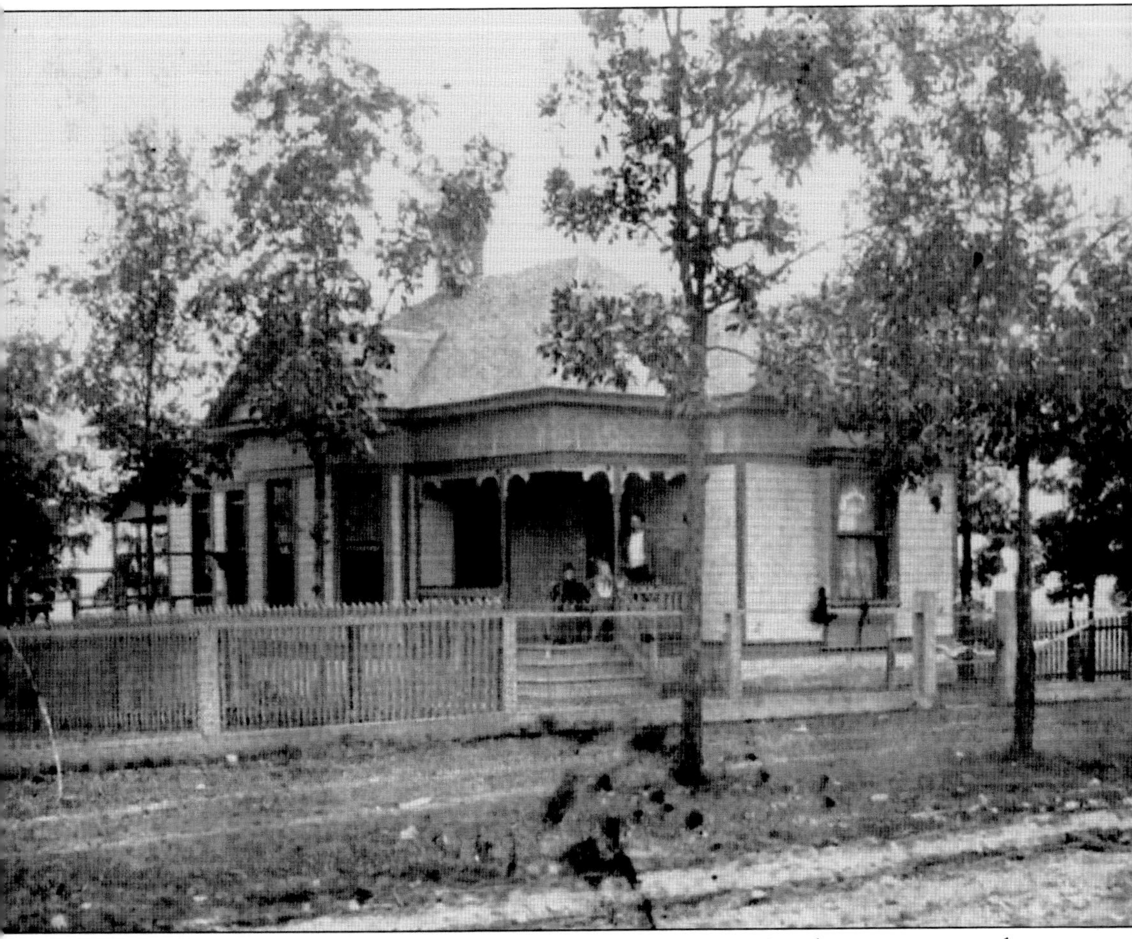

RESIDENCE OF L. H. CAUGH. The 1897 Directory lists Laurence H. Caugh as a carpenter who lived at 733 West Pratt Street. (Photograph courtesy DeSoto Public Library.)

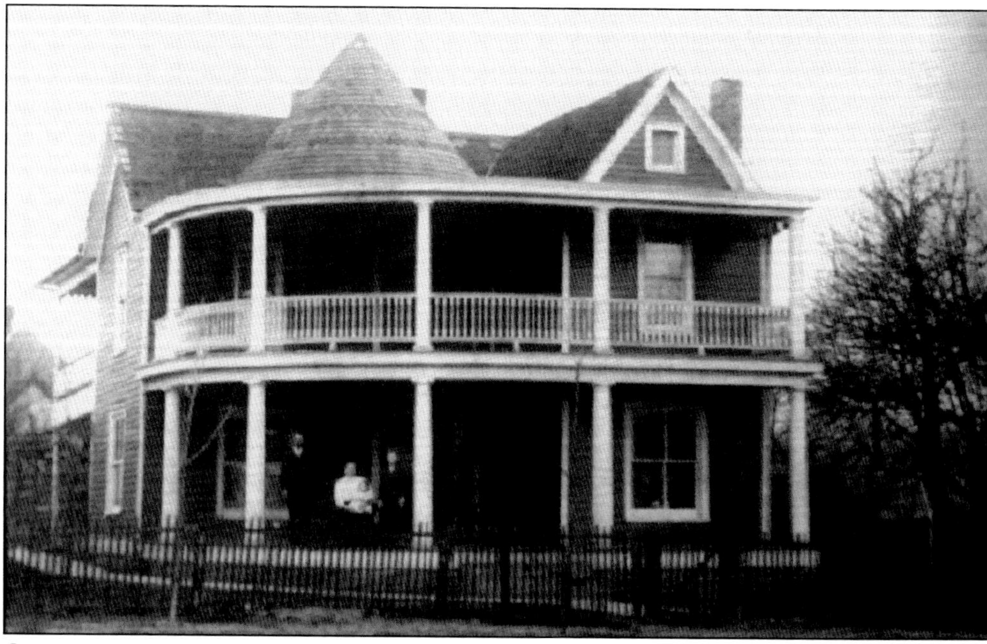

OLEVIA HOSPITAL, MAIN STREET. The original building, located on South Main Street, was erected in 1898 by George and Olevia Hobby. After several revisions, it was transformed into a 25-bed hospital named after Olevia Hobby, the first registered nurse in Jefferson County. During World War II, it became the first nursing home in DeSoto. The house remained in the Hobby family for 79 years, after which it was sold. At present there are apartments in the building. (Photograph courtesy DeSoto Public Library.)

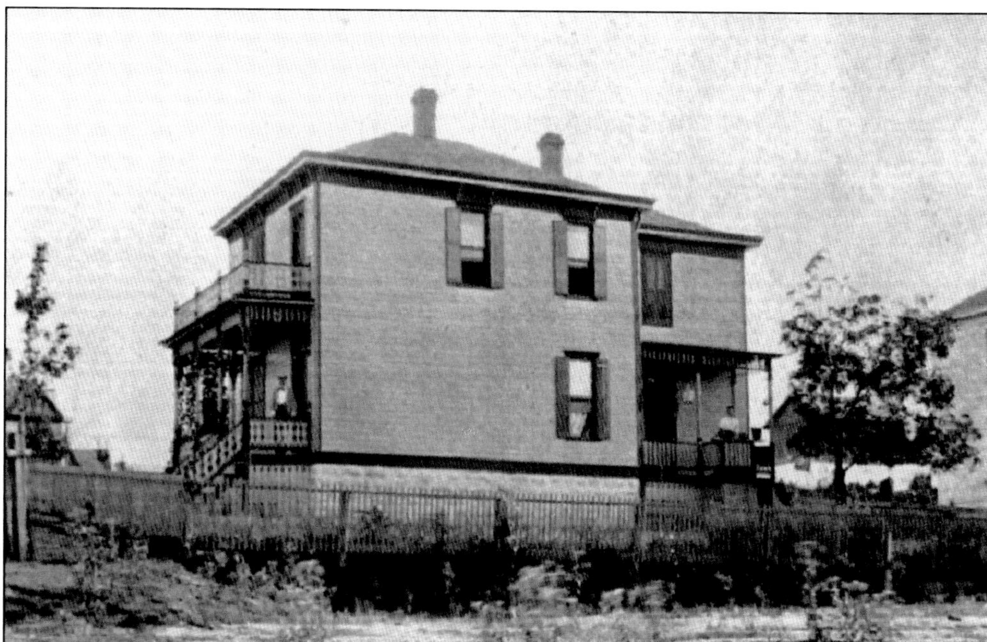

G. F. CARD RESIDENCE. According to the Directory of 1897, G. F. Card was a stenographer and lived at 300 South Sixth Street. (Photograph courtesy DeSoto Public Library.)

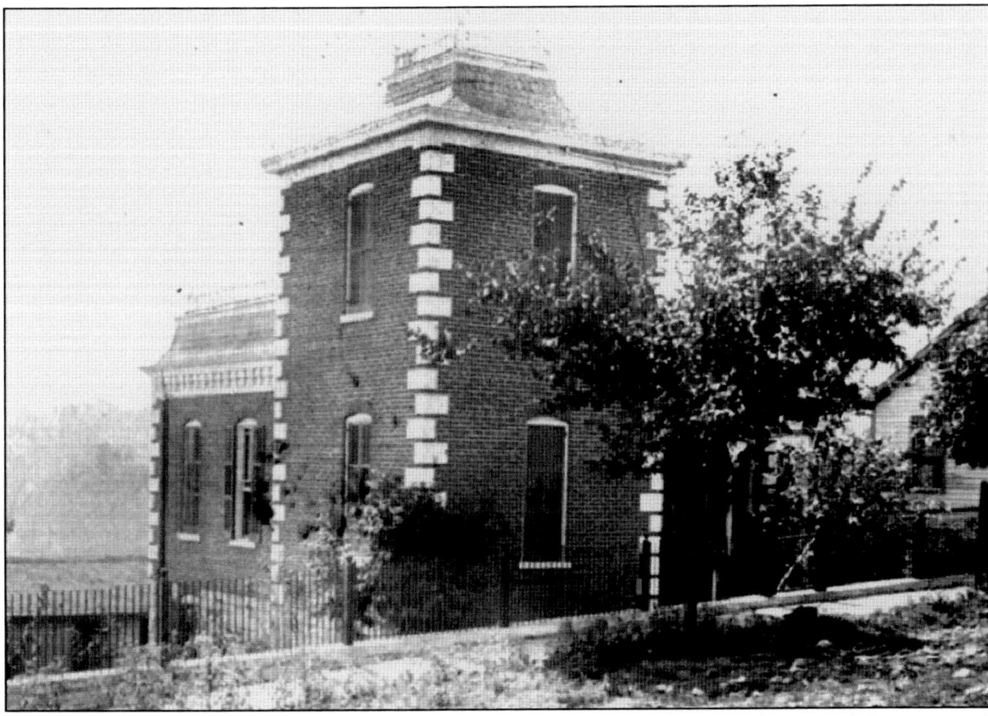

RESIDENCE OF GUST HAMEL. This distinctive structure, located on South Second Street, is still used as a residence today. (Photograph courtesy DeSoto Public Library.)

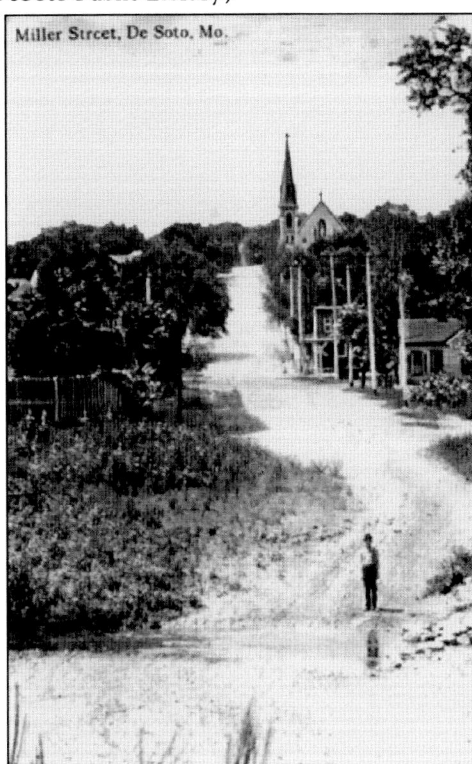

MAIN AND MILLER STREETS. This view of Main and Miller Streets shows a man by Joachim Creek before the bridge over the creek was erected. St. Rose of Lima Church can be seen in the background. (Photograph courtesy DeSoto Public Library.)

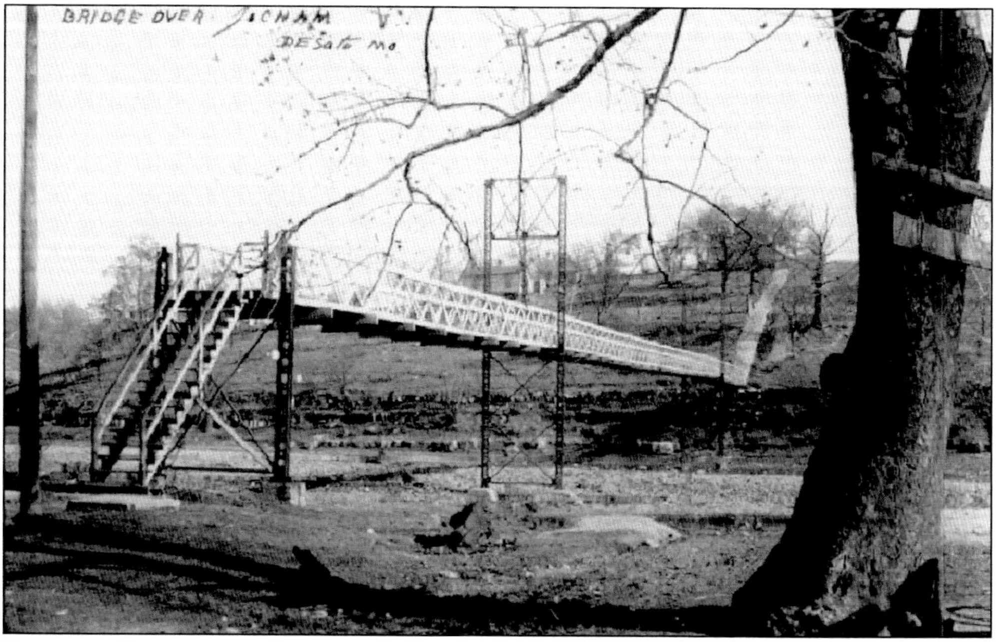

SWINGING BRIDGE OVER JOACHIM CREEK. Joachim Creek had several bridges. This pedestrian bridge was a favorite of many DeSotoans. (Photograph courtesy DeSoto Public Library.)

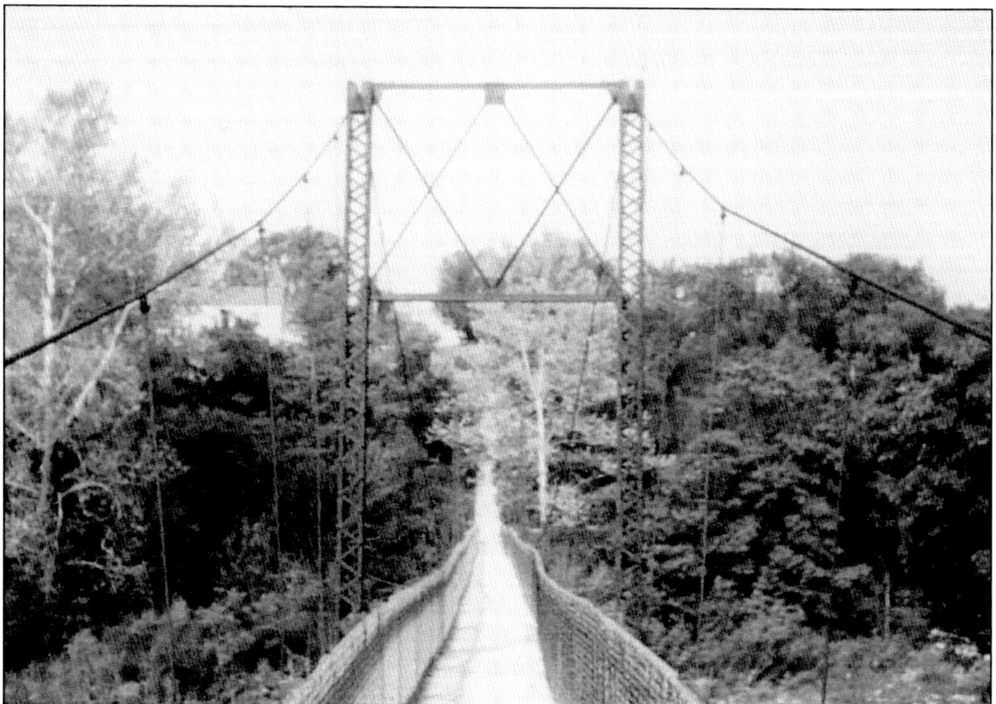

SWINGING BRIDGE. This is another view of the bridge that was located on East Clement Street. (Photograph courtesy DeSoto Public Library.)

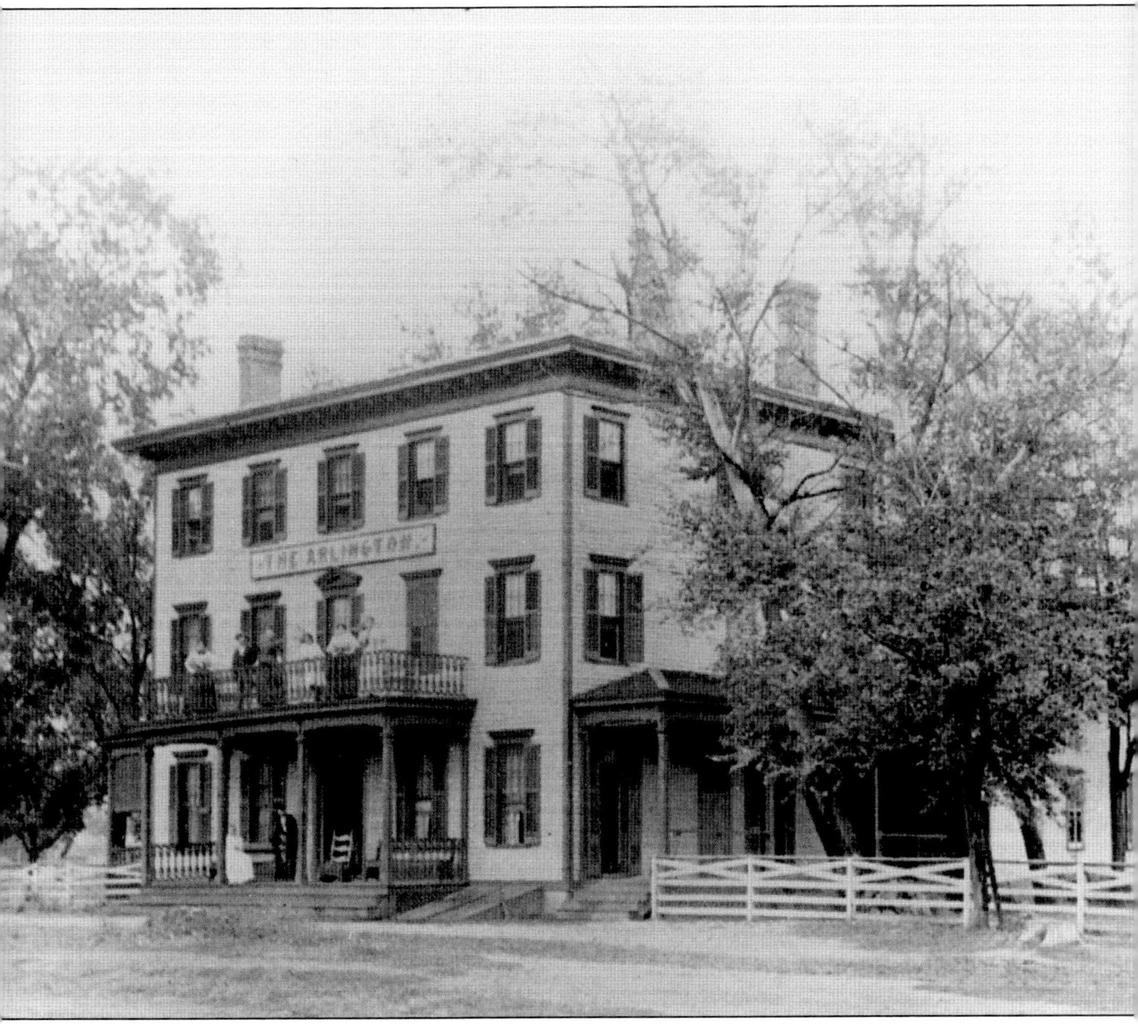

ARLINGTON HOTEL. This historic structure was built in the mid-1800s and was frequently used by passengers on the railroad. It welcomed many visitors to DeSoto, including Jefferson Davis. Presently it is a bed and breakfast operated by Don and Diana Johnson. (Photograph courtesy DeSoto Public Library.)

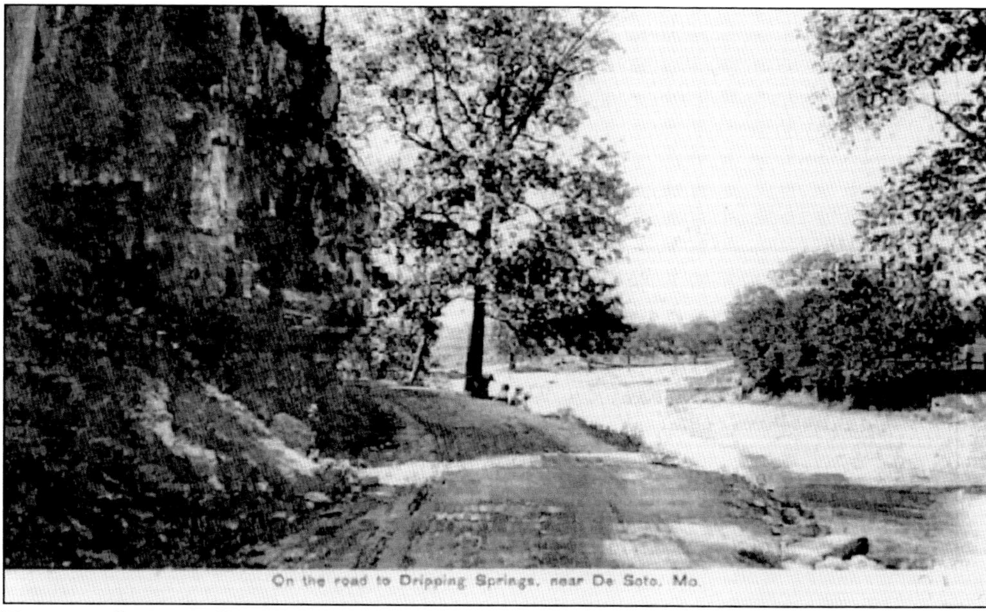

DRIPPING SPRINGS. Dripping Springs was located near DeSoto and was a favorite vacation spot in the early days. (Photograph courtesy DeSoto Public Library.)

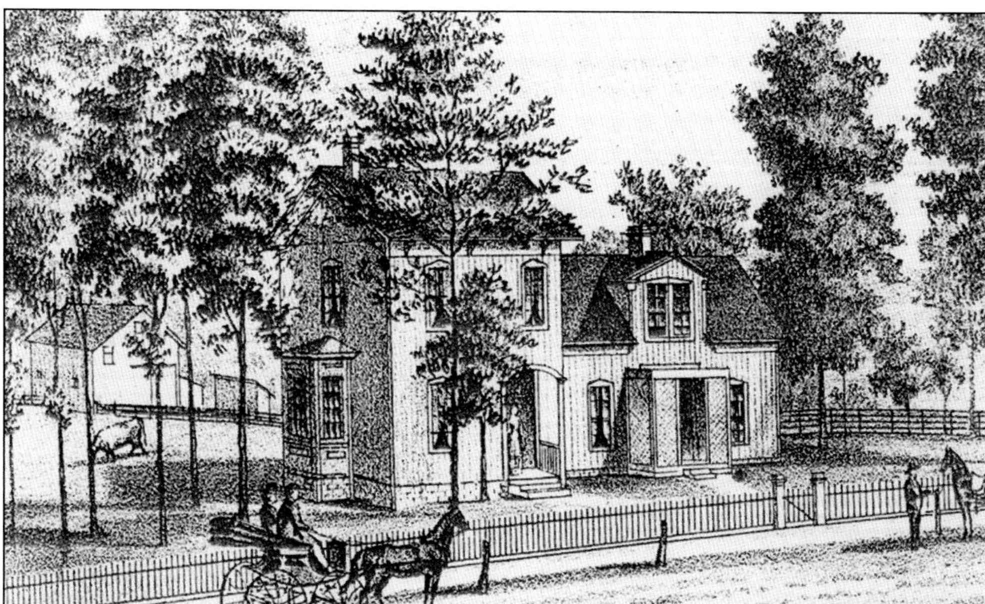

PEARL COTTAGE, 607 WEST MILLER STREET. Considered the oldest residence in DeSoto, the original structure was built in 1832 and purchased with British gold. Additions were made in 1870. For some time it was used as the Episcopal parsonage. (Photograph courtesy DeSoto Public Library.)

HENRY KEMP RESIDENCE, 508 SOUTH SECOND STREET. This house was built in 1879 and was kept in the Kemp family until 1963. The carpenters were Hopson and Paul, and the bricklayer was Otto Hermann. Hermann's work is seen in the way he finished his brickwork at the top of his buildings. Many houses in DeSoto still bear Hermann's distinctive mark. Pictured in this photograph are Louisa Kemp, holding Mildred Kemp Mahn (wife of Bernard Mahn). (Photograph courtesy DeSoto Public Library.)

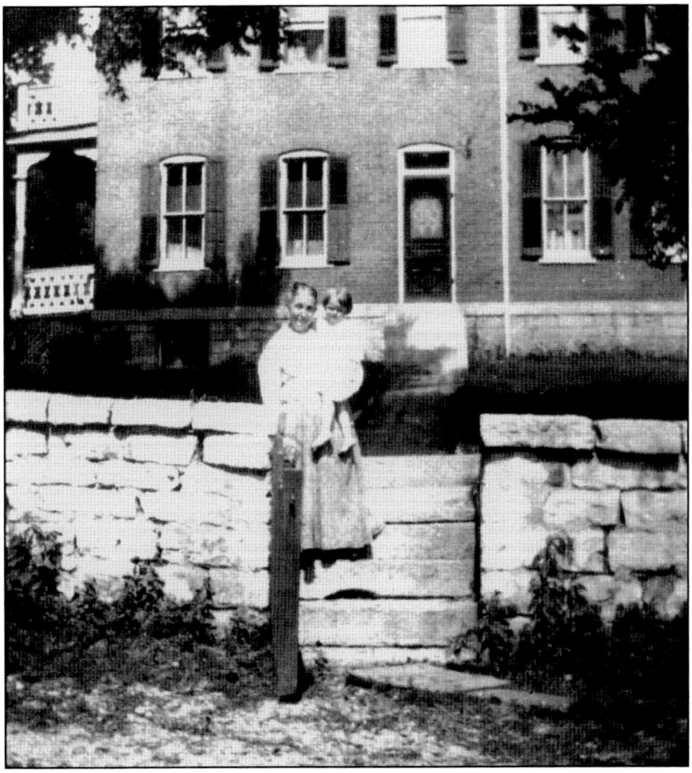

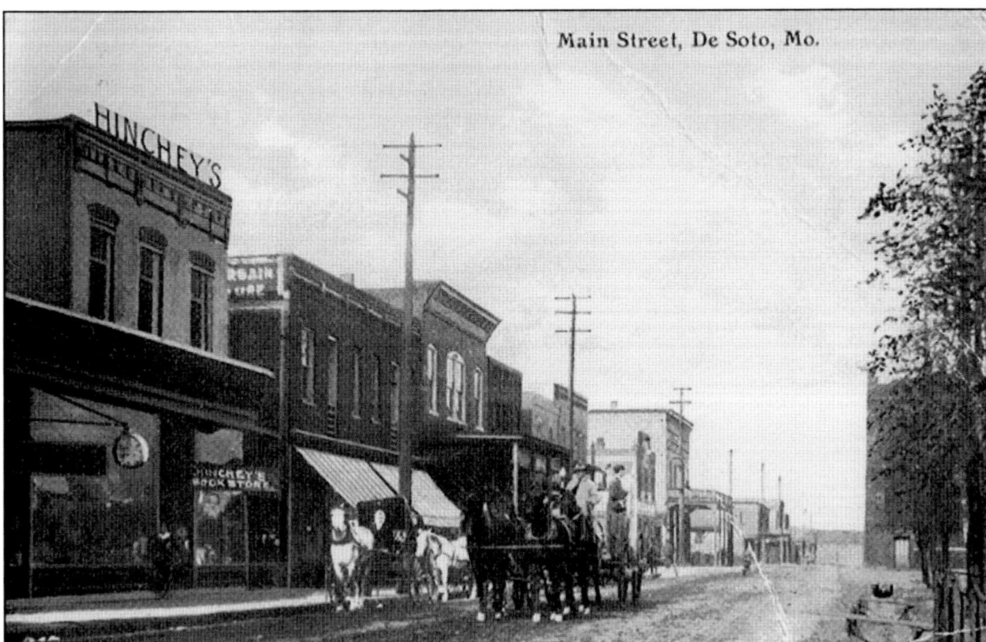

AN EARLY VIEW OF MAIN STREET. Unpaved Main Street and horse-drawn wagons are visible in this photograph. Some of the local buildings are still in existence. (Photograph courtesy DeSoto Public Library.)

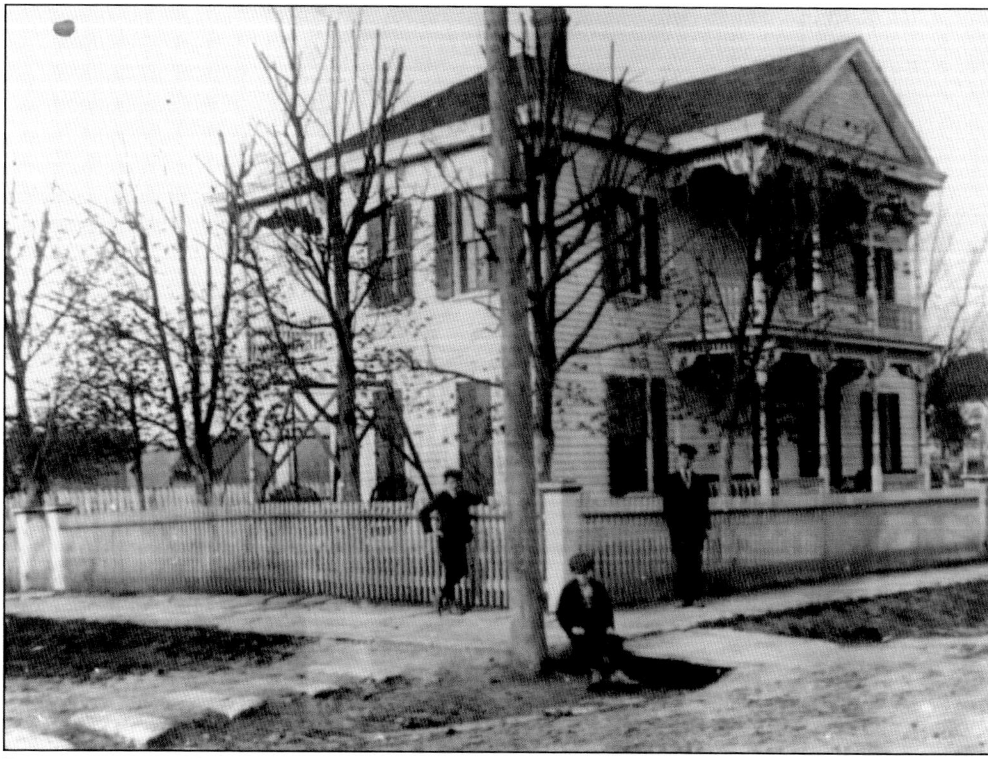

Residence of W. C. Ellis. According to the Directory of 1897, William C. Ellis was a conductor on the railroad and lived at 901 South Second Street. (Photograph courtesy DeSoto Public Library.)

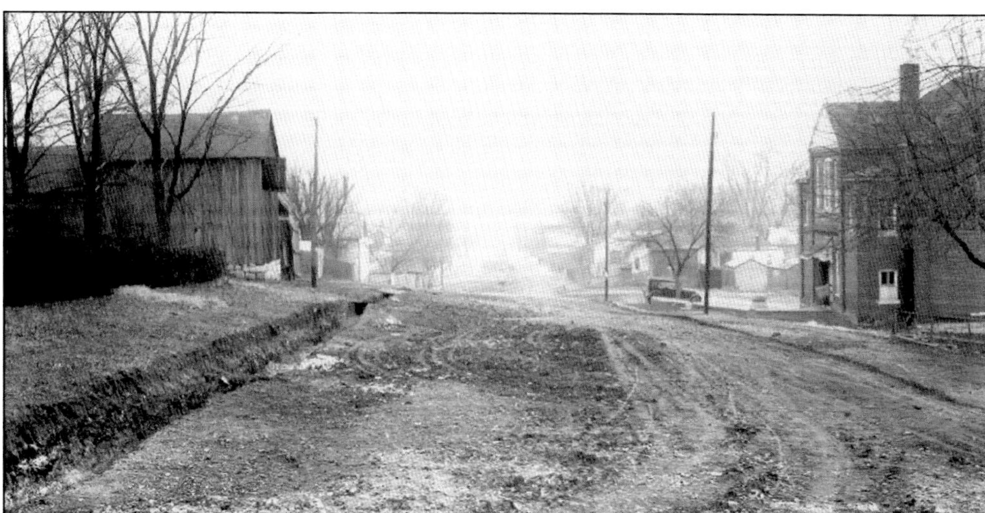

Amvets Drive. Amvets Drive is seen here in its earlier days, before it was paved. The former Ward School, now a residence, can be identified on the right. (Photograph courtesy DeSoto Public Library.)

Two

The Railroad

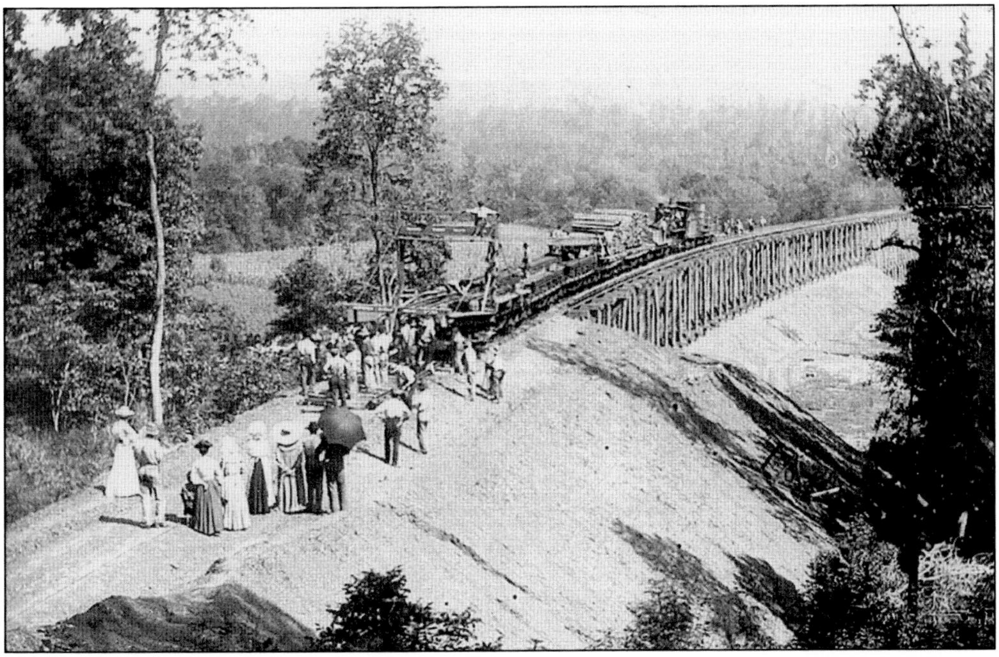

Laying Track. Track was laid on the Iron Mountain Railroad near DeSoto in preparation for train travel. (Photograph courtesy DeSoto Public Library.)

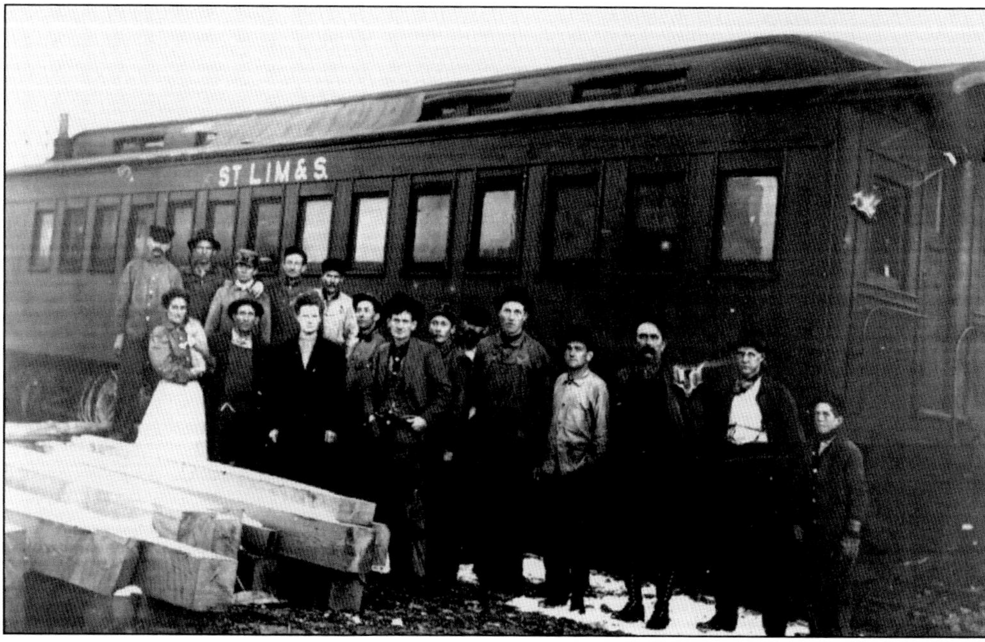

ST. LOUIS AND IRON MOUNTAIN CONSTRUCTION CREW. The St. Louis and Iron Mountain Railroad was the first railroad in DeSoto. The women in this photo were possibly cooks for the crew. (Photograph courtesy DeSoto Public Library.)

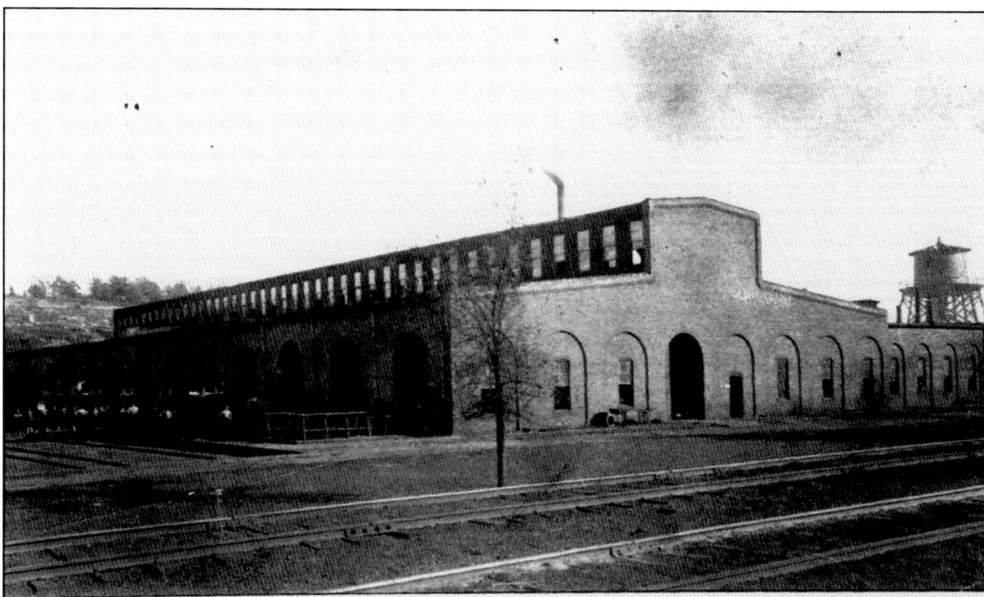

VIEW OF ST. L. I. M. & S. RAILWAY MACHINE SHOPS, DE SOTO.

MACHINE SHOPS OF THE ST. LOUIS, IRON MOUNTAIN AND SOUTHERN RAILWAY. These shops were among the first major businesses in DeSoto. (Photograph courtesy DeSoto Public Library.)

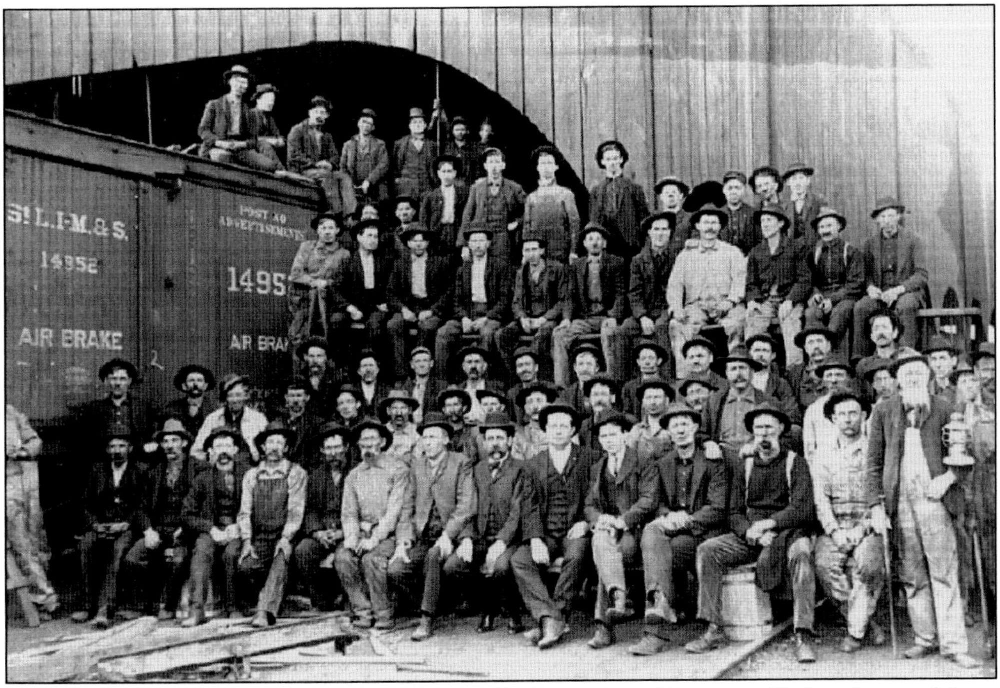

RAILROAD WORKERS. These workers for the St. Louis Iron Mountain Railroad paused from their work for this photograph. (Photograph courtesy DeSoto Public Library.)

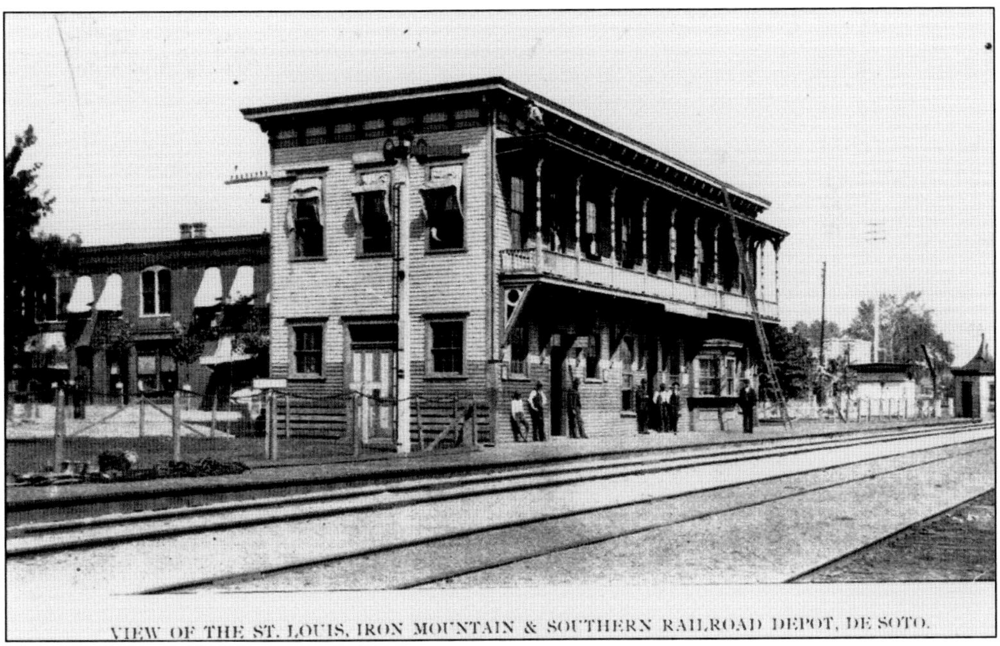

DESOTO DEPOT. The old DeSoto Depot, built by Fletcher and Rankin, had a major function in the operation of the railroad in the early 1900s. This building is now on Second and Pratt Streets and is occupied by the St. Vincent de Paul Store. (Photograph courtesy DeSoto Public Library.)

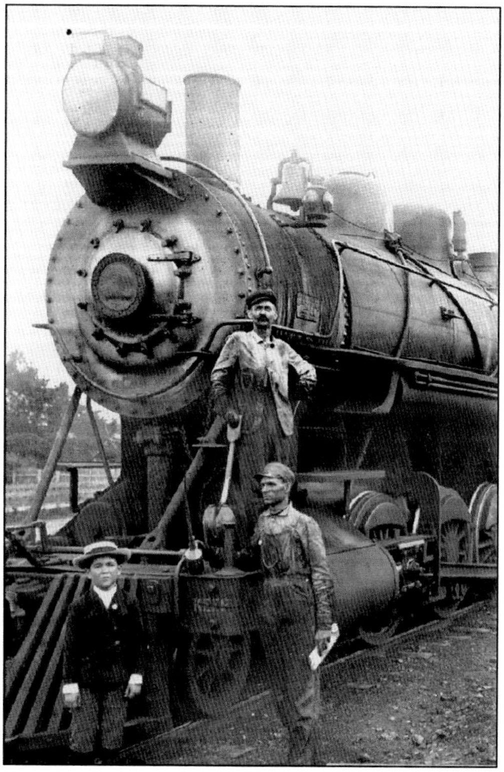

STEAM ENGINE. The railroad had many engines powered by steam that were in use in the early days. (Photograph courtesy DeSoto Public Library.)

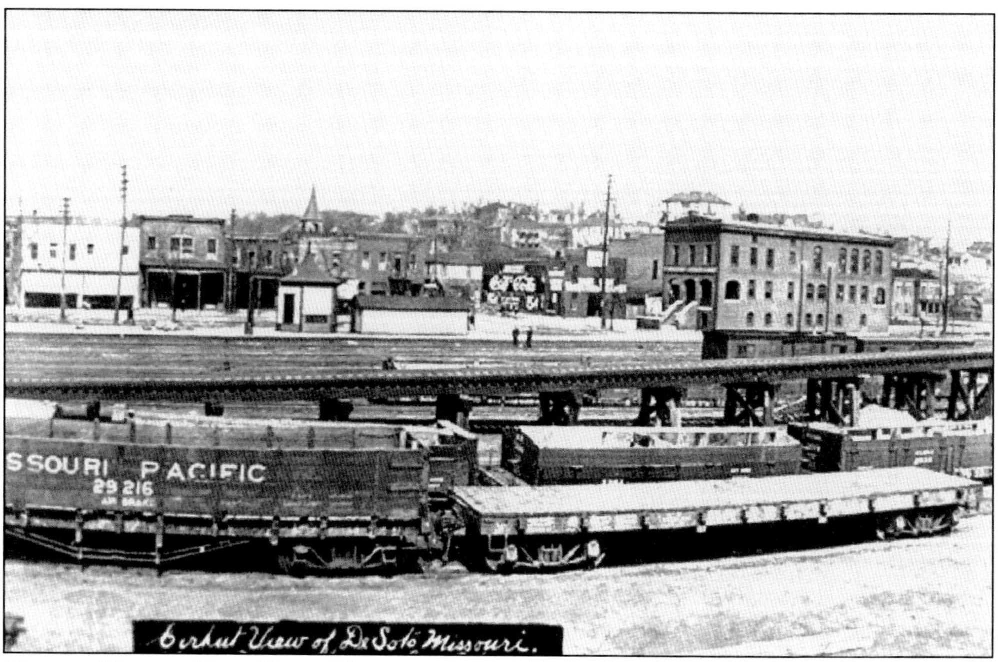

CIRCUIT VIEW OF RAIL YARD. This circuit view of the rail yard was taken in 1913. The YMCA building, located next to the tracks, is seen in the background. (Photograph courtesy DeSoto Public Library.)

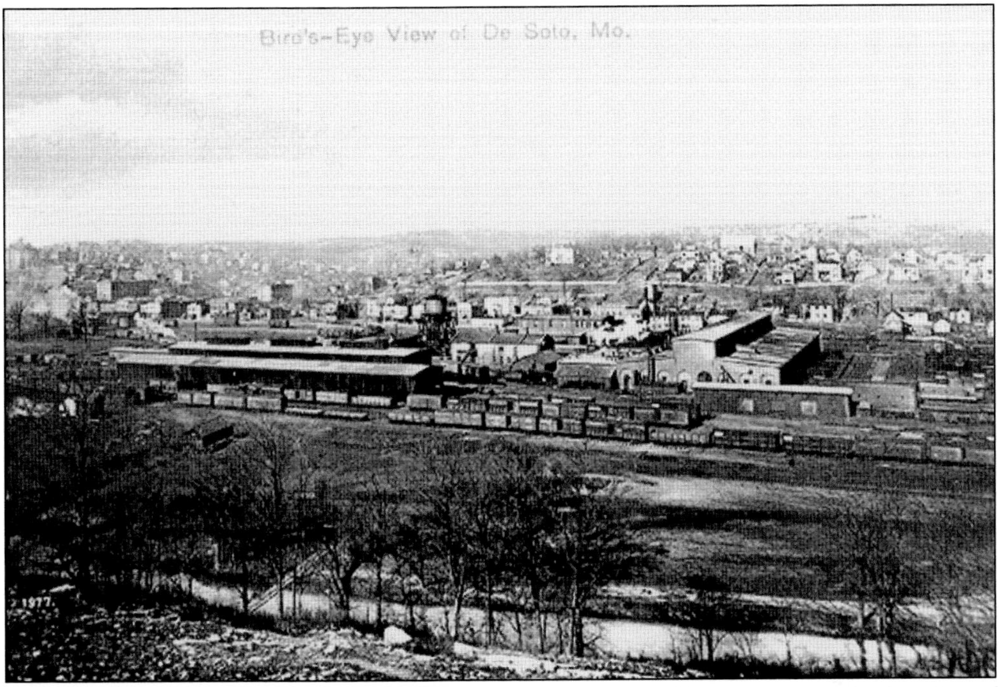

GENERAL VIEW. This general view of the railroad and surrounding area shows the location of the railroad industry in DeSoto. (Photograph courtesy DeSoto Public Library.)

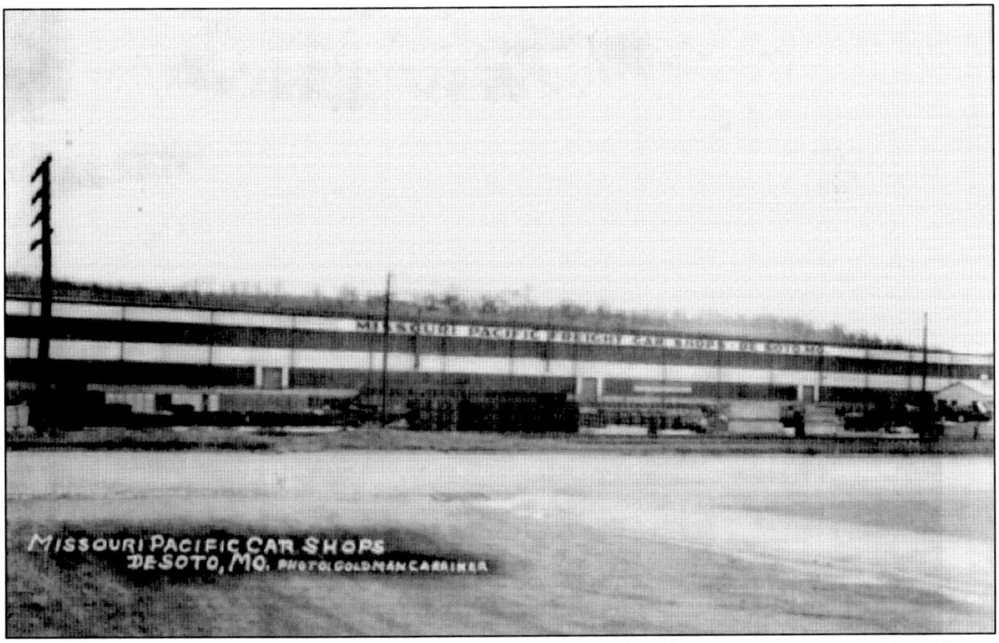

THE SHOPS. The railroad shops, where rail cars are repaired and returned to service, have been a constant source of employment for DeSoto. (Photograph courtesy DeSoto Public Library.)

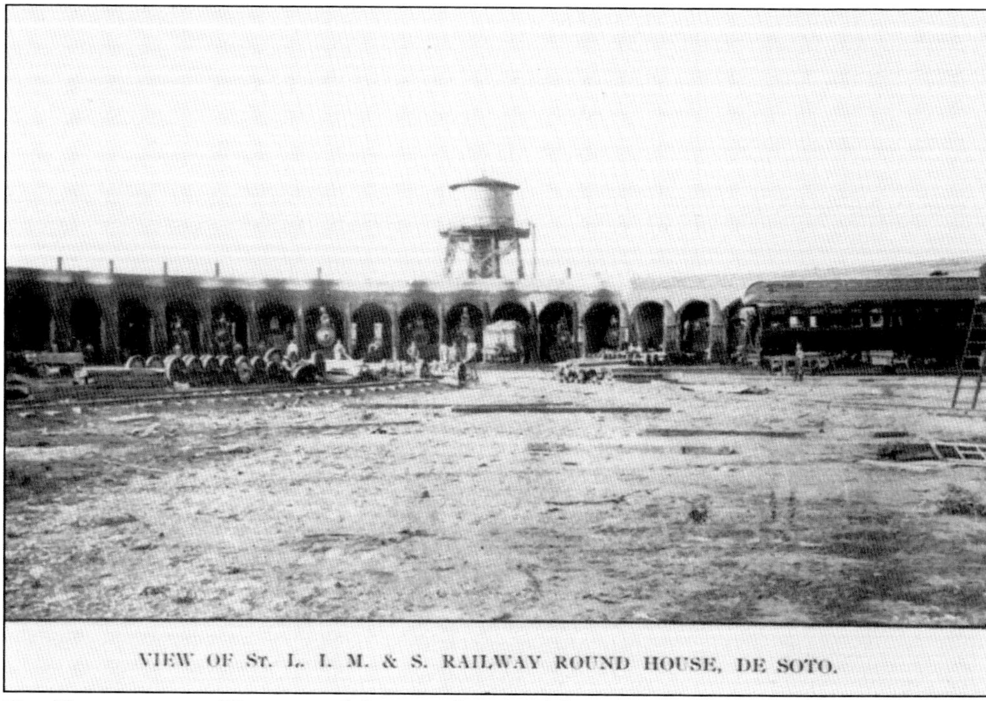

THE ROUNDHOUSE. This view of the roundhouse of the St. Louis and Iron Mountain Railroad was taken in 1881. (Photograph courtesy DeSoto Public Library.)

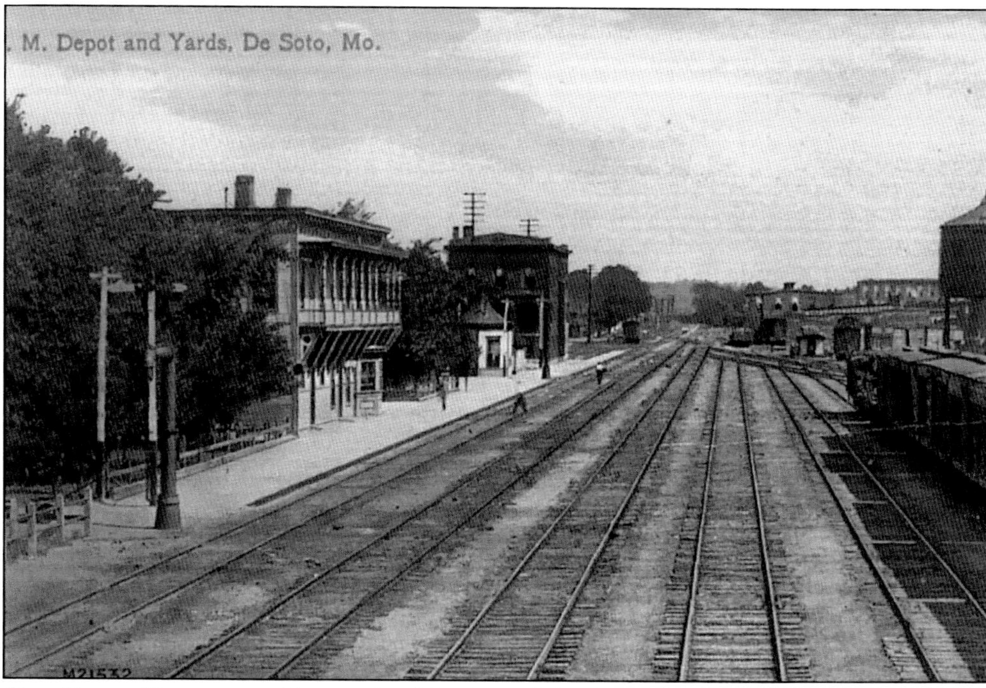

OLD TRAIN DEPOT AND YARDS. In this view of the Iron Mountain Depot and Yards, the Booster Hall can be seen at the left and the old water tower is visible on the right. (Photograph courtesy DeSoto Public Library.)

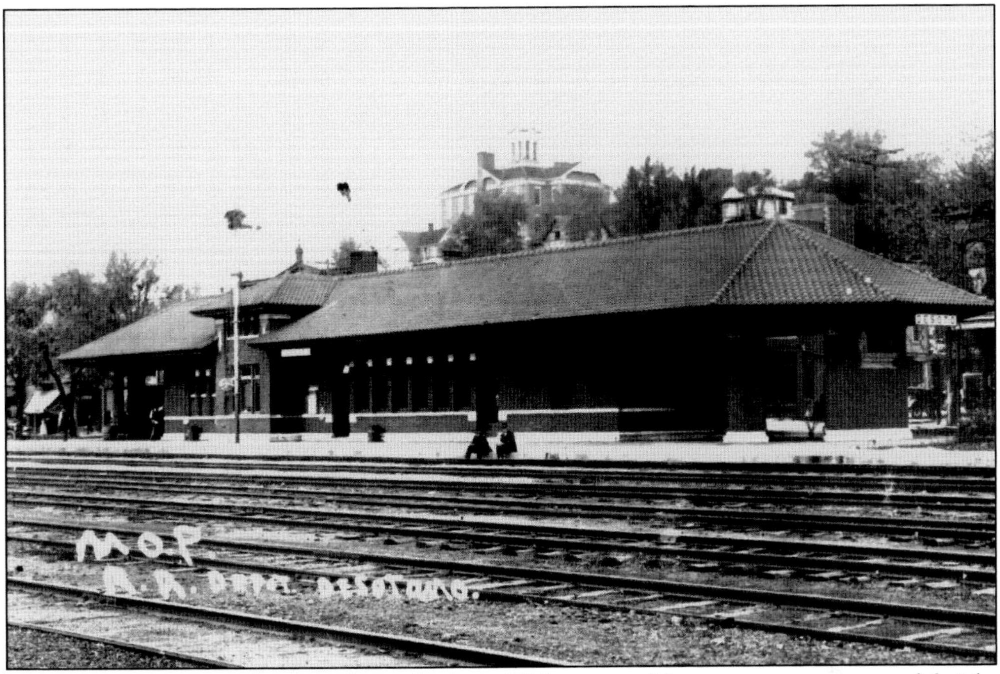

NEW TRAIN DEPOT. This new depot, built in 1916, was used by many passengers and freight trains that traveled through DeSoto on a daily basis. The building was demolished in order to widen Main Street. (Photograph courtesy DeSoto Public Library.)

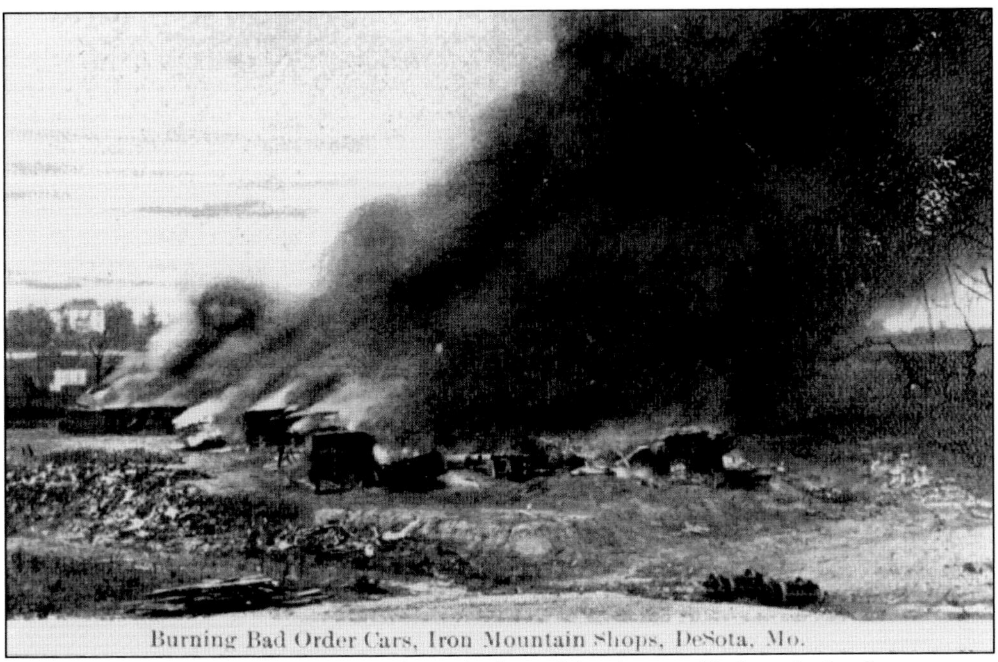

BURNING OF BAD ORDER CARS. In the early days of the shops in DeSoto, bad order cars were burned at the site. (Photograph courtesy DeSoto Public Library.)

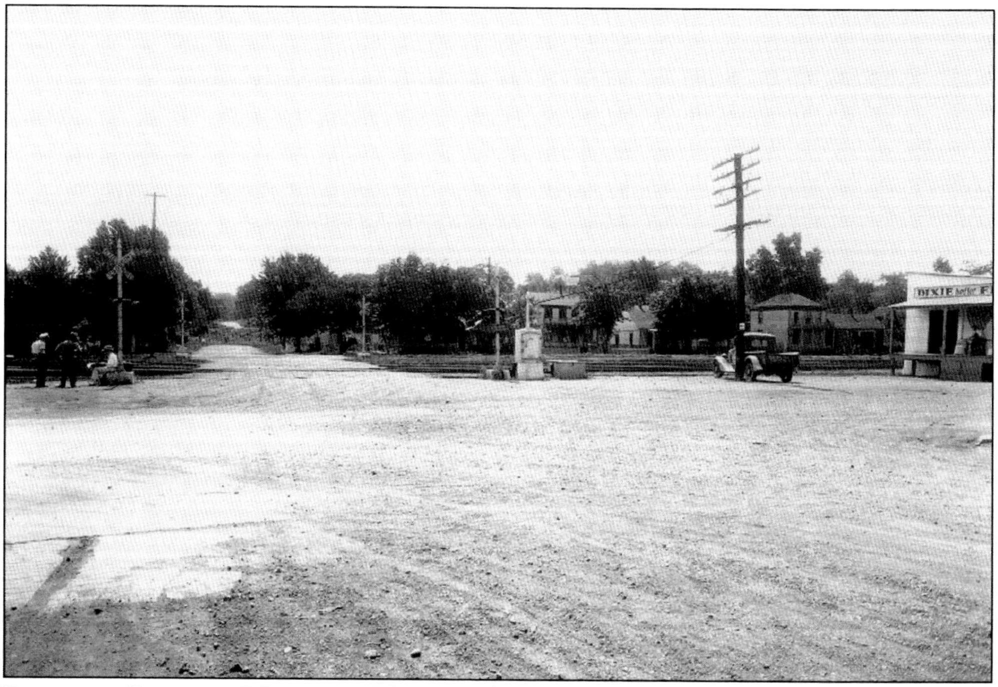

RAILROAD CROSSING, MAIN AND MILLER. This photograph of the railroad crossing at Main and Miller Streets, looking south, was made in the early 1930s. (Photograph courtesy DeSoto Public Library.)

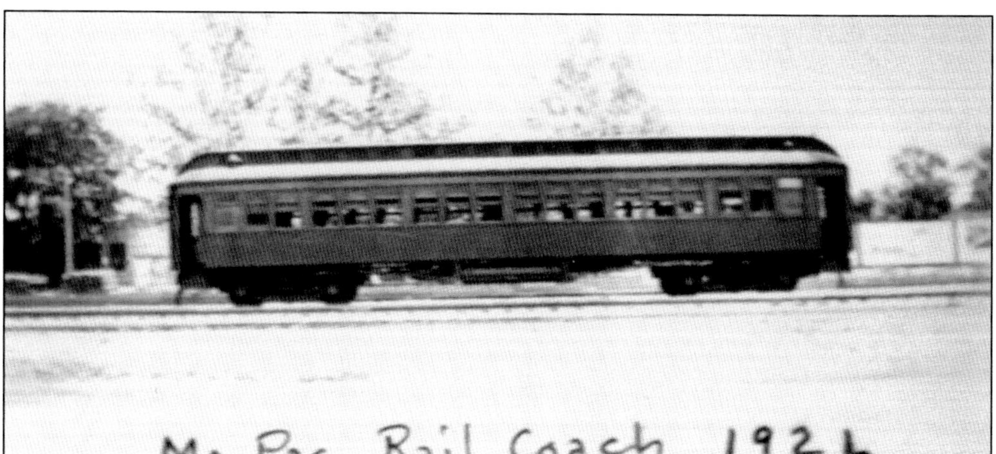

RAILROAD COACH ON THE TRACKS. This railroad car was typical of the type of coaches used for travel by train. (Photograph courtesy DeSoto Public Library.)

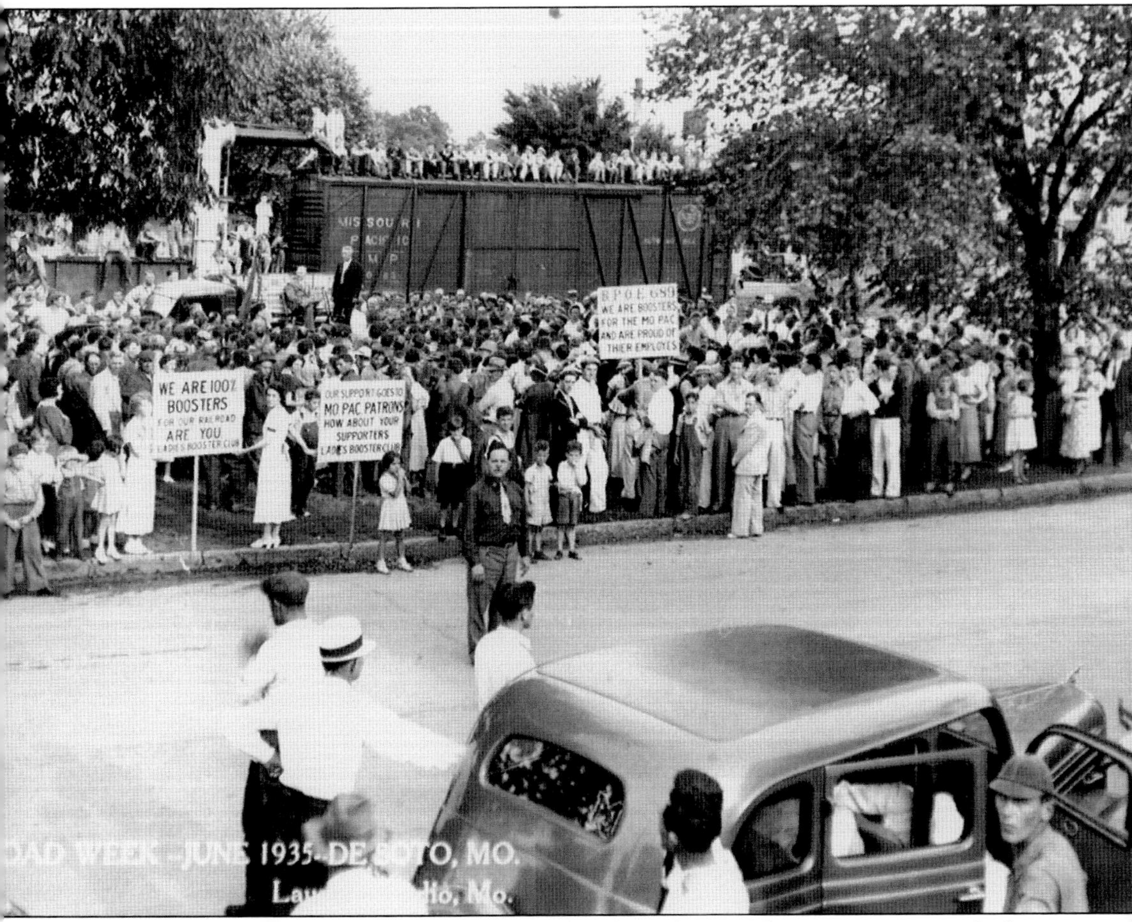

RAILROAD BOOSTER DAY. DeSoto celebrated Railroad Week in 1935 in conjunction with the Missouri Pacific Railroad and had a special Railroad Booster Day during that week. The man in the middle of the street is Ed Eaton. (Photograph courtesy DeSoto Public Library.)

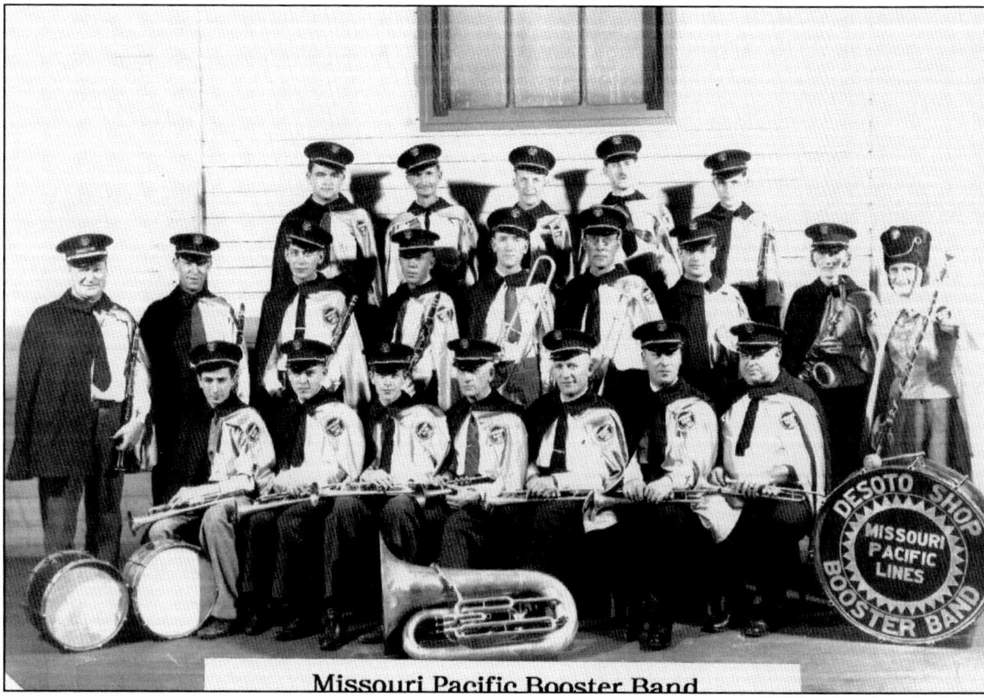

MISSOURI PACIFIC BOOSTER BAND. Among those pictured here are Adolph "Max" Schwaegerle, Walter Schwaegerle, Joe Withington, and Roy Lee Lewis. (Photograph courtesy DeSoto Public Library.)

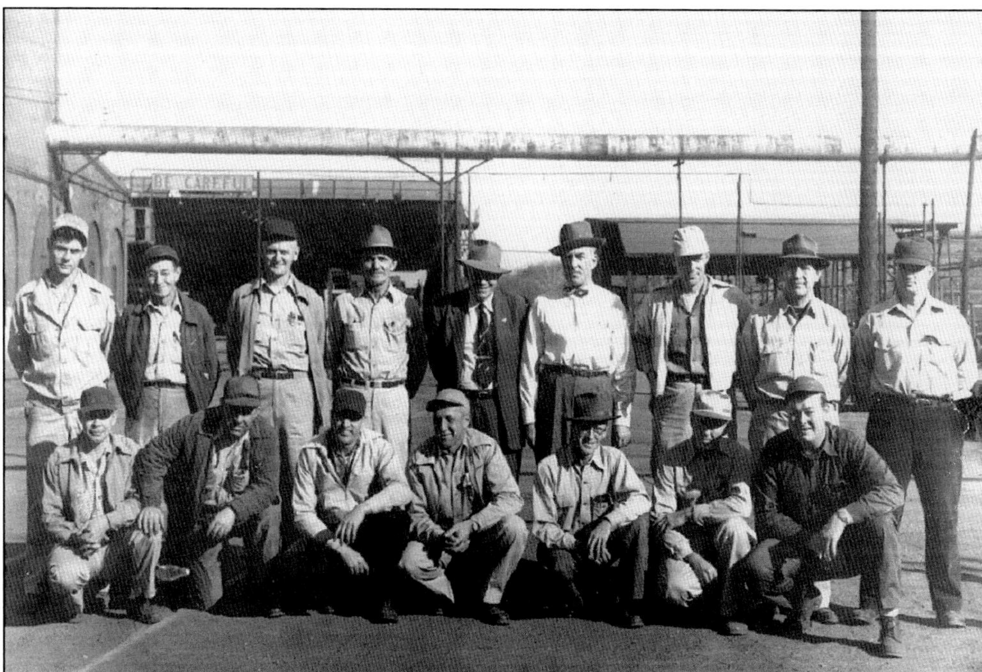

RAILROAD WORKERS. A group of workers at the Missouri Pacific Shops stand close to the sign, "Be Careful." (Photograph courtesy DeSoto Public Library.)

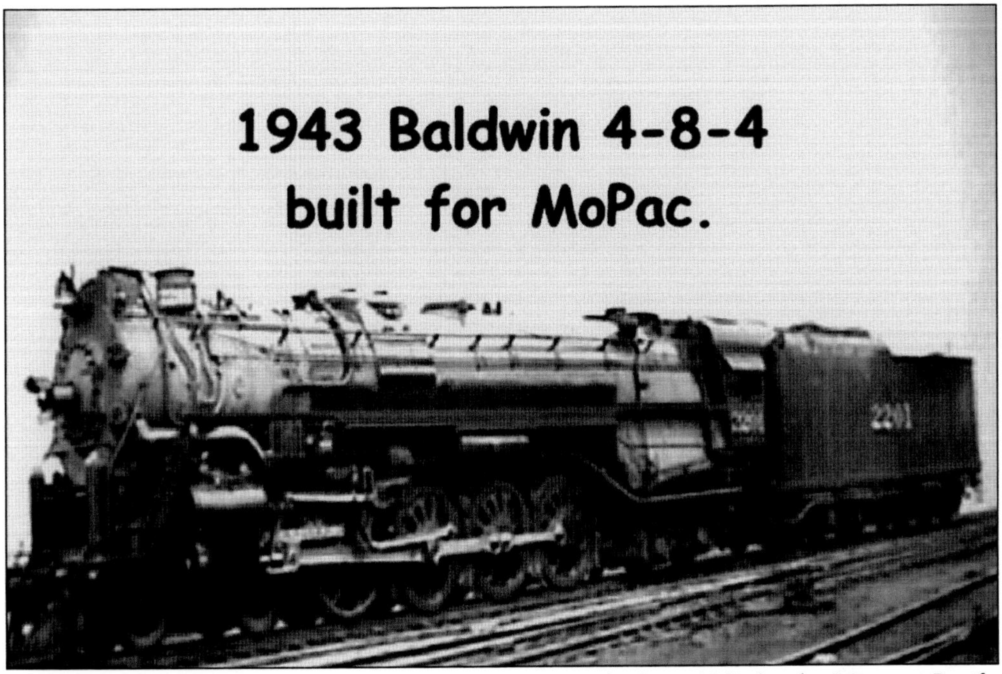

BALDWIN LOCOMOTIVE. The Baldwin Locomotive was built in 1943 for the Missouri Pacific Railroad. It provided much service to the railroad when it was in use. (Photograph courtesy Dave Williamson.)

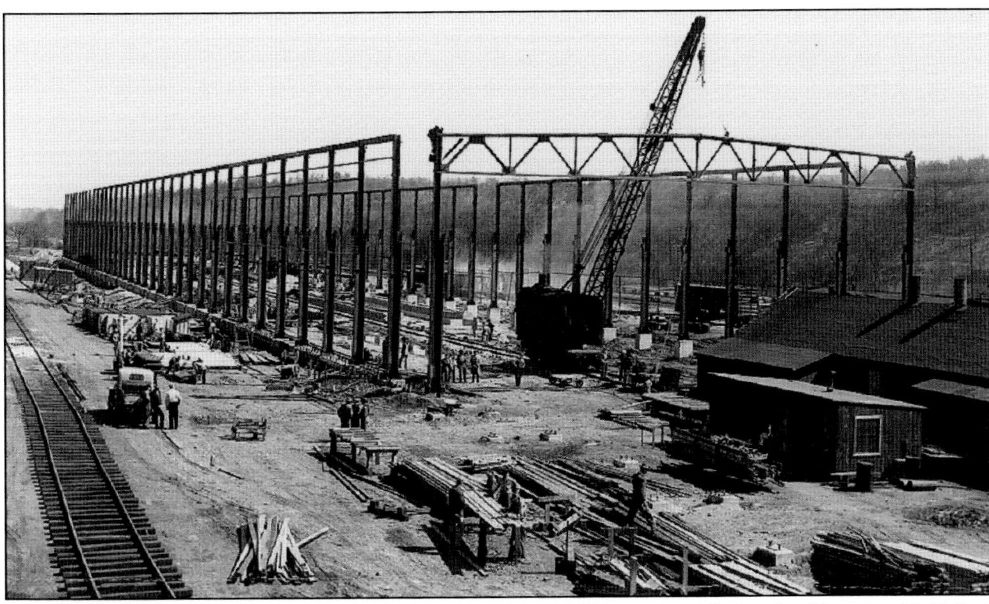

MISSOURI PACIFIC CAR SHOPS. The Missouri Pacific Shops erected this building in 1947. It is 110 feet wide by 700 feet long and contains two tracks extending the length of the building. The building has work stations on both tracks for repair work on railroad cars. (Photograph courtesy DeSoto Public Library.)

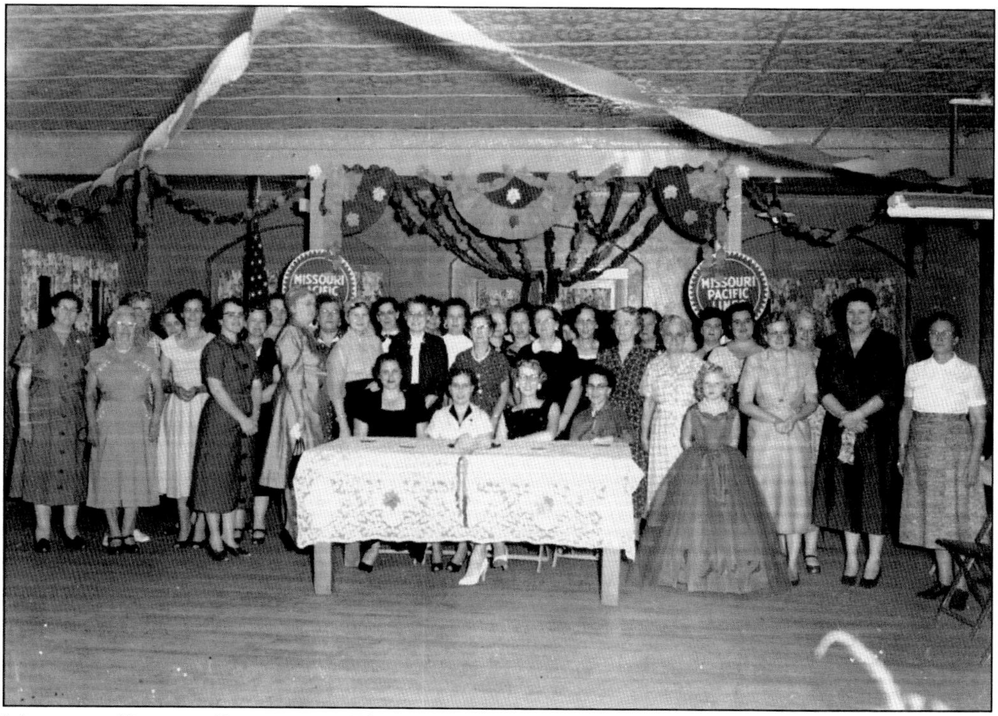

Missouri Pacific Boosters. This organization has assisted the railroad in many ways throughout the years. (Photograph courtesy DeSoto Public Library.)

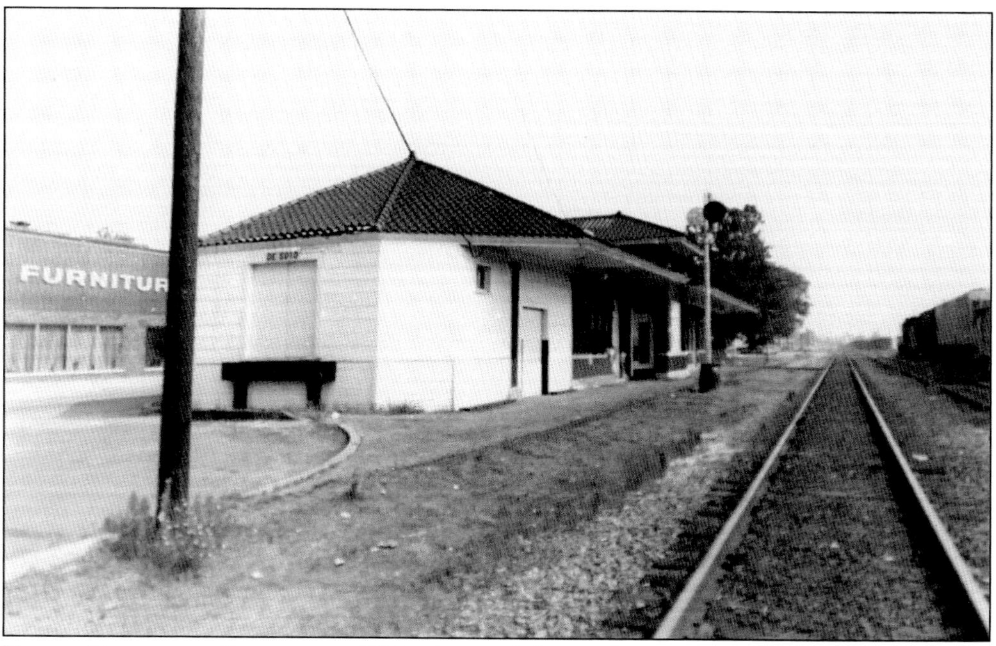

Depot, View from Southeast. This view is of the southeast section of the DeSoto Depot. (Photograph courtesy DeSoto Public Library.)

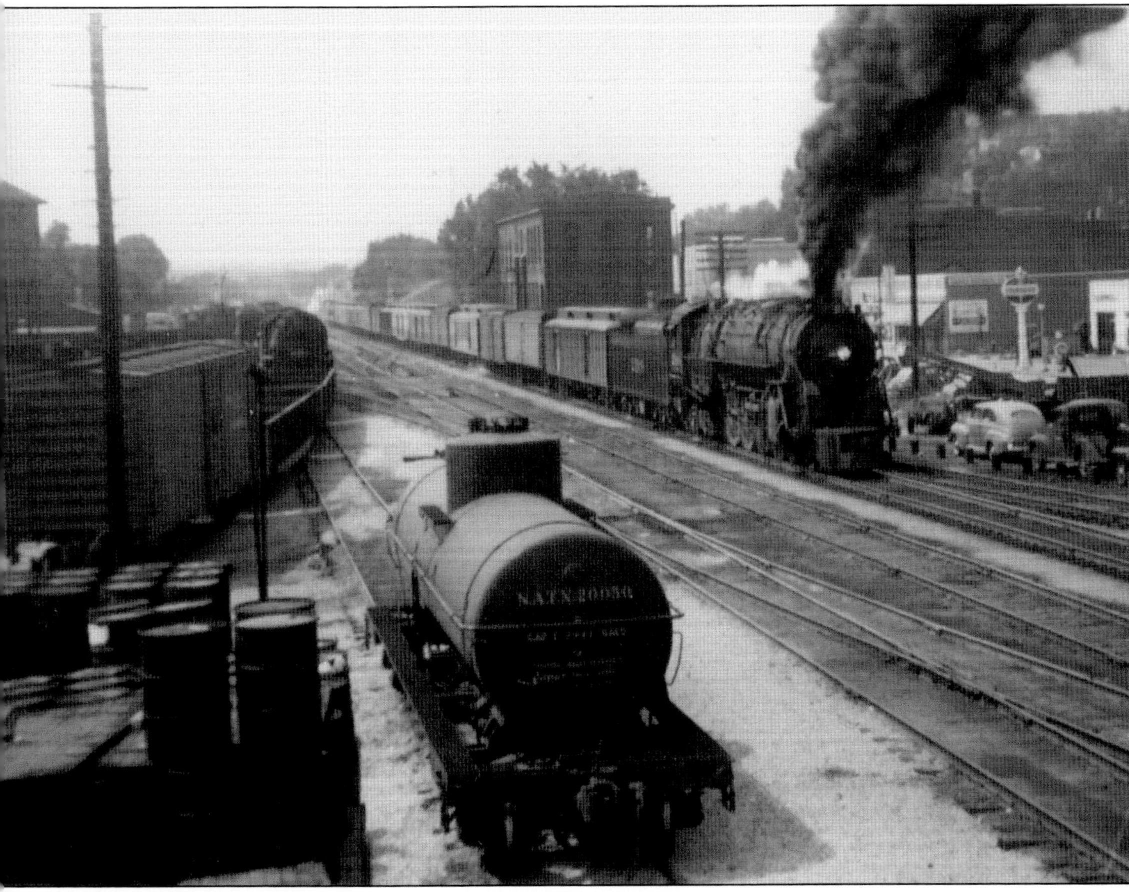

LAST STEAM TRAIN. This photo captured the final steam train that traveled through DeSoto in 1958. The photograph was taken by Stewart Street in DeSoto. (Photograph courtesy Dave Williamson.)

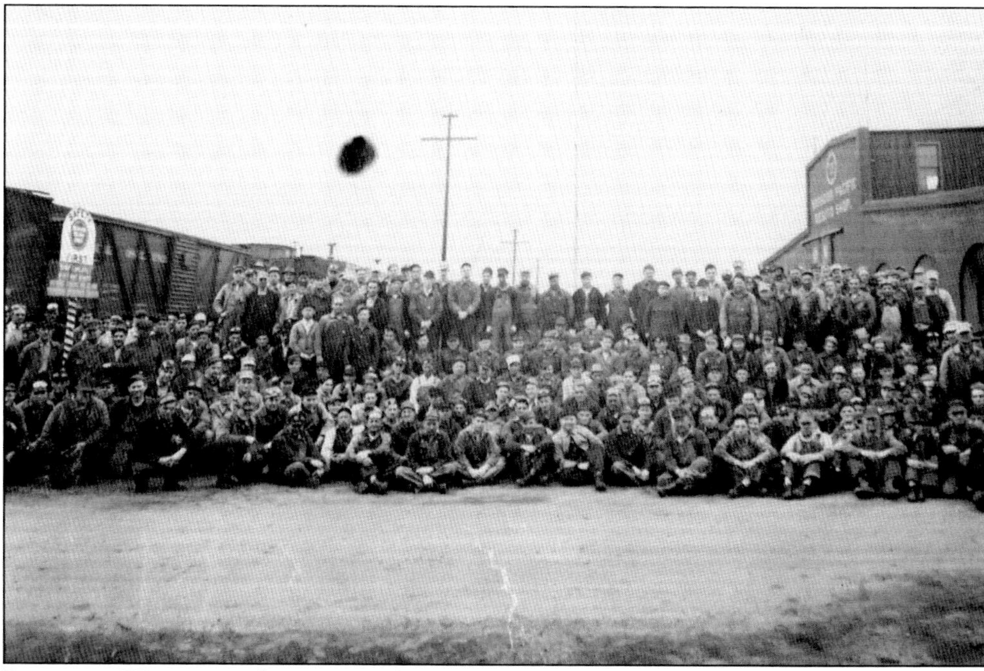

Railroad Workers. The many workers at the shops in DeSoto paused for their photograph next to the tracks. (Photograph courtesy Dave Williamson.)

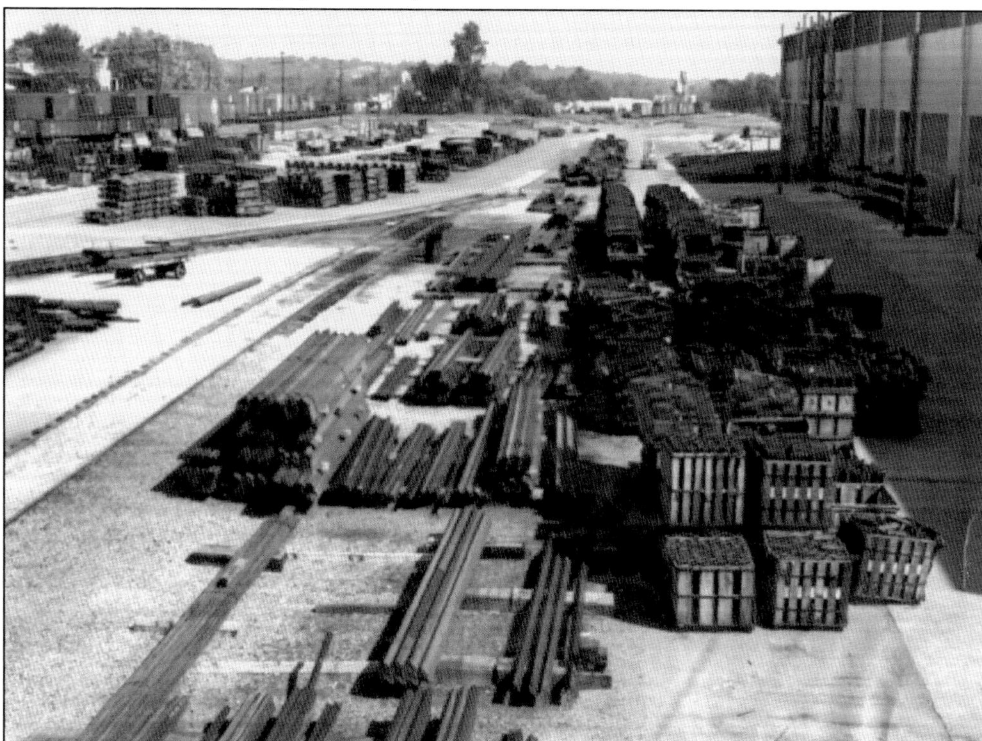

Supplies for the Mo Pac Line. These supplies for the railroad were gathered next to the building of the Missouri Pacific Shops. (Photograph courtesy Dave Williamson.)

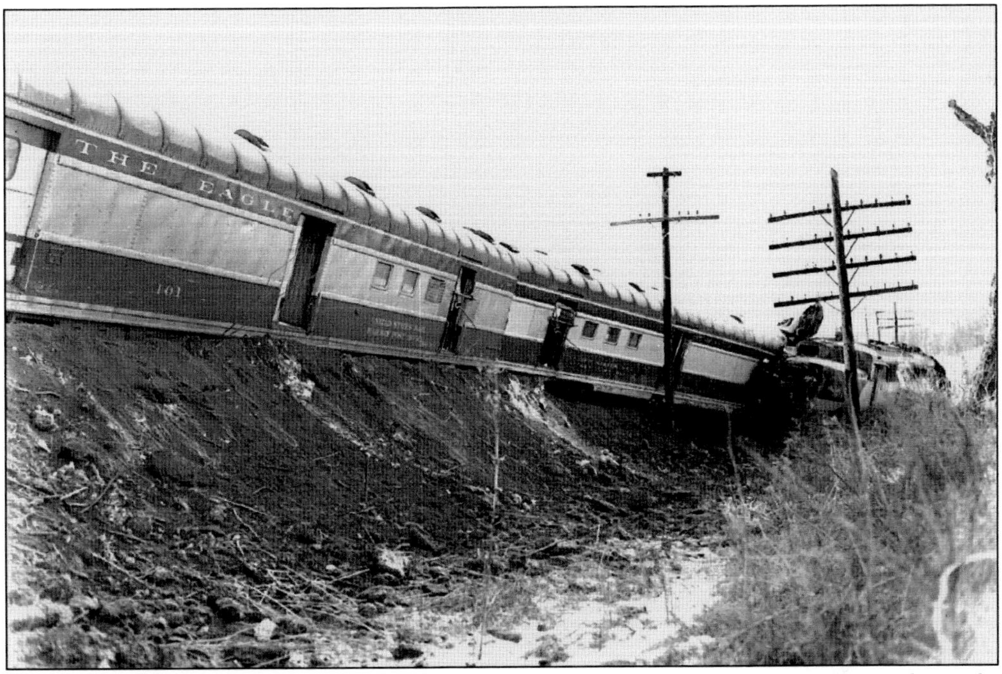

WRECK ON MISSOURI PACIFIC RAILROAD. The wreck of the Missouri Pacific train, *the Eagle*, occurred at Mooney's Bridge, north of DeSoto, in January 1962. (Photograph courtesy DeSoto Public Library.)

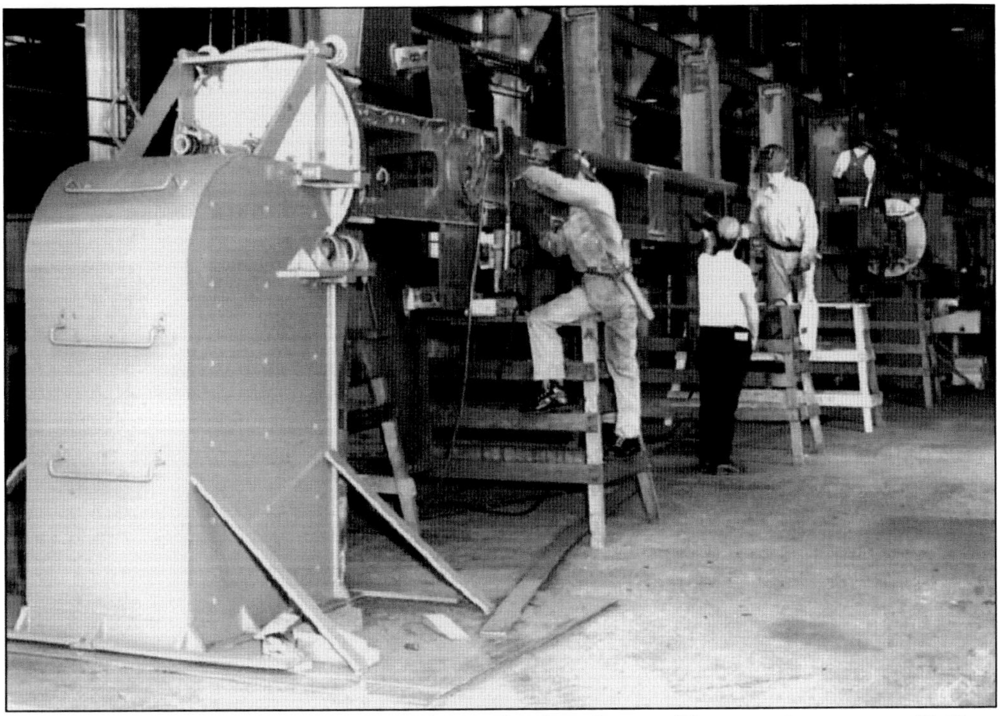

WELDERS. These welders are at work inside the shops. (Photograph courtesy DeSoto Public Library.)

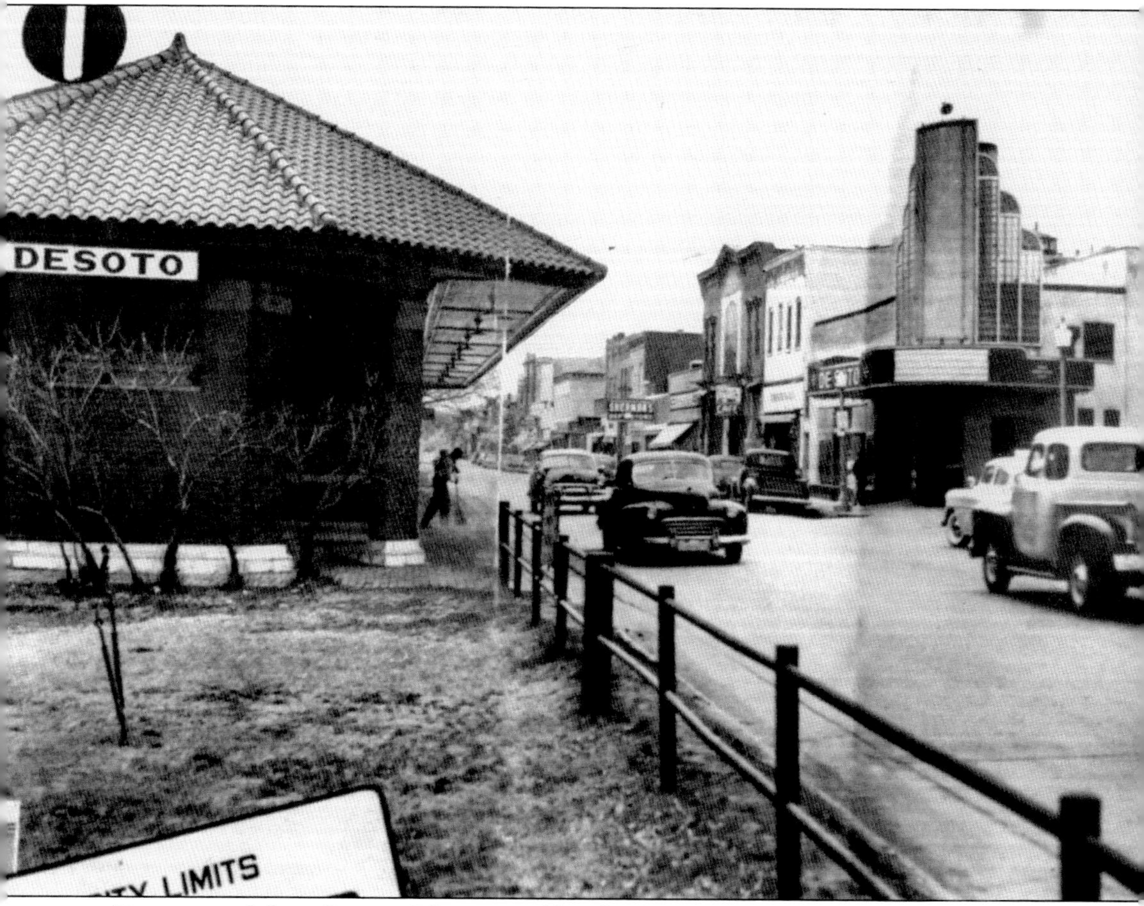

DEPOT AND MAIN STREET. This view of South Main Street was probably taken in the 1950s. (Photograph courtesy DeSoto Public Library.)

Three

Churches and Schools

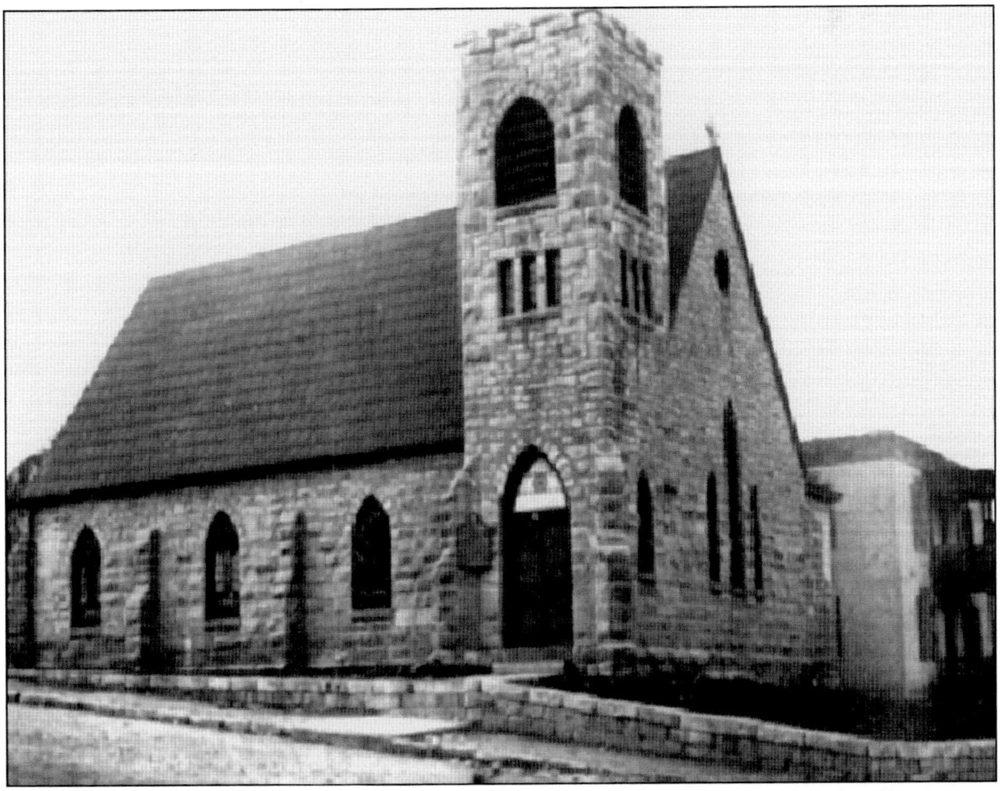

Trinity Episcopal Church. Trinity Episcopal Church, located at Second and Miller Streets, was built in 1871. Weekly services are still held in this historic structure. (Photograph courtesy DeSoto Public Library.)

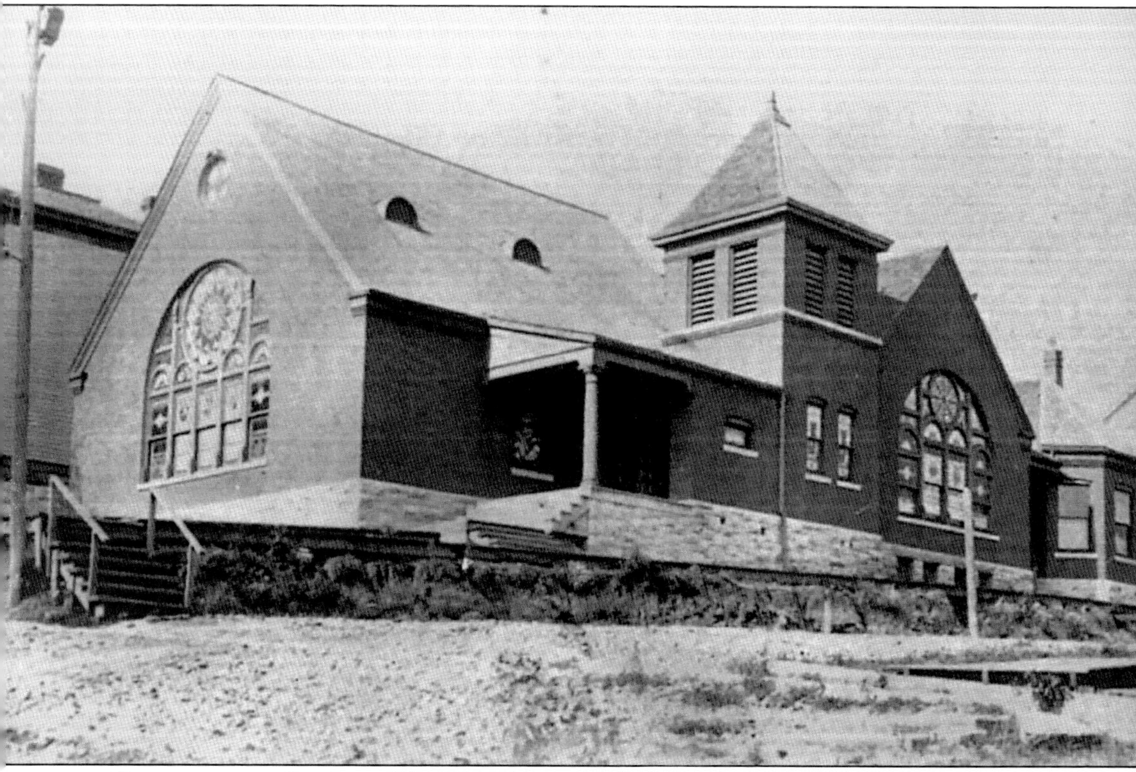

PRESBYTERIAN CHURCH. This church, originally located at Second and Easton Streets, has been razed. (Photograph courtesy DeSoto Public Library.)

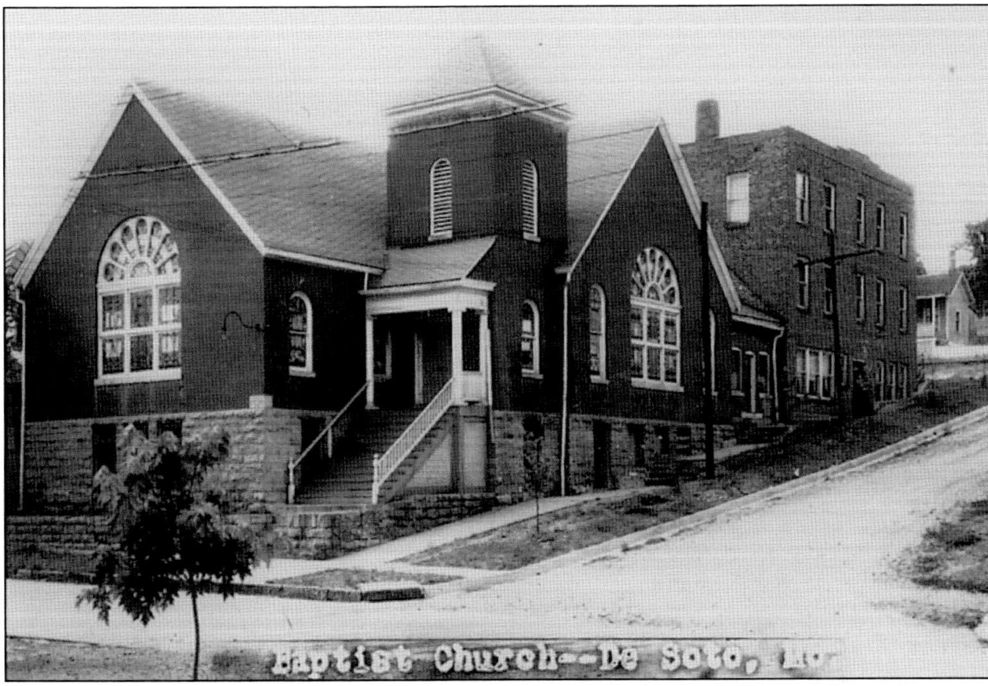

Baptist Church. This church, built in 1900, was located at Second and Stone Streets in DeSoto. (Photograph courtesy DeSoto Public Library.)

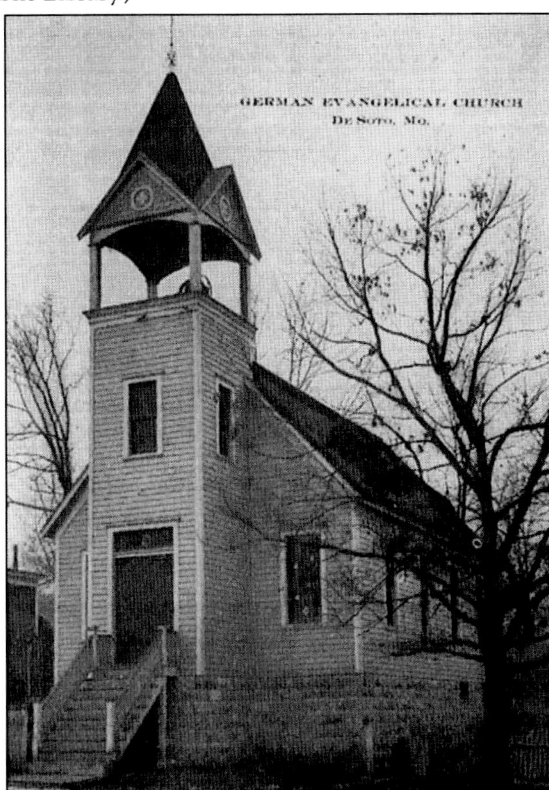

Church at Third and Boyd Streets. Formerly the DeSoto Christian Church, this building is no longer used as a church. (Photograph courtesy DeSoto Public Library.)

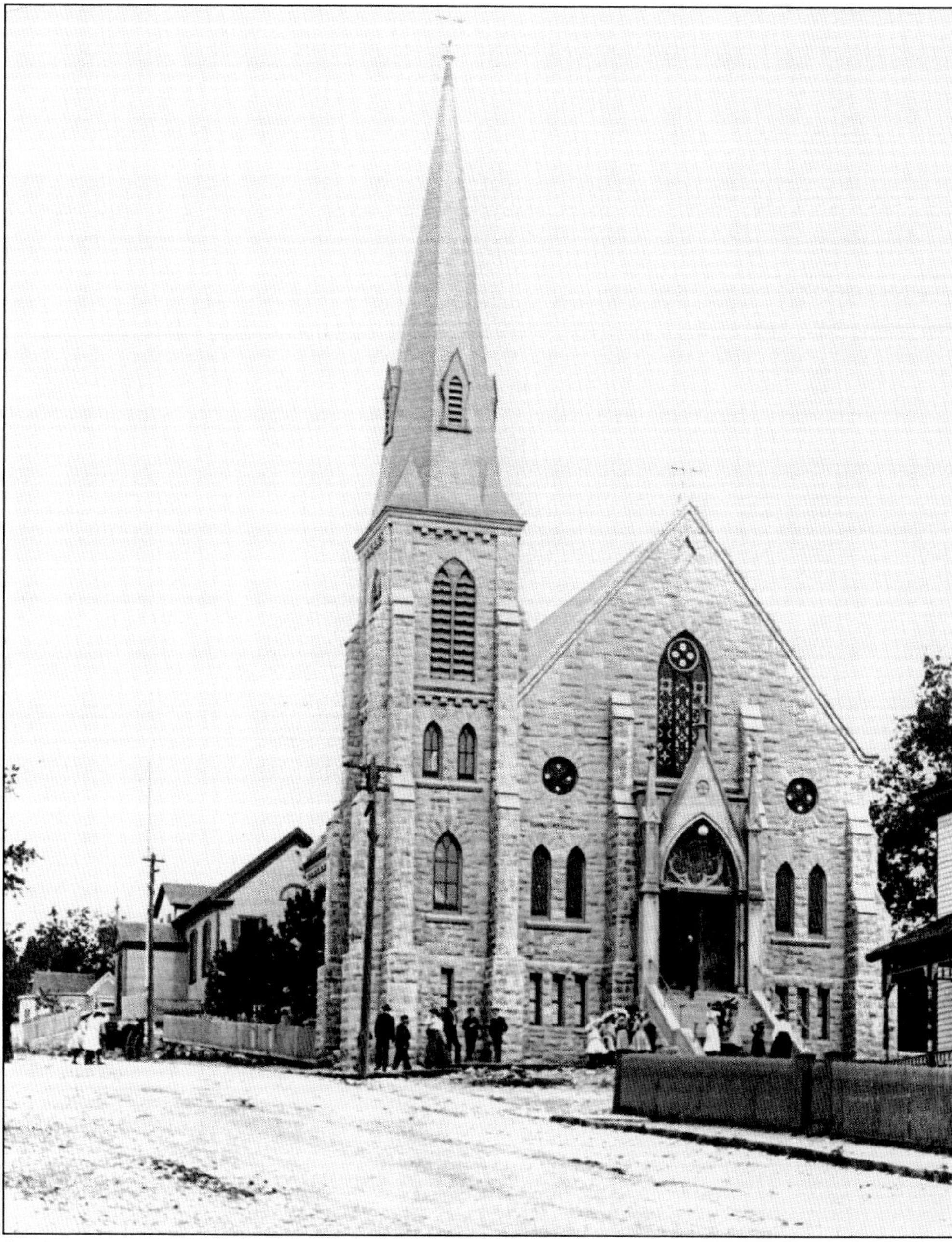

St. Rose of Lima Church. This Gothic-style stone structure of St. Rose of Lima Church was built in 1883 of limestone quarried from the old stone quarry located at the end of West Kelley Street. This limestone was transported to the church site on wagons pulled by a team of oxen. An earlier church made of wood served the parish from the mid-1850s until the present church was built. (Photograph courtesy DeSoto Public Library.)

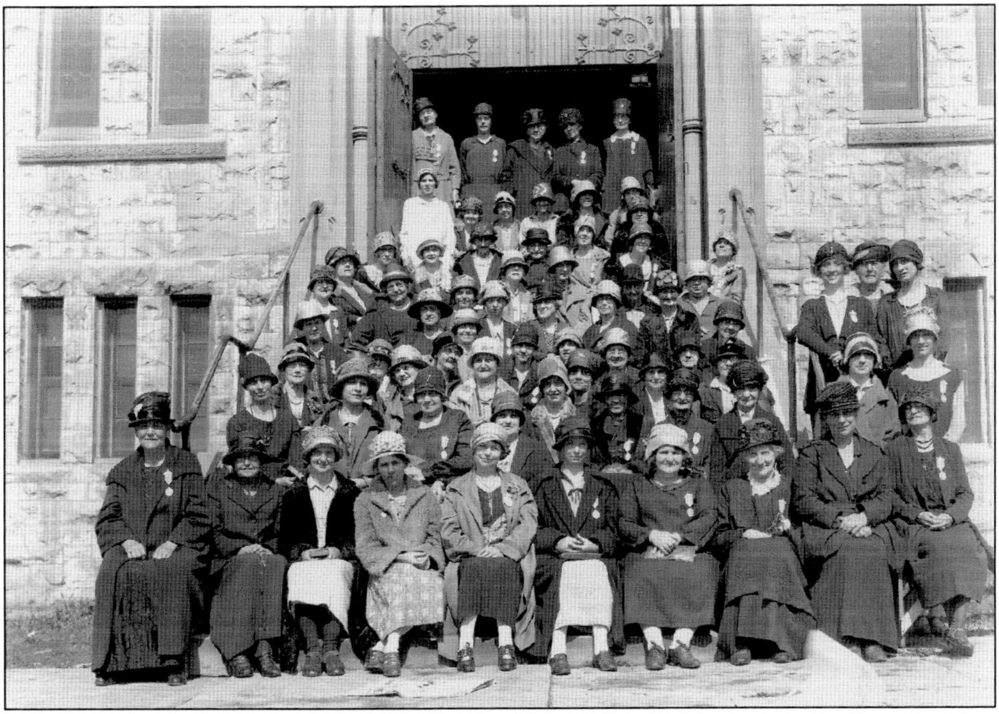

LADIES OF ST. ROSE OF LIMA CHURCH. This group of ladies, members of St. Ann Sodality, pose for their photograph on the front steps of St. Rose of Lima Church in the early 1930s. (Photograph courtesy DeSoto Public Library.)

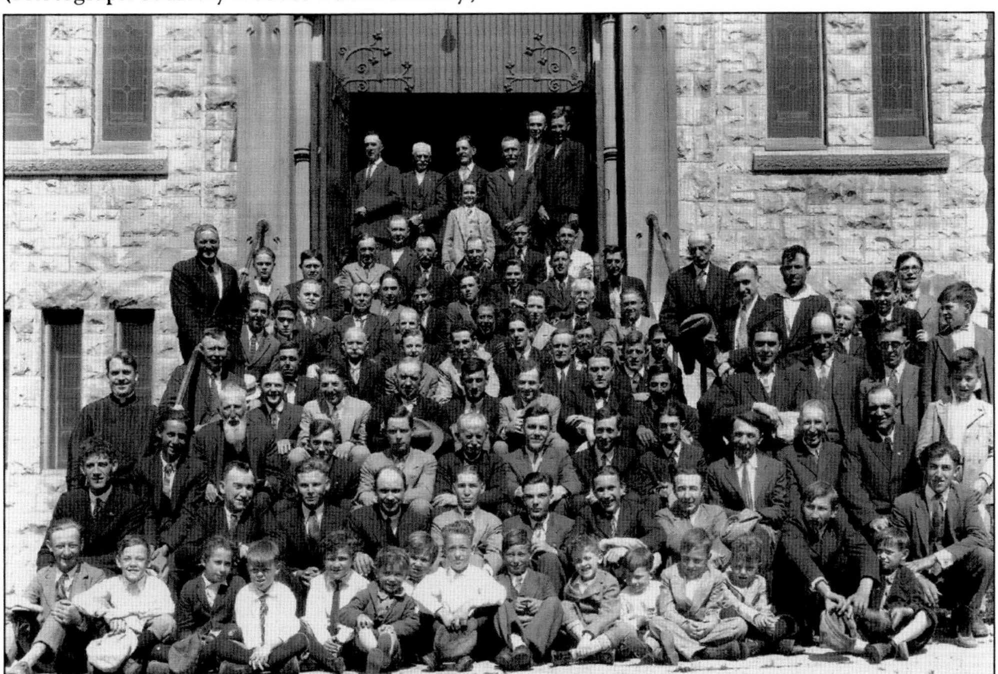

MEN OF ST. ROSE OF LIMA CHURCH. These men from St. Rose of Lima Church also use the front steps of the church for their photograph. (Photograph courtesy DeSoto Public Library.)

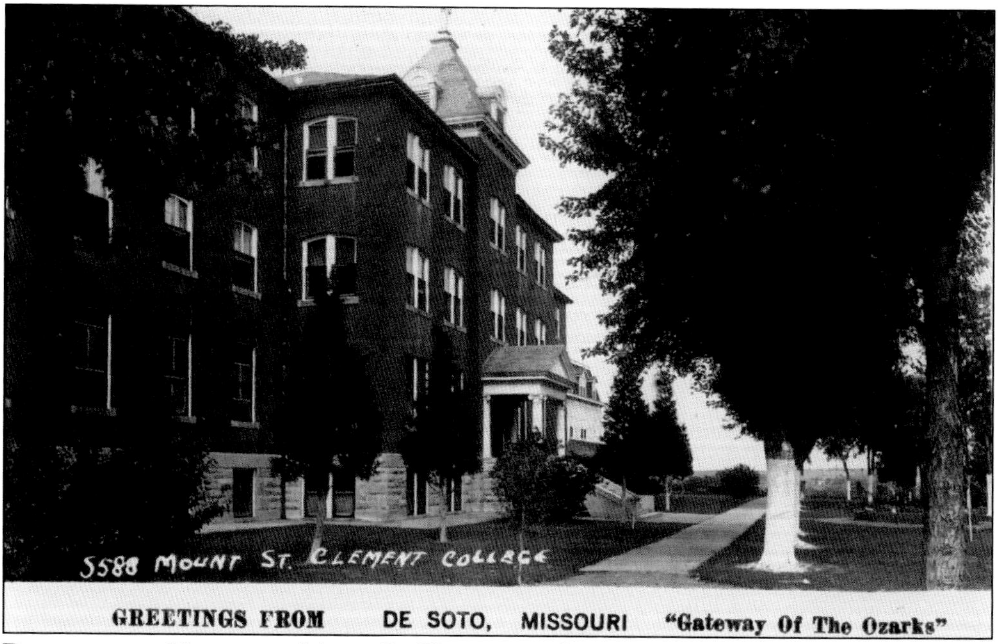

REDEMPTORIST NOVITIATE. Mount St. Clement was the novitiate for the Redemptorist Fathers. This building, destroyed by fire in 1966, was located on the present site of Vineland Elementary School. (Photograph courtesy DeSoto Public Library.)

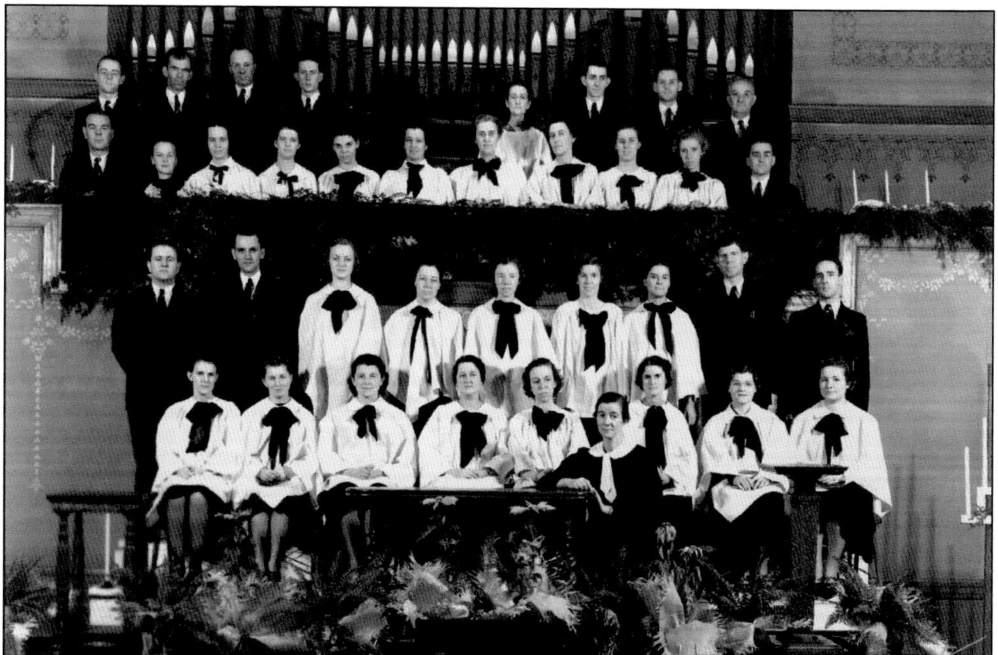

CHURCH CHOIR, 1938. Among those pictured are Gertrude Coil (director), Helen Theobold (organist), Rebekah Fraser, Margaret Fraser, Dorothy Wilson Jones, Estelle Couch Pierce, Geraldine Fauth, Paul Klein, Celia Ingels, Henrietta Niehoff, John Baker, Robert McKay, Erna A. Seemel, Vesper Dodd, Frances Calliatt, Julia Bell Richardson, Gertrude Burgess, O. T. Gibbons, Harrison Williams, and Oscar T. Coil. (Photograph courtesy DeSoto Public Library.)

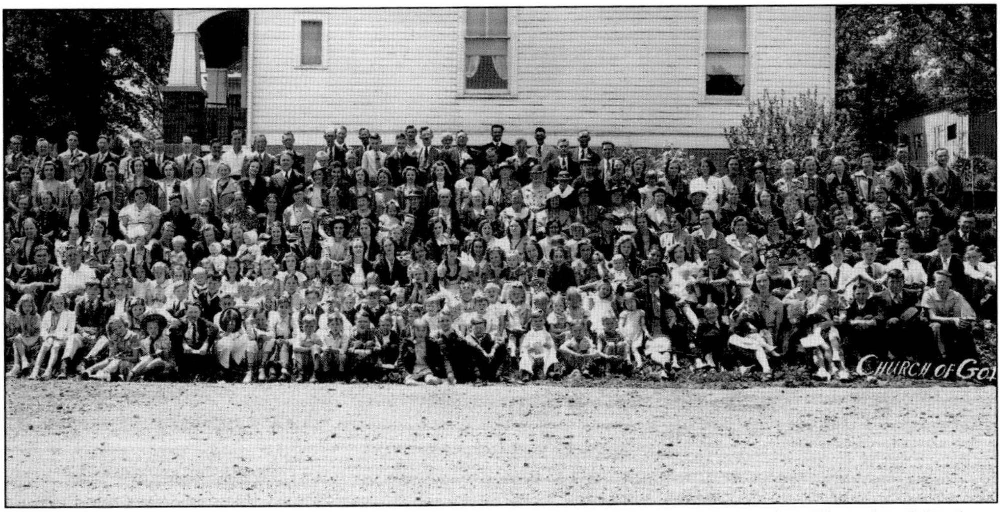

CHURCH OF GOD. Pictured is a large gathering of churchgoers in 1939 at the Church of God on Third Street. (Photograph courtesy DeSoto Public Library.)

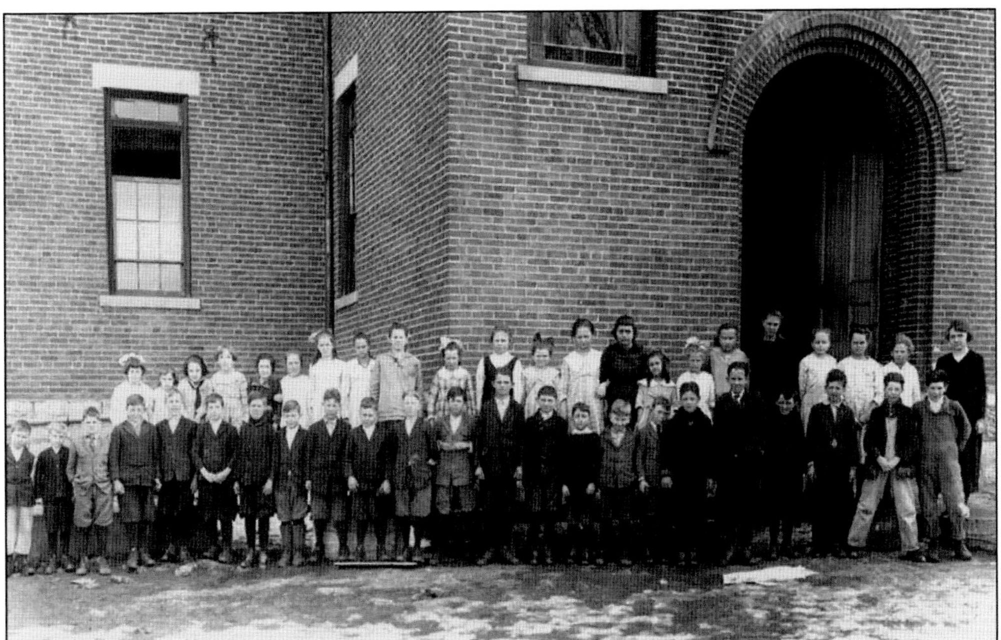

DESOTO SCHOOL AND CHILDREN. This photograph shows students standing in front of the school building on Third Street. (Photograph courtesy DeSoto Public Library.)

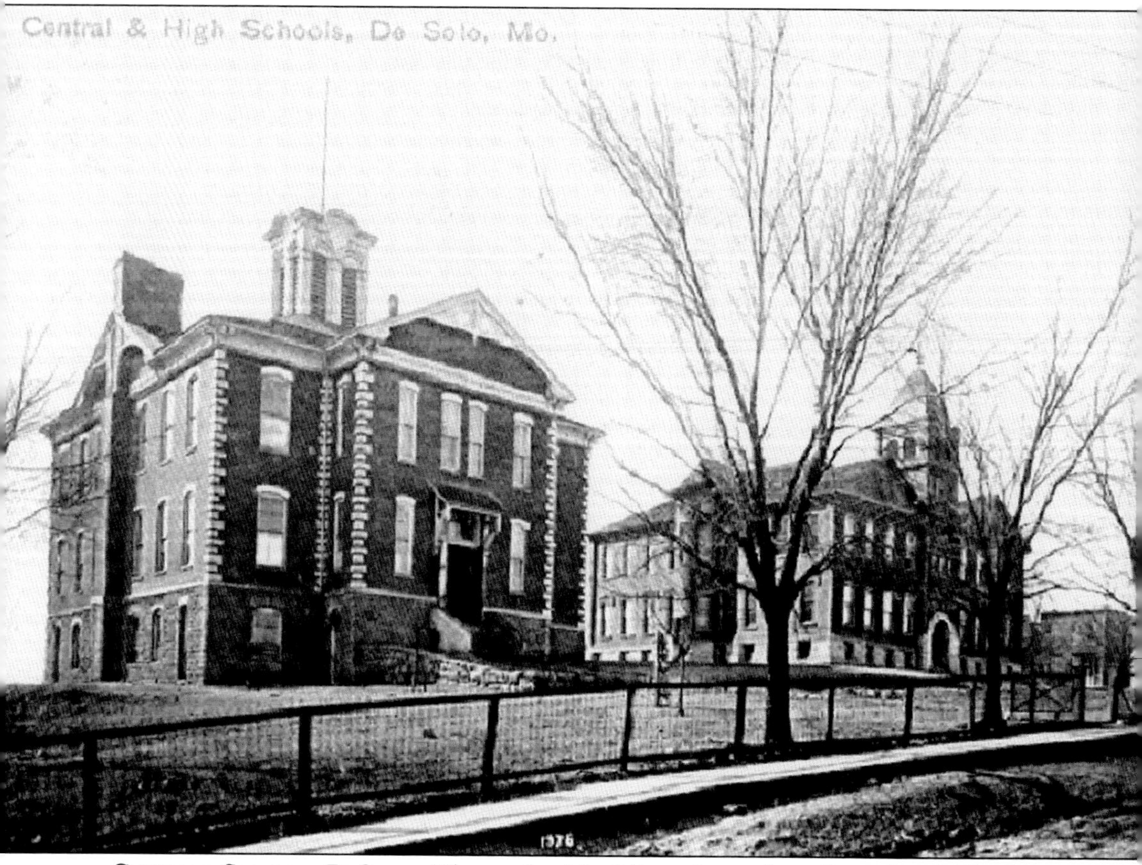

CENTRAL SCHOOL, DESOTO. These school buildings, located on Second and Third Streets, were replaced by the school buildings on Amvets Drive in DeSoto. (Photograph courtesy DeSoto Public Library.)

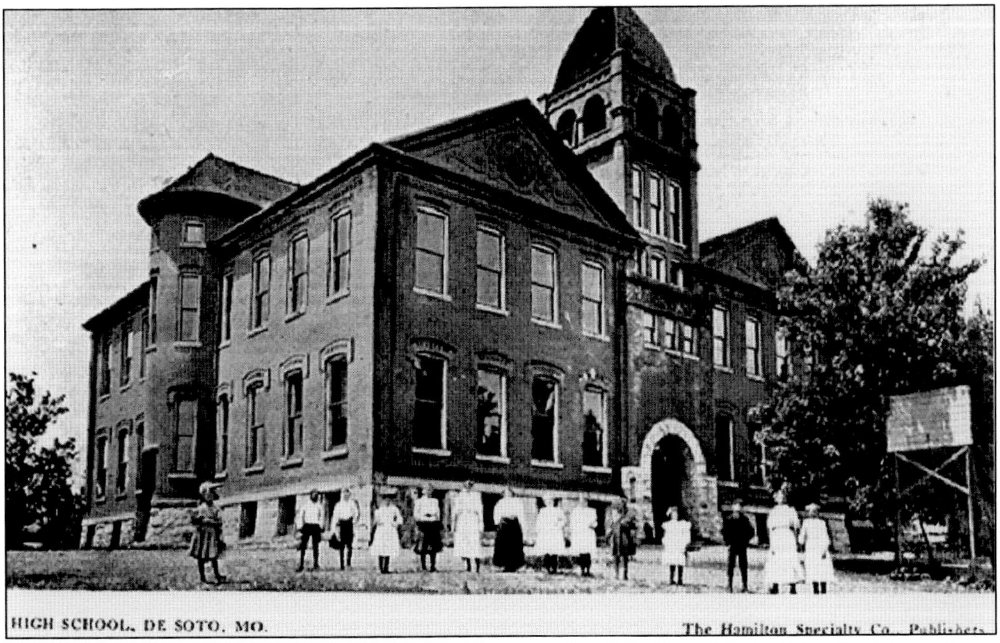

DESOTO HIGH SCHOOL. Shown here is a photograph of DeSoto High School with students standing in front of the building. (Photograph courtesy DeSoto Public Library.)

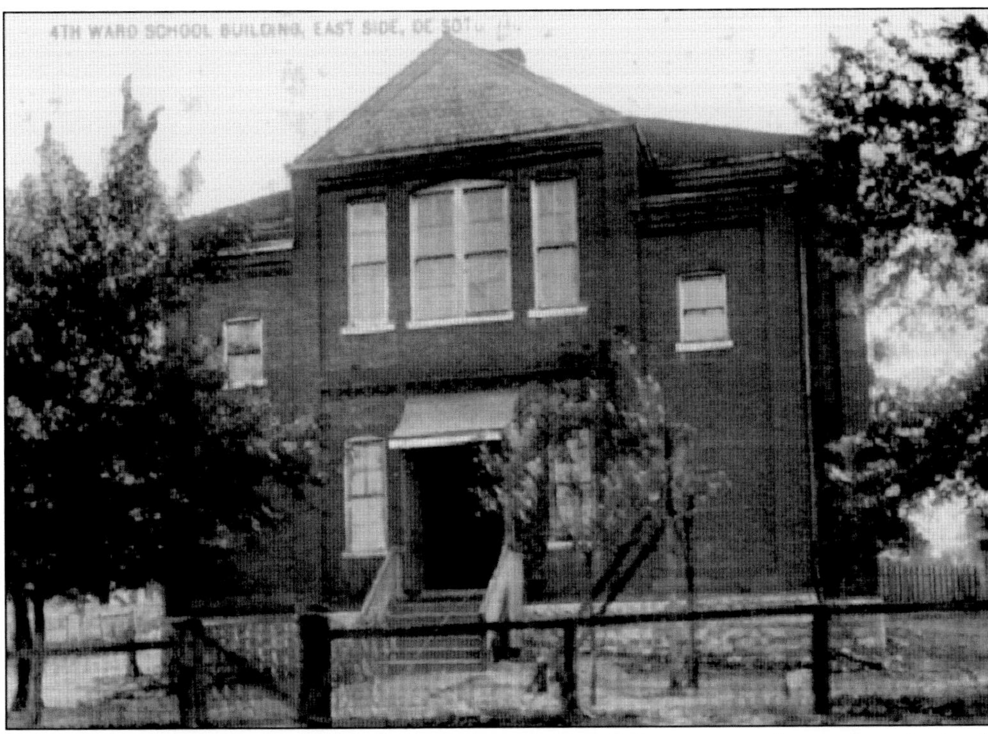

EAST WARD SCHOOL. This building, located on the East Side, was one of several ward schools in DeSoto. It is no longer used as a school. (Photograph courtesy DeSoto Public Library.)

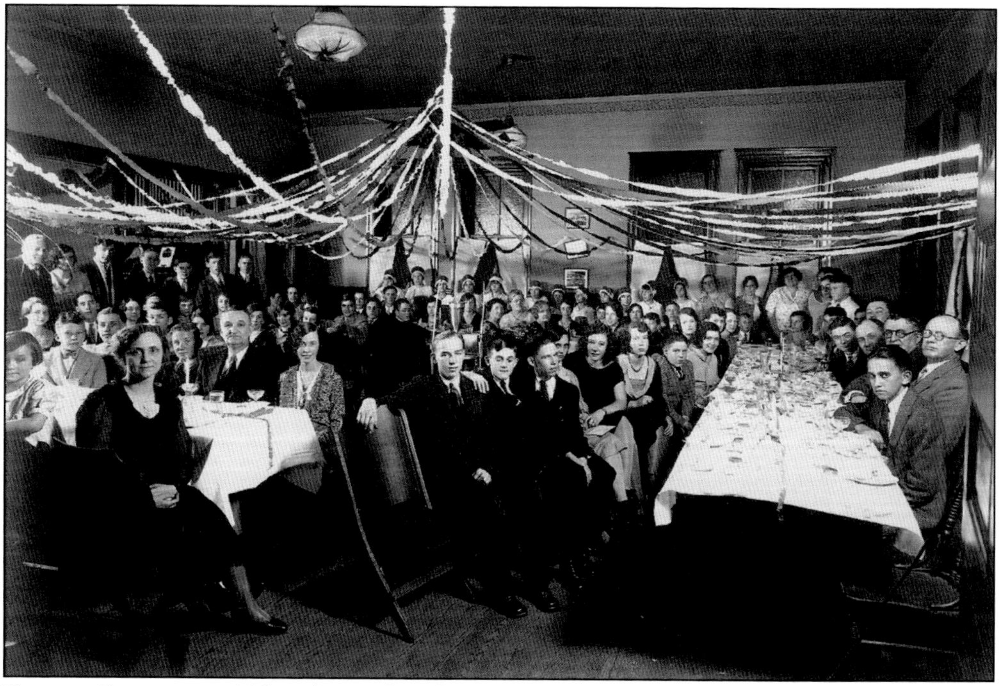

FESTIVE FUNCTION. Although no identification is given for this photograph, it is believed to be a gathering of students from DeSoto High School celebrating their graduation. (Photograph courtesy Fo-Jo Studio.)

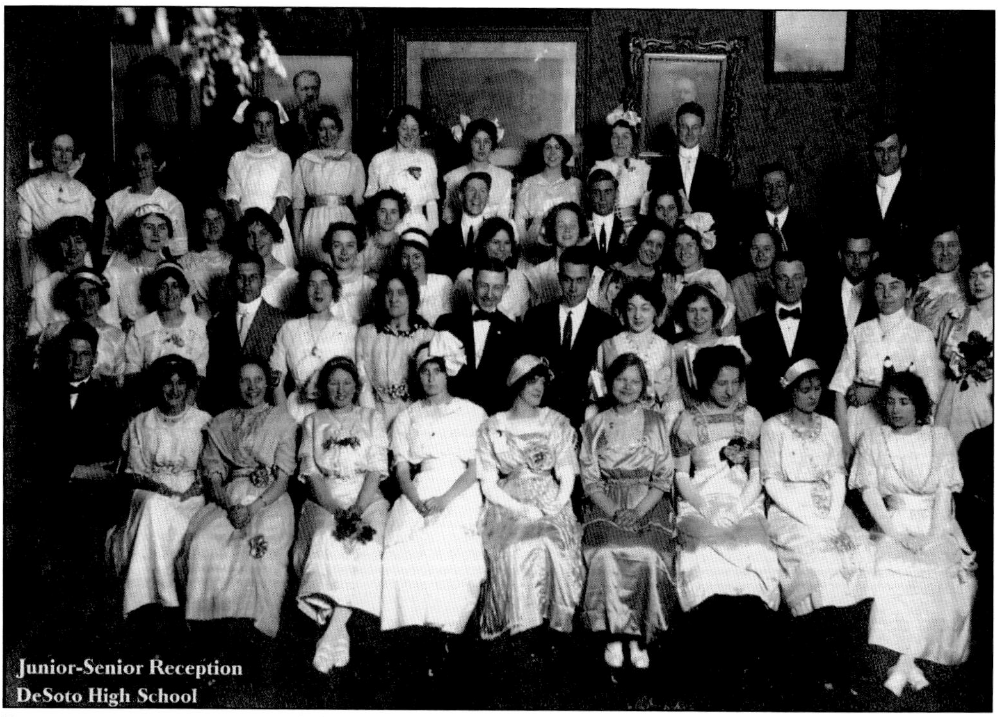

RECEPTION, 1913. Pictured here is the Junior-Senior Reception of DeSoto High School. (Photograph courtesy Fo-Jo Studio.)

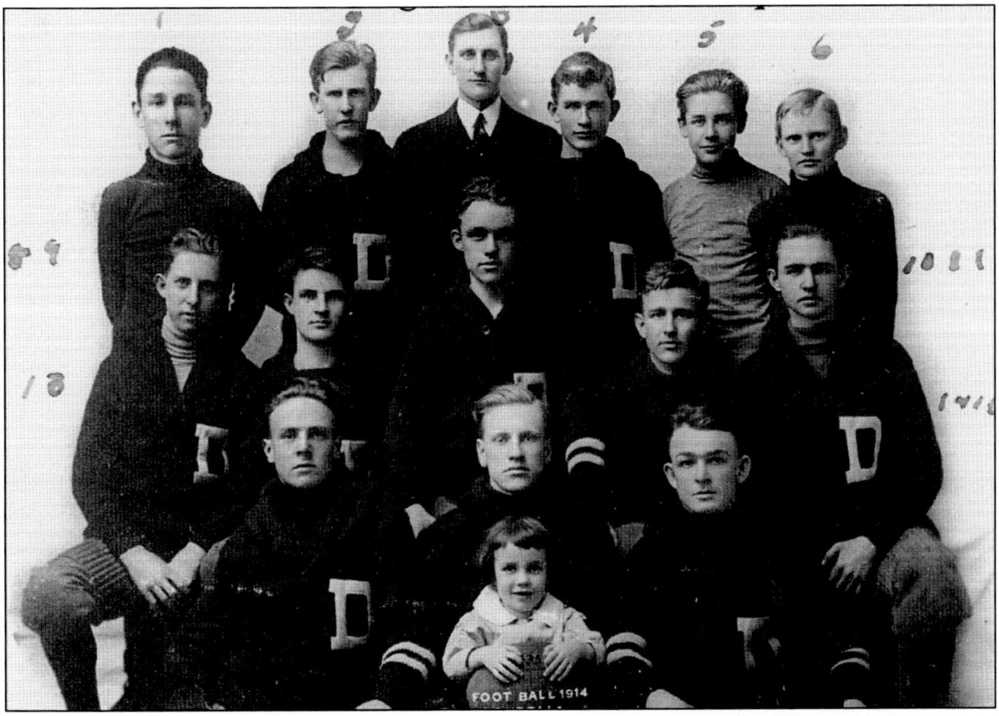

FOOTBALL TEAM, 1914. The football team poses for their photograph. (Photograph courtesy Fo-Jo Studio.)

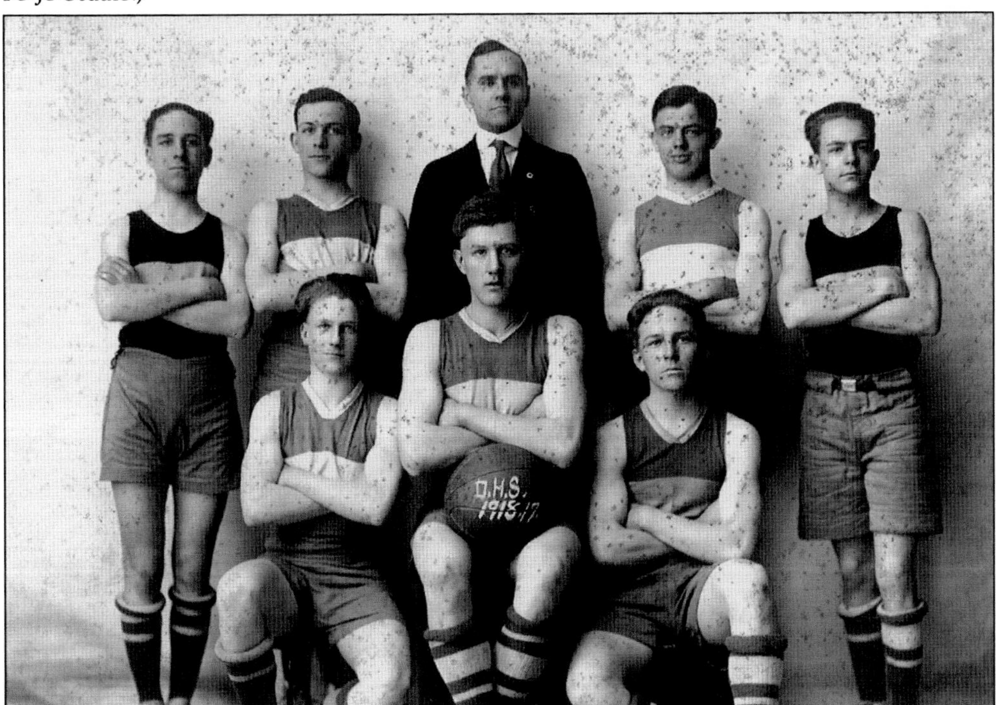

FOOTBALL TEAM. The football team of 1916 is pictured here. (Photograph courtesy Fo-Jo Studio.)

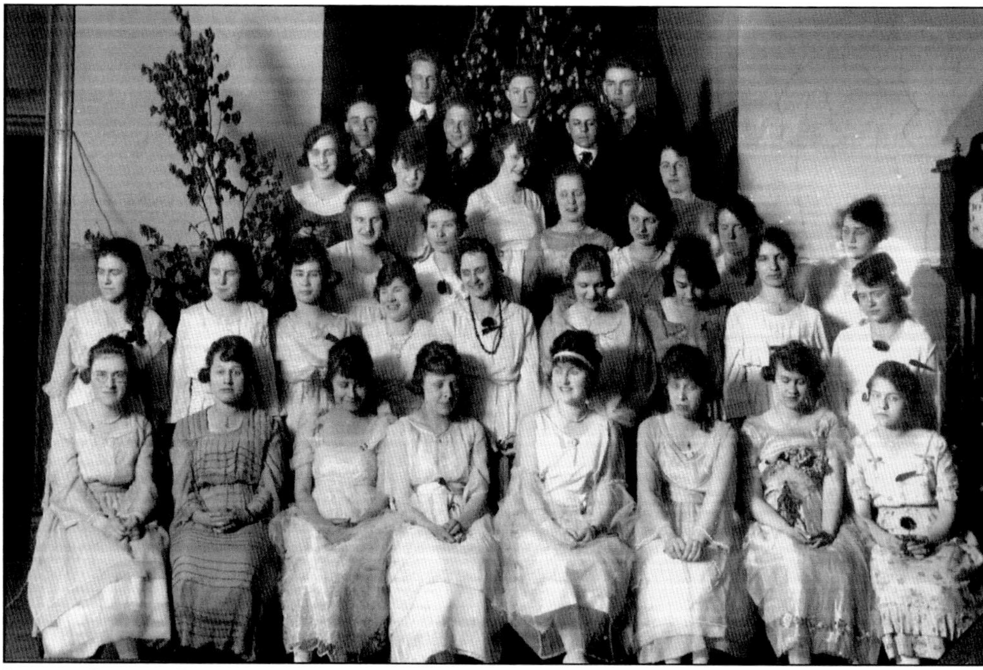

JUNIOR-SENIOR CHRISTMAS PARTY, 1919. Among the students attending this party are Marie Outman, Kathleen McBride, Hazel Haverstick, Hazel Kennedy, Alfreda Karte, Martha Mae Boyer, Marian Zorn, Marguerite Roop Schwaegerle, Clara Knauer Ritterbush, Lula Matthews, Rachel Farley, Gertrude Farley, Harold Brackman, Helen Wyler, Elmer Belew, Fred Mews, Chick Hopson, and Roy Blanton. (Photograph courtesy DeSoto Historical Society.)

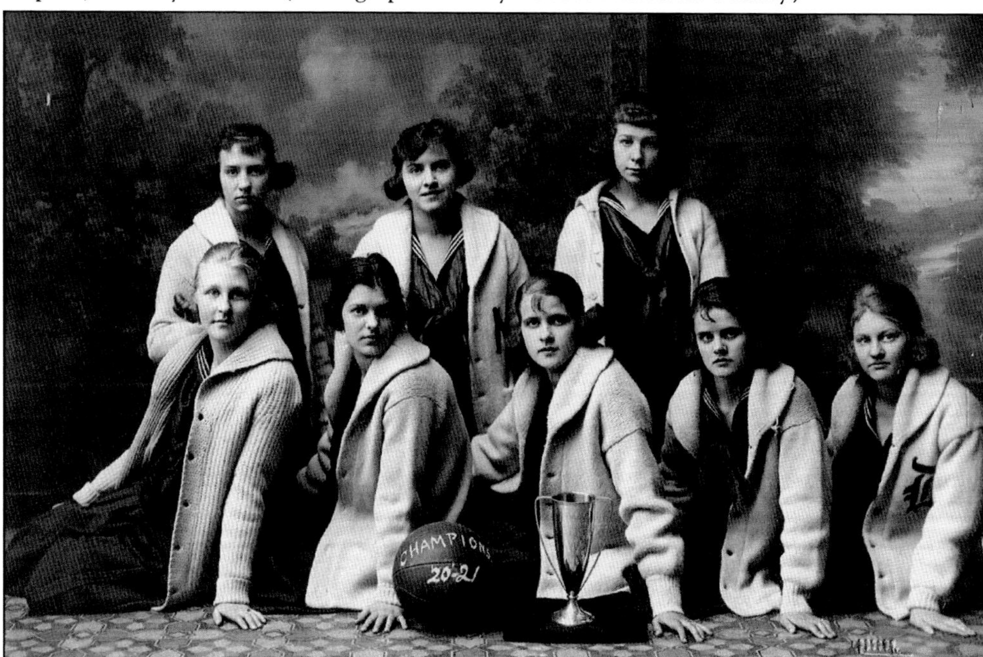

GIRLS' TEAM, 1920. This DeSoto girls basketball team were champions in 1920–1921. (Photograph courtesy Fo-Jo Studio.)

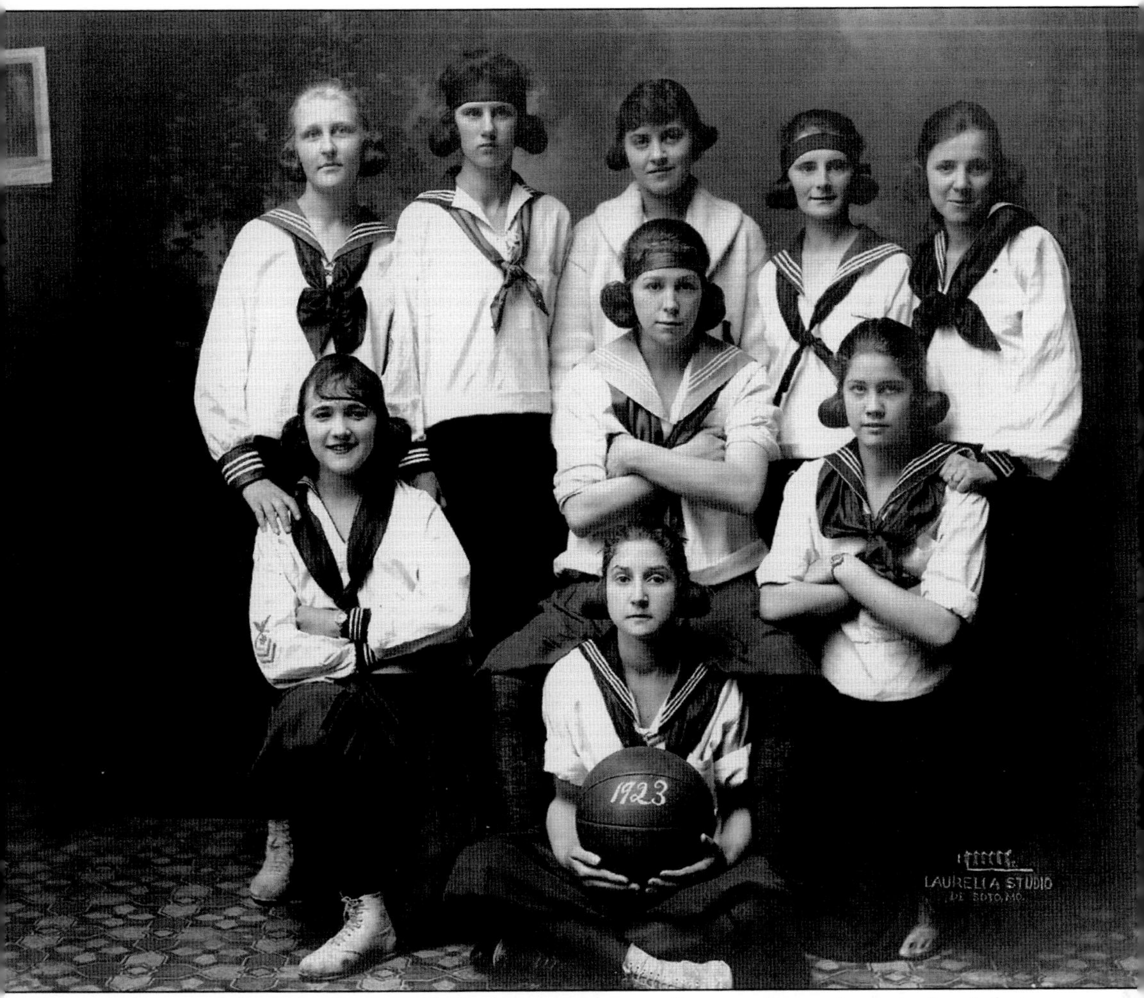

GIRLS' TEAM, 1923. The DeSoto High School girls proudly pose for a photograph of their basketball team. (Photograph courtesy Fo-Jo Studio.)

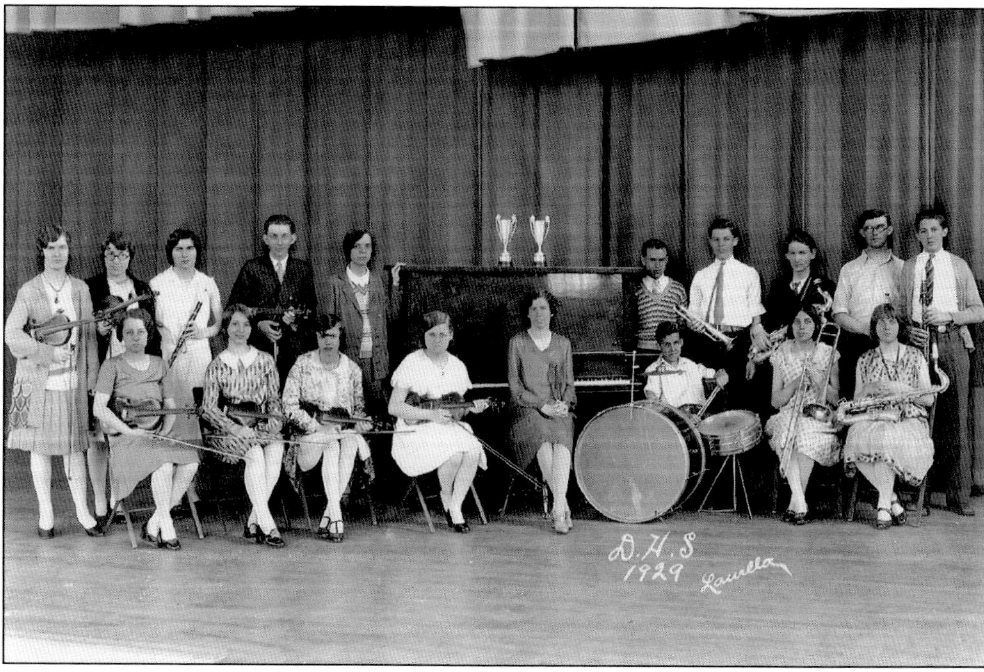

DESOTO SENIOR HIGH ORCHESTRA, 1929. The members of the DeSoto Senior High Orchestra and their instructor pose for their photograph. Trophies on the piano indicate honors received by this group. (Photograph courtesy Fo-Jo Studio.)

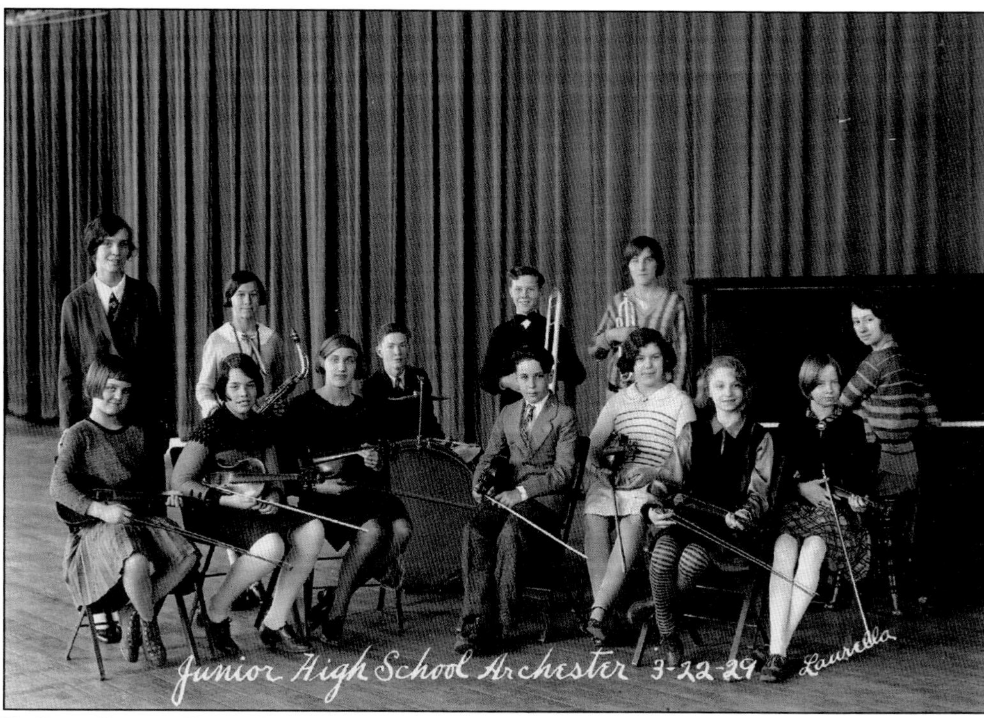

DESOTO JUNIOR HIGH ORCHESTRA, 1929. Pictured here is the Junior High School Orchestra with instruments in hand. (Photograph courtesy Fo-Jo Studio.)

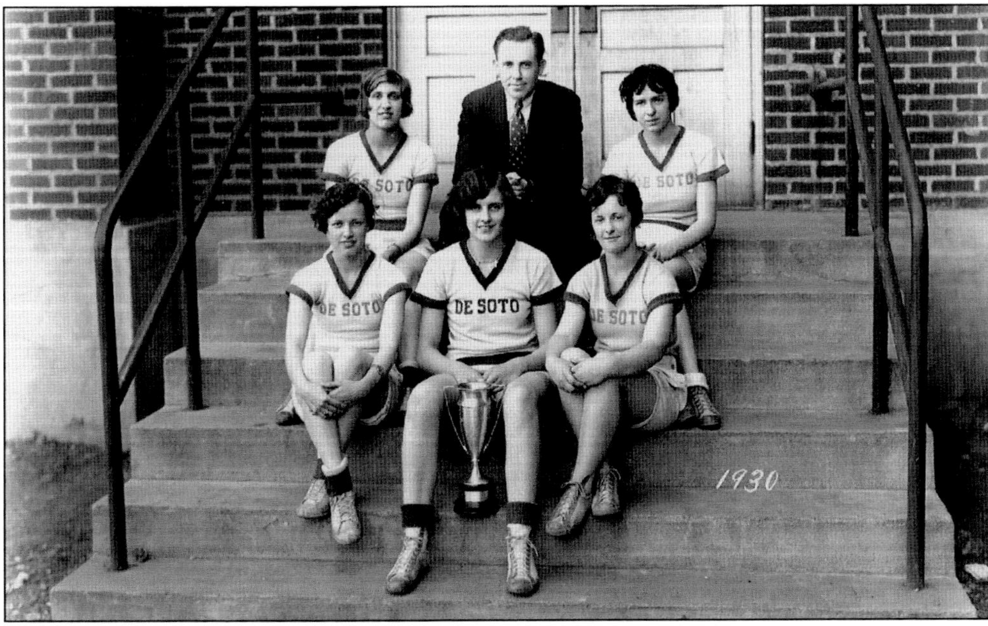

GIRLS ON STEPS, 1930. These five athletes pose with their coach and with their coveted trophy. Identified here are Grace Mills, Lois Rohlfing, Una Baygents, Marie Hacke, Ralph Pool, and Alice Underwood. (Photograph courtesy Fo-Jo Studio.)

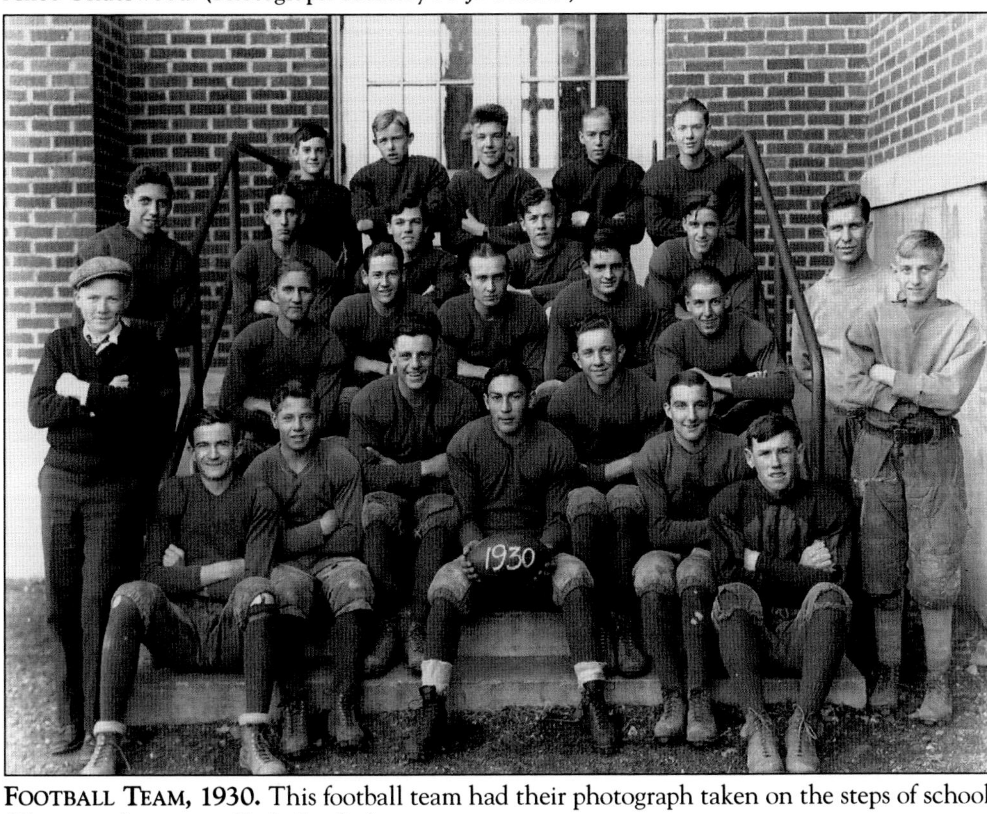

FOOTBALL TEAM, 1930. This football team had their photograph taken on the steps of school. (Photograph courtesy Fo-Jo Studio.)

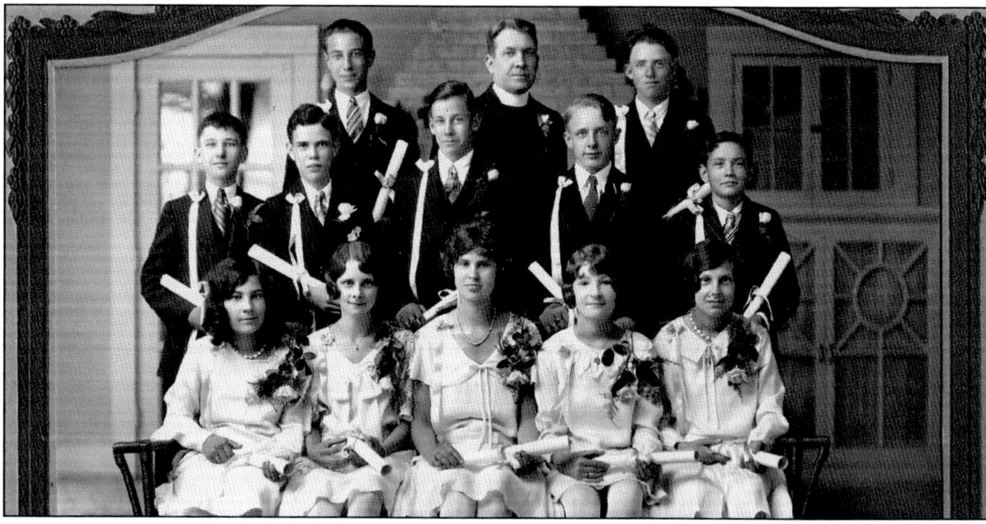

St. Rose of Lima Eighth-Grade Graduation Class, 1930. The graduates pictured here are, from left to right, (first row) Lillian Pieschel, Dorothy Ponzar, Adelaide Camp, Erma Bayer, and Bernice Solomon; (second row) Oscar Baer, Dwight Milfeld, Walter Page, Henry Christ, and unidentified; (third row) Michael Datillo, Rev. Edward Rogers, and Harry Pope. (Photograph courtesy DeSoto Historical Society and Cathy Camp Roop.)

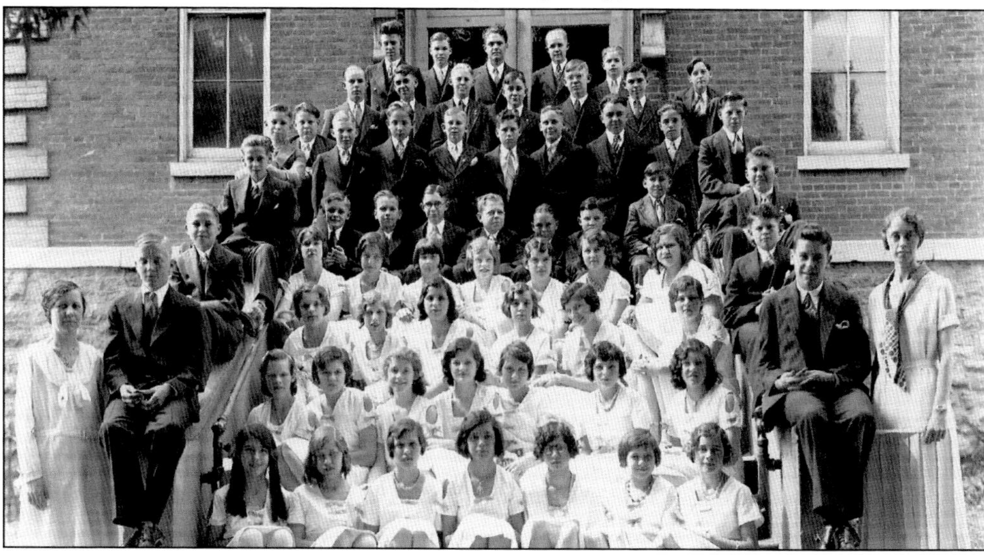

DeSoto Eighth-Grade Graduation Class, 1931. The students include (first row) Ruth Landau, Lisa Elmore, and Alice Hughes; (second row) Alpha Wall, Florence Merseal, Georgia Ann Dickey, Maxine Huskey, and Doris Burgess; (third row) Alma Miller; (fourth row) Evelyn Shepherd, Marie Houston, Helen Van Huesen, Ernestine Couch, Maxine Forrester, and Ruth Maness; (fifth row) Roy Huskey, Howard Hawkins, Enlo Boyer, and Eddie Bauer; (sixth row) Poston Whitehead, Ernest Kempe, J. R. Marshall, Curtis Cooper, Kenneth Blank, and Toby Reynolds; (seventh row) Forrest Mountford, Charles Clark, Cecil Covington, Frederick Hacke, Bill Ellis, and Kenneth Cheatham; (eighth row) Kenneth Fisher, and Wesley Lewis. Seated on left railing are Russell Goff, N. O. Boyer, Willard Leutzinger, and Karl Boyd. Seated on the right railing are Harrison Gibbon, Walter Walton, and Paul Dover. The teachers are Mary Rose Clyde (left) and Olive Fitch. (Photograph courtesy DeSoto Historical Society.)

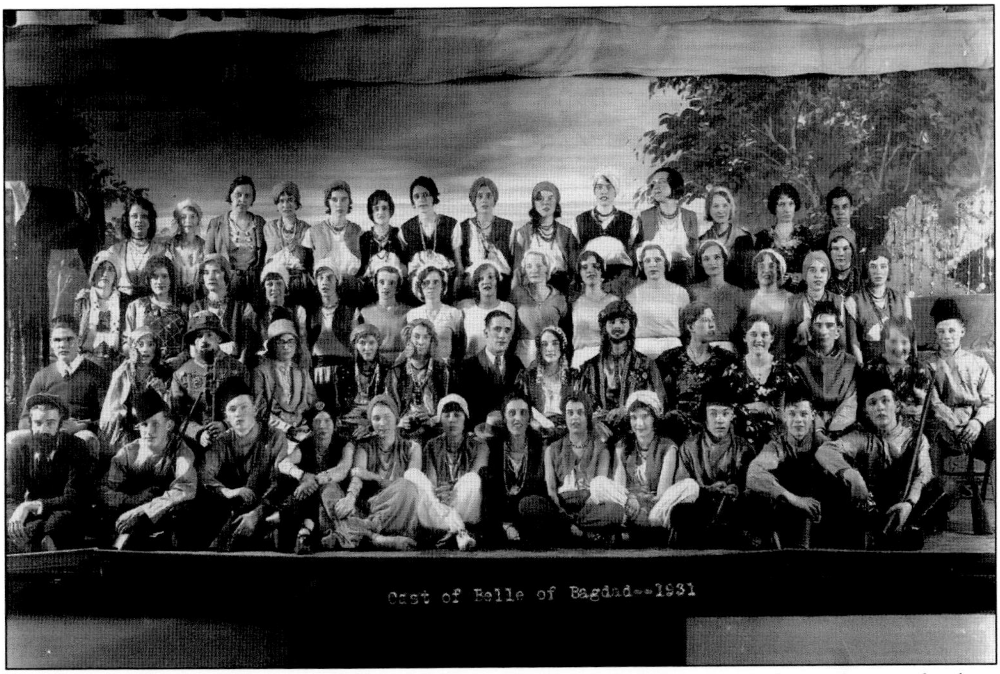

OPERETTA, "BELLE OF BAGDAD." The cast of the "Belle of Bagdad," presented in 1931, pose for their photograph on the stage at DeSoto High School Auditorium. (Photograph courtesy Fo-Jo Studio.)

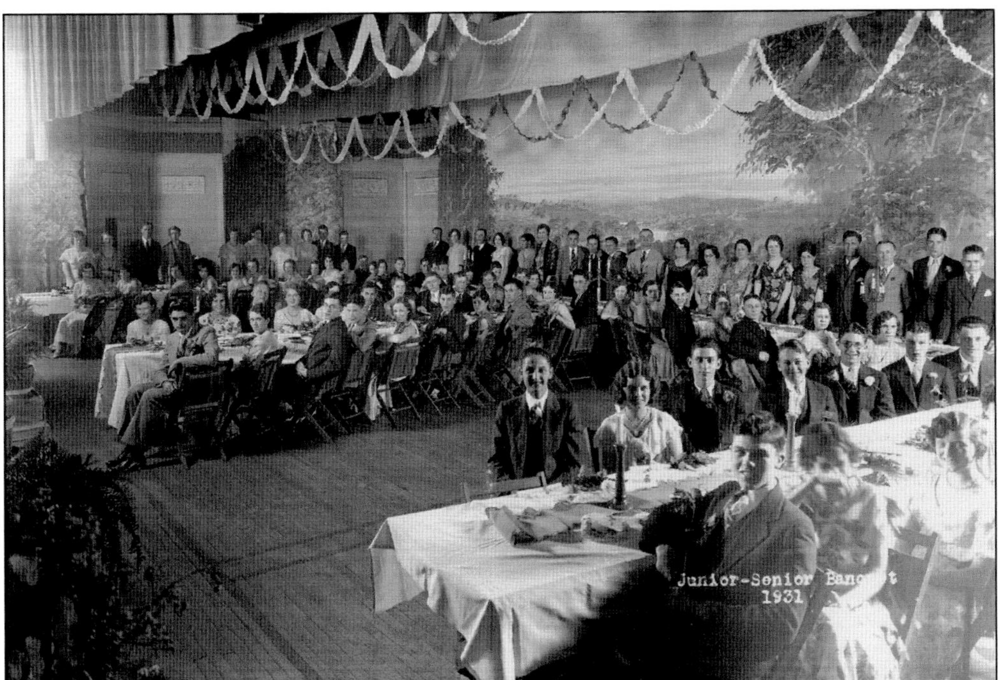

DESOTO HIGH JUNIOR-SENIOR BANQUET, 1931. This annual function took place on the stage of the auditorium in the high school, now Central Auditorium. (Photograph courtesy Fo-Jo Studio.)

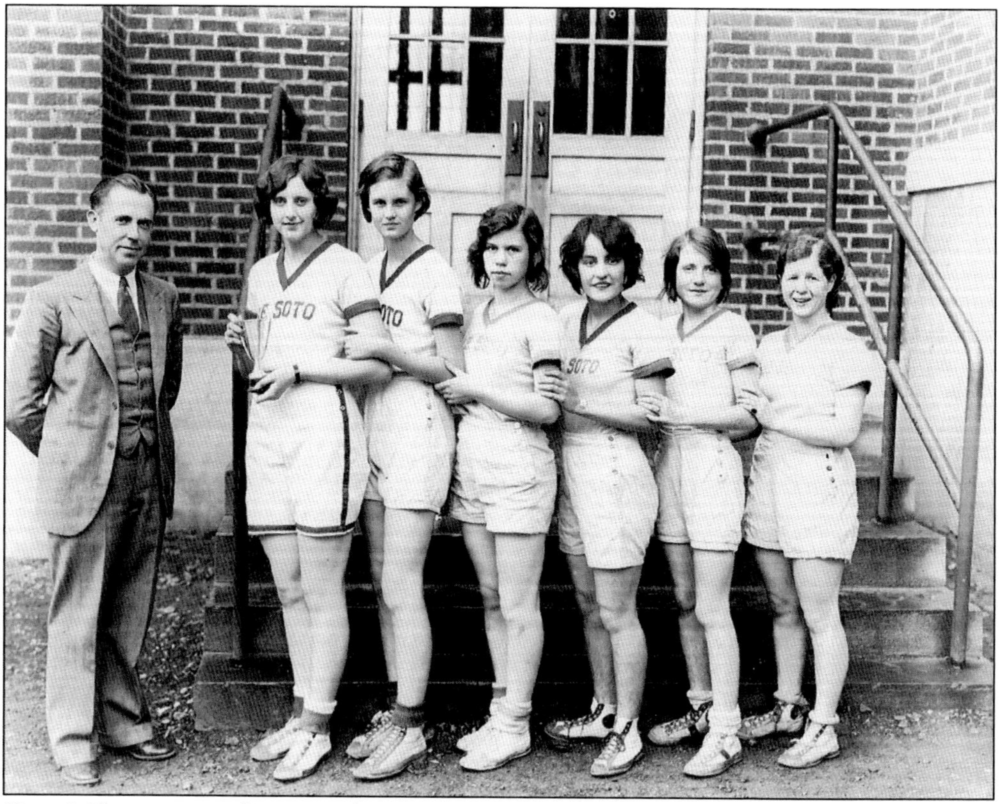

GIRLS' TEAM, WITH COACH. These six girls pose with their coach. (Photograph courtesy Fo-Jo Studio.)

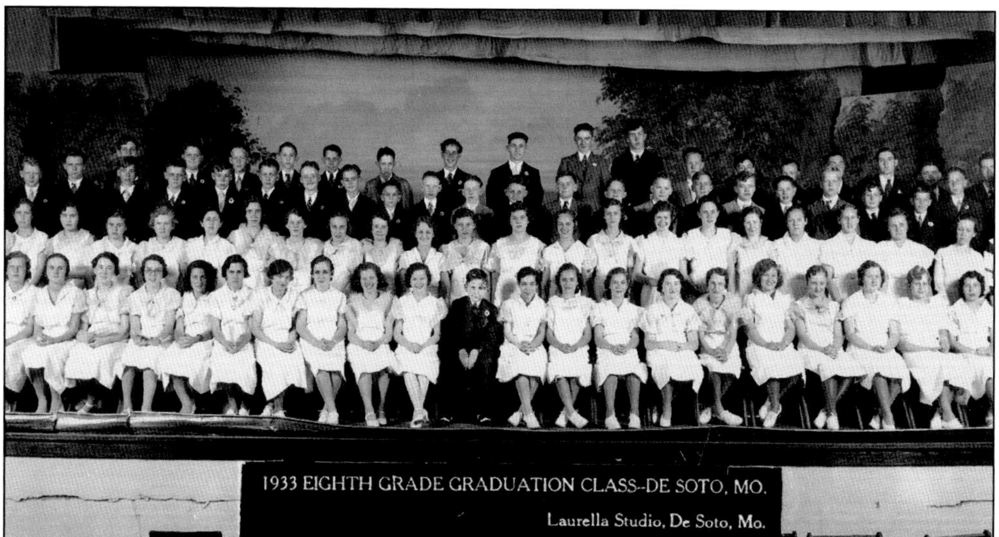

DESOTO GRADUATION CLASS, 1933. This photograph was taken on the stage of the auditorium in the high school, now Central Auditorium. (Photograph courtesy DeSoto Historical Society.)

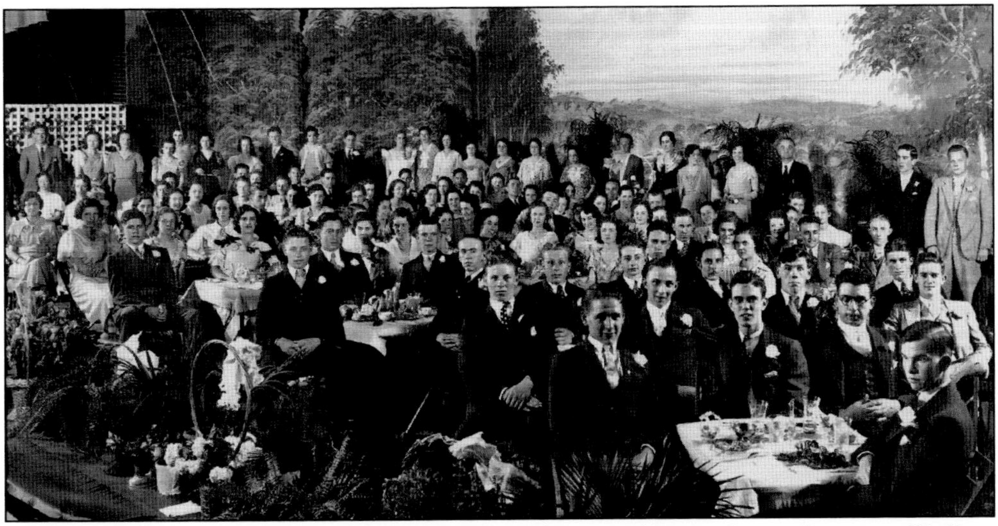

DESOTO HIGH JUNIOR-SENIOR BANQUET, 1933. The annual Junior-Senior Banquet of DeSoto High School students was held on the stage of the high school auditorium. (Photograph courtesy Fo-Jo Studio.)

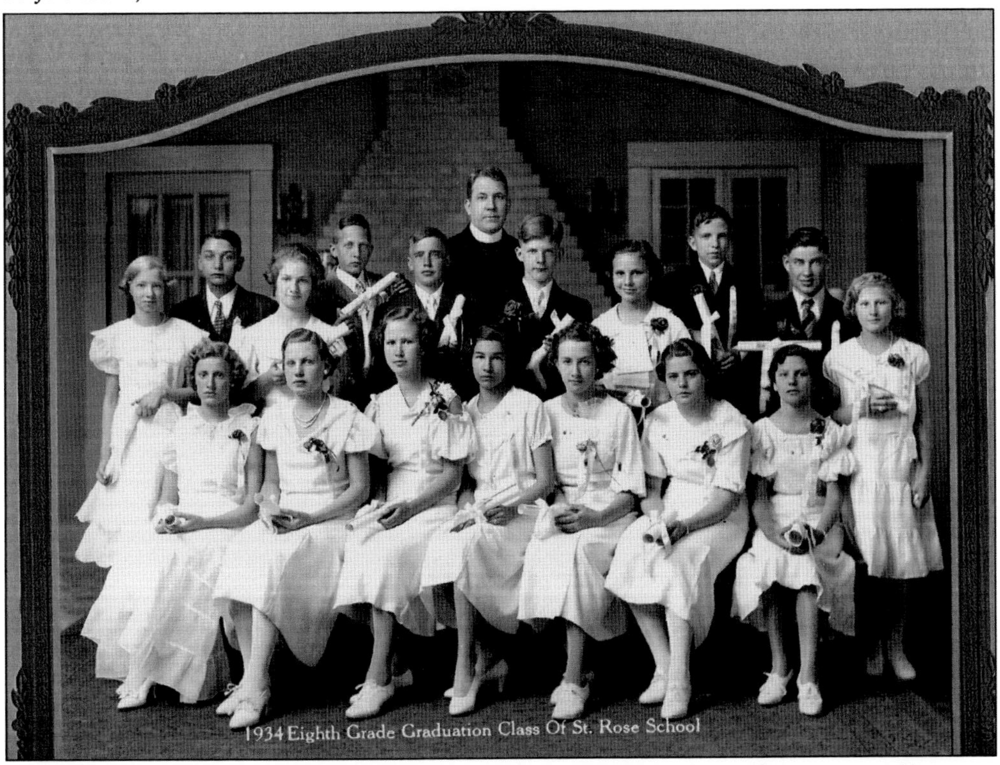

ST. ROSE OF LIMA EIGHTH-GRADE GRADUATION CLASS, 1934. The graduates pictured here are, from left to right, (first row) Lorraine Windmoeller, Mildred Simon, Marian Camp, Josephine Pieschel, Margaret Burt, Ellen O'Rourke, and Evelyn Washburn; (second row) Agatha Cook, Mary Elizabeth Duffner, Christopher Westhoff, Edwin Gebken, Theresa Kraus, and unidentified; (third row) Raymond Hellwig, Jack Steffen, Rev. Edward Rogers (pastor), Paul Aubuchon, and Robert Lacey. (Photograph courtesy DeSoto Historical Society and Cathy Camp Roop.)

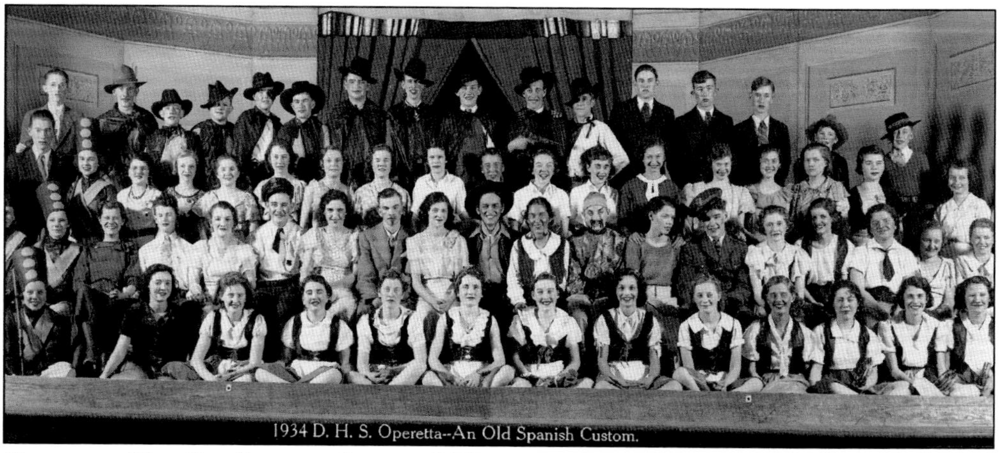

OPERETTA, "AN OLD SPANISH CUSTOM." This musical operetta was presented on the stage of the high school auditorium in 1934. (Photograph courtesy Fo-Jo Studio.)

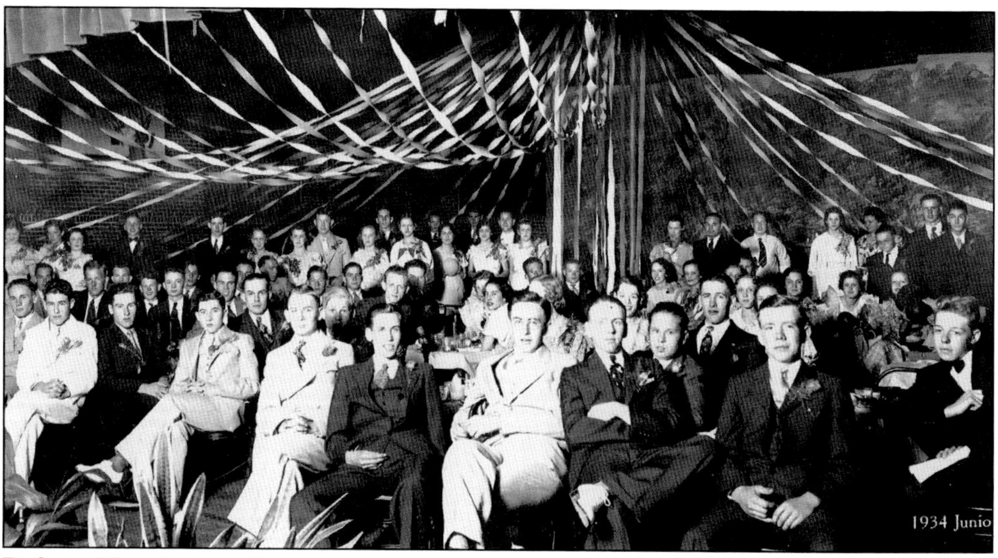

DESOTO HIGH JUNIOR-SENIOR BANQUET, 1934. The members of the Junior-Senior classes enjoy their annual banquet in the auditorium of the high school. (Photograph courtesy Fo-Jo Studio.)

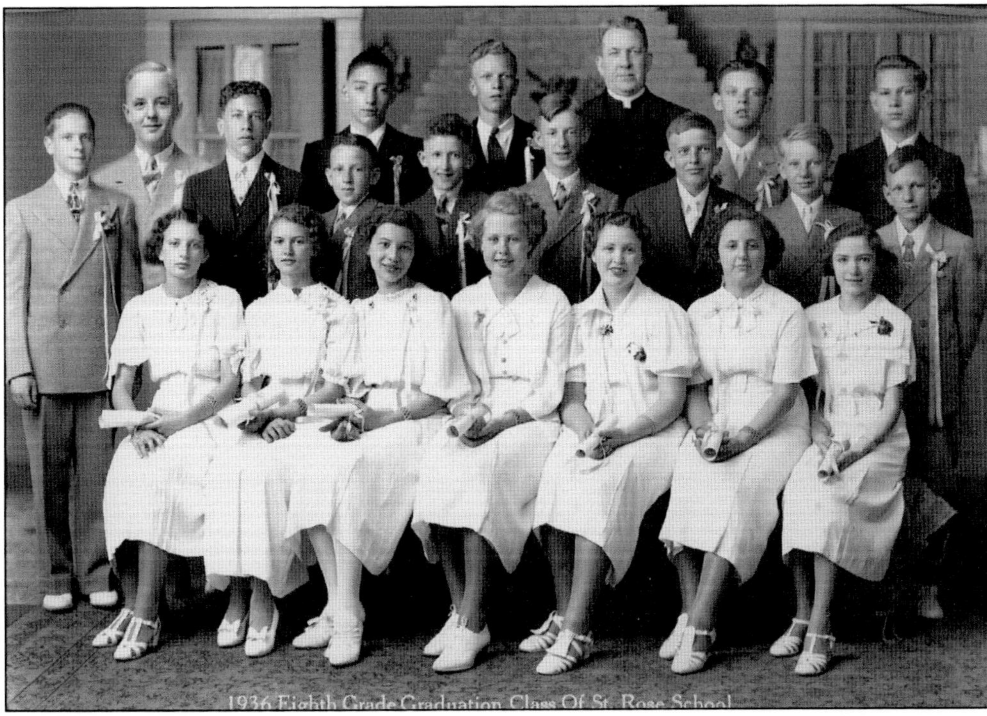

ST. ROSE OF LIMA EIGHTH-GRADE GRADUATION CLASS, 1936. The graduates pictured here are, from left to right, (first row) Dorothy Bayer, Mary Theresa Poncet, Marie Pieschel, Catherine Camp, Kathleen Recar, Helen Wilson, and Mildred Burke; (second row) Herbert Washburn, Andrew Datillo, Eugene Wilson, William Mahn, Joseph Rosenthal, Paul Westhoff, William Bayer, and Kevin Ohlman; (third row) James Collins, Frank Micke, Philip Bradford, Rev. Edward Rogers (pastor), Edward Pope, and Clarence Ponzar. (Photograph courtesy DeSoto Historical Society and Cathy Camp Roop.)

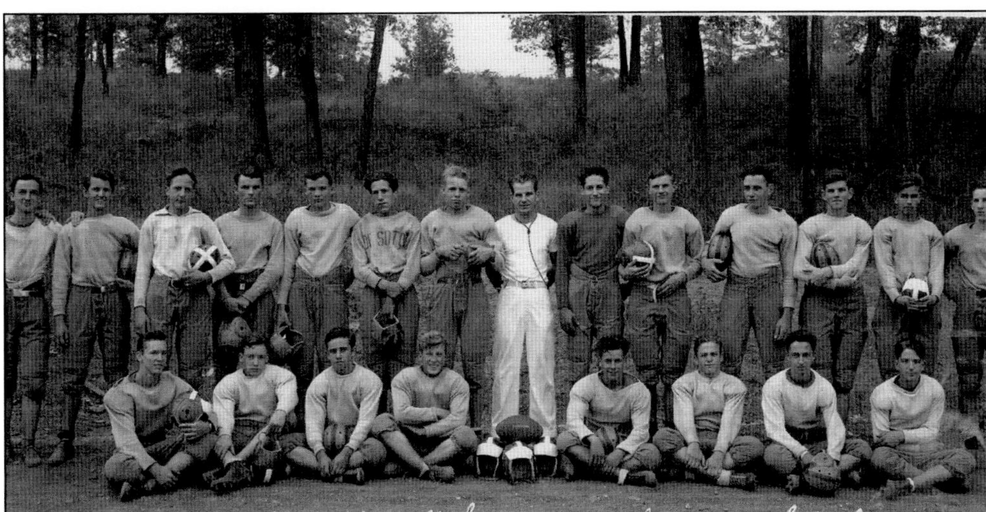

FOOTBALL TEAM, 1937. The football squad pose with their coaches on the field for this photograph. (Photograph courtesy Fo-Jo Studio.)

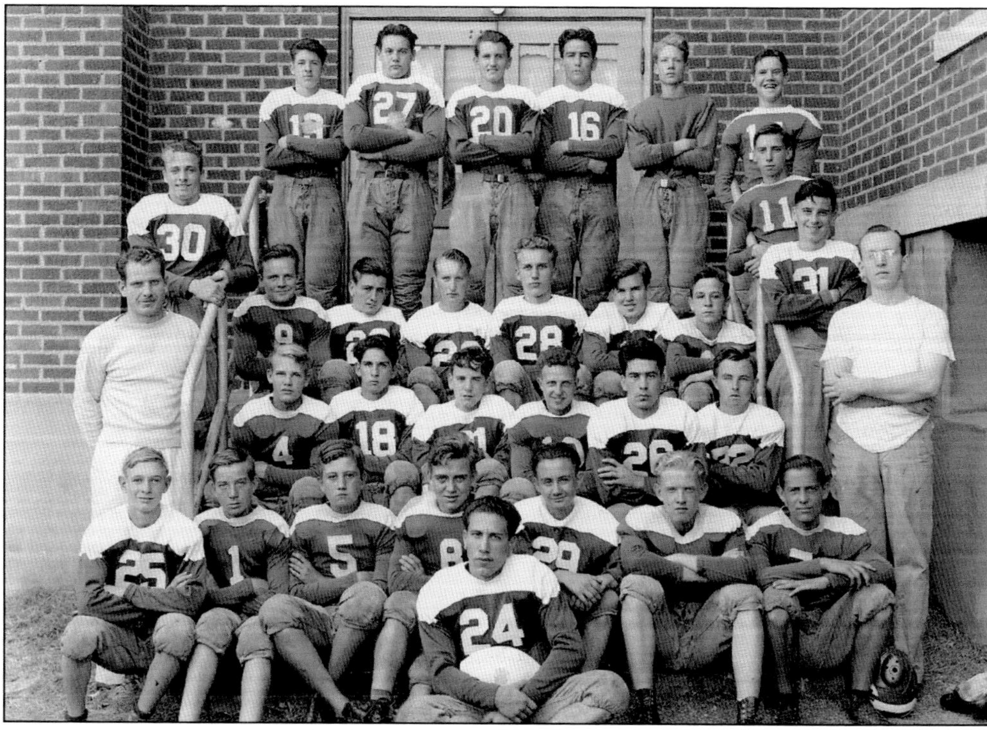

FOOTBALL TEAM, 1939. The football squad are seen here with their coaches on the side steps of the school. (Photograph courtesy Fo-Jo Studio.)

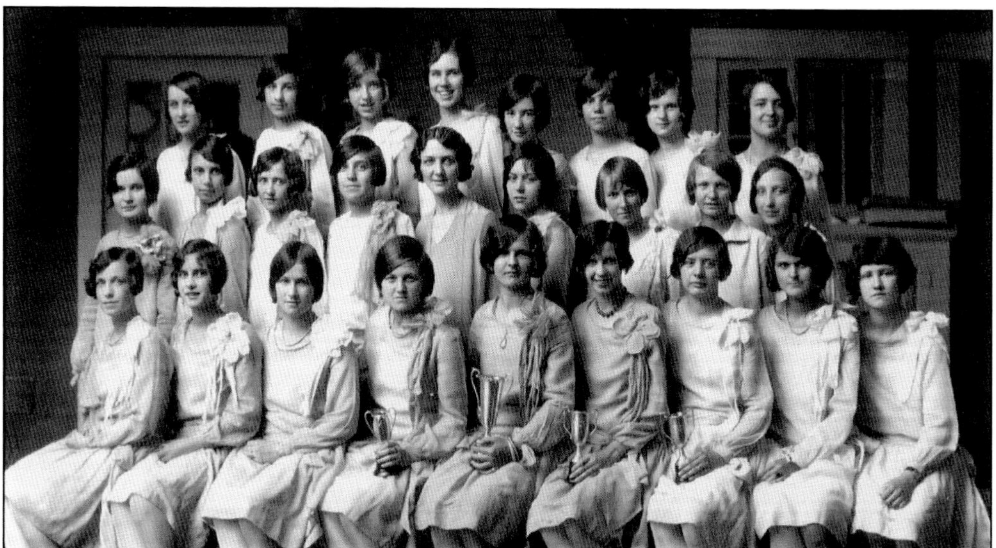

DESOTO HIGH SCHOOL GLEE CLUB. The students pictured here are, from left to right, (first row) Violet Whaley, Virginia Lewis, Winnie Frasier, Louise Merseal, Flora Slade, Ada Whaley, Marian Gibbins, Geraldine Fauth, and Dora Milton; (second row) Virginia Donald, Janette Jones, Clara Tibbits, Virginia Hazard, V. Benson, Ercel Murphy, Dorothy Brady, Viola Day, and Mary Akins; (third row) Wilma Dorlac, Louise Courtway, Shirley Bell, Julia Bell, Alpha Scoggins, Sadie Claire Crow, Rebecca Boyd, and Ruth Rosenburg. (Photograph courtesy Fo-Jo Studio.)

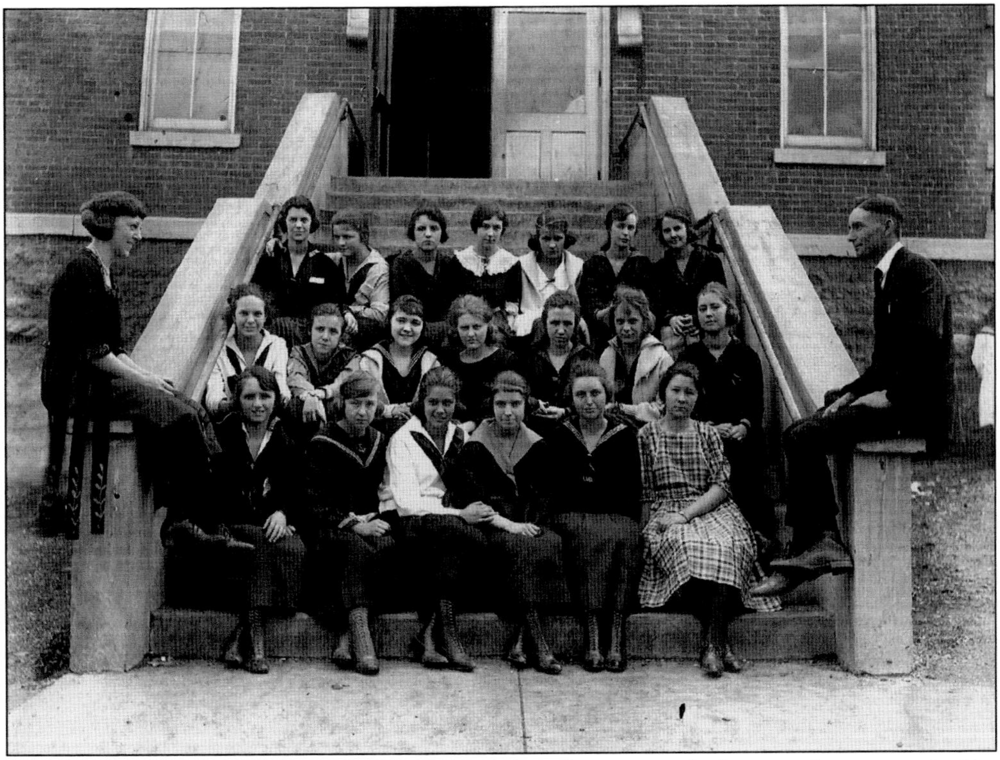

Student Group. This group of students, seated on the steps with their teachers on each side, are not identified except for Erna Seemel Culwell in the second row and Estelle Couch Pierce in the fifth row. (Photograph courtesy Fo-Jo Studio.)

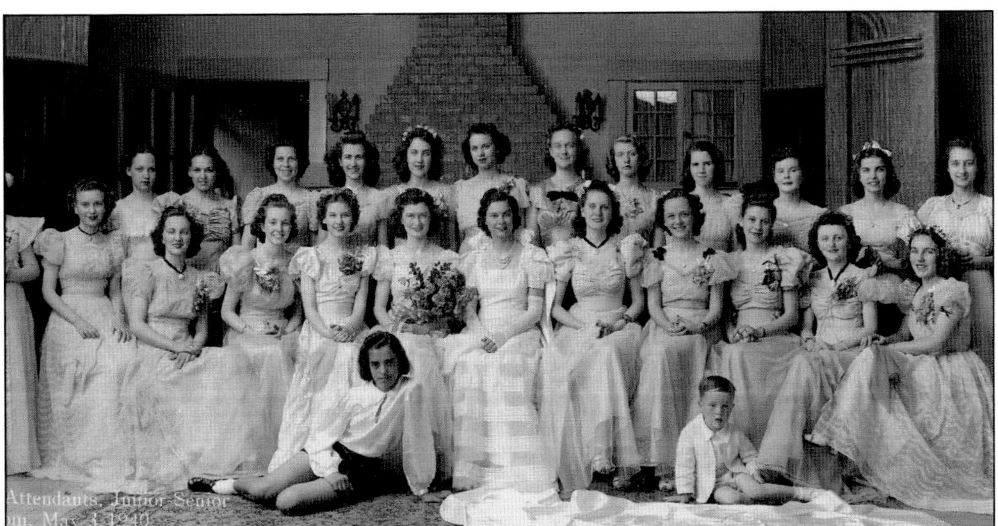

Junior-Senior Prom Queen, 1940. The Prom Queen and her attendants pose for a formal photograph to mark their memorable event. (Photograph courtesy Fo-Jo Studio.)

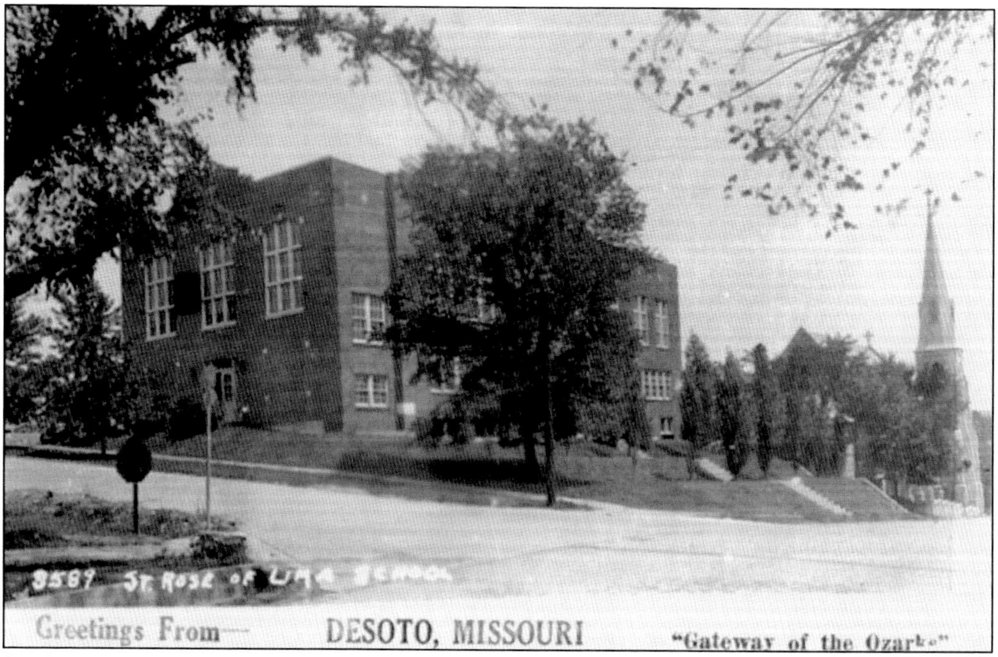

St. Rose of Lima School. St. Rose of Lima School started teaching classes in 1891 by the Ursuline Sisters from St. Louis. The present school building, located at Fourth and Miller Streets, was built in 1929. (Photograph courtesy DeSoto Public Library.)

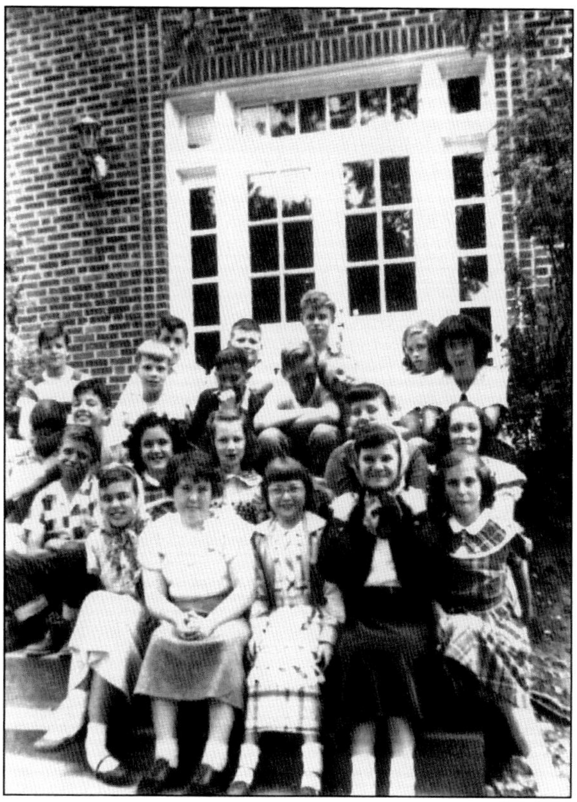

Students on Steps at St. Rose. These students were photographed on the steps of St. Rose of Lima School at the Miller Street entrance. (Photograph courtesy DeSoto Historical Society.)

Four

BUSINESSES

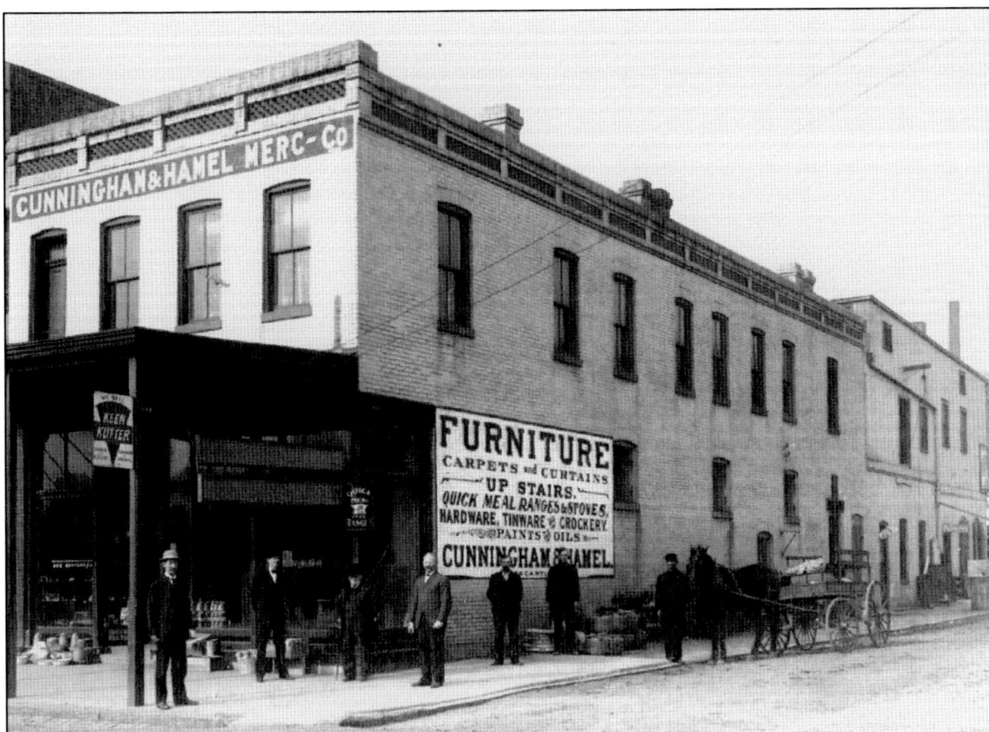

CUNNINGHAM AND HAMEL, MAIN AND PRATT STREETS. The men in this 1905 photo of the Cunningham and Hamel Store include Ward Cunningham, Ward A. Hamel, Gust Hamel, and Arch Blanks. (Photograph courtesy DeSoto Public Library.)

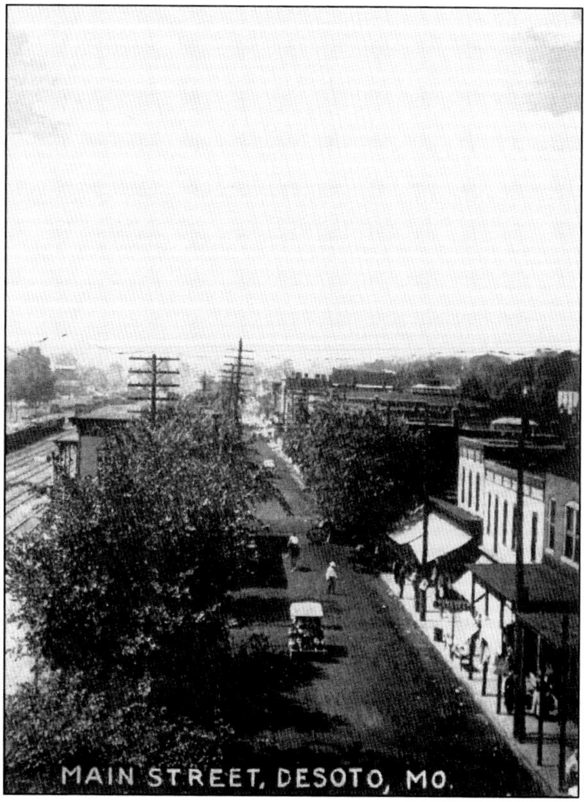

MAIN STREET, 1911. This photograph of Main Street shows the railroad station visible at the left. (Photograph courtesy DeSoto Public Library.)

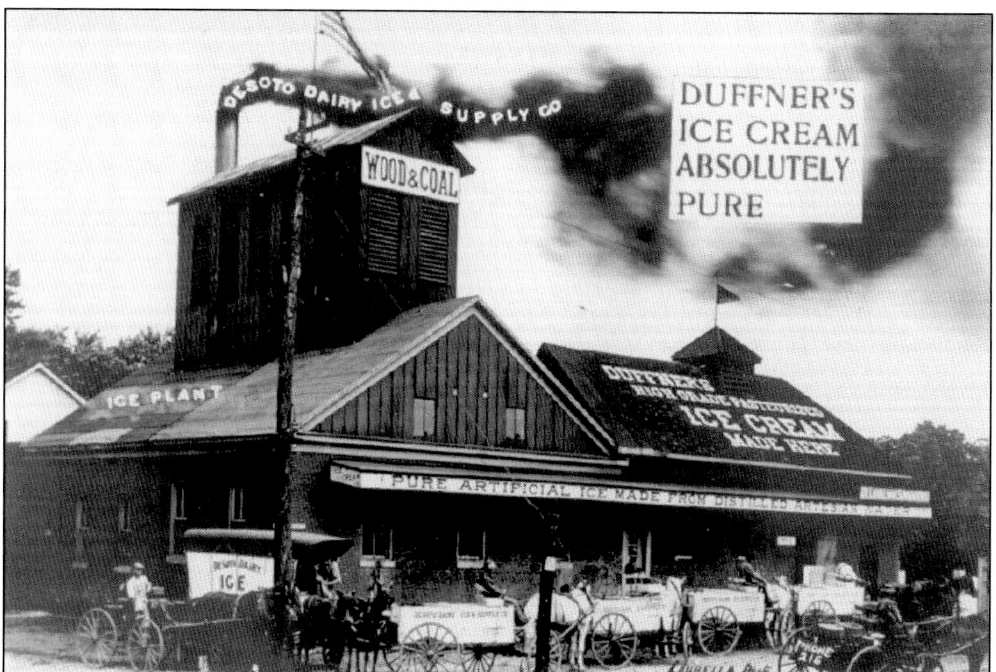

DUFFNER'S DAIRY. In 1911, this local dairy was an important source for ice cream and other dairy products. (Photograph courtesy DeSoto Public Library.)

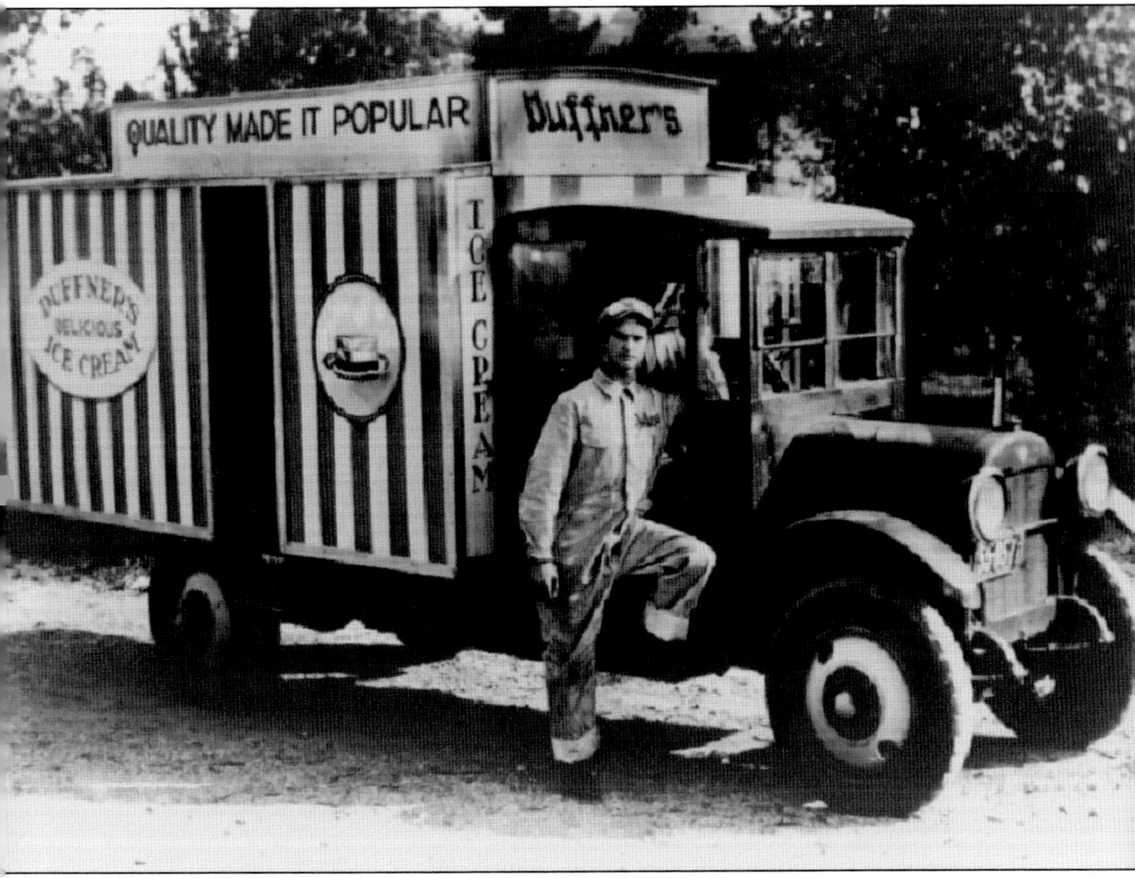

DUFFNER'S DAIRY TRUCK. The driver of this Duffner's Dairy Truck is Julius Finkins. The delivery of milk and other dairy products was an important feature of the Duffner Dairy. (Photograph courtesy DeSoto Public Library.)

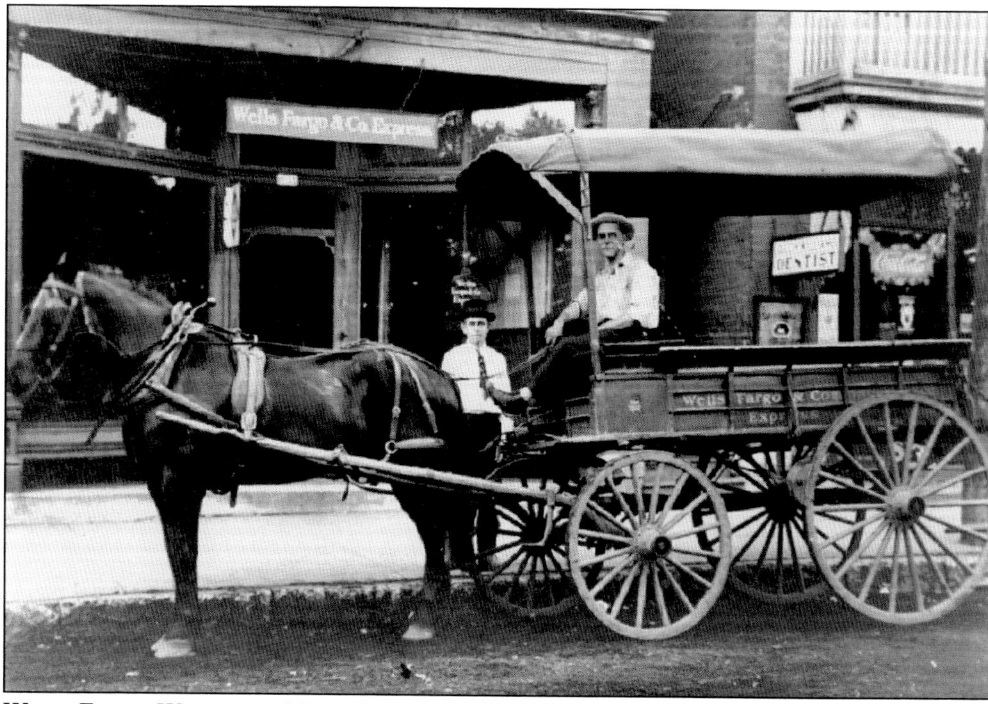

WELLS FARGO WAGON ON MAIN STREET. Wells Fargo Company had a location on Main Street in 1915 or 1916. The man pictured in this wagon is Ed Eaton. (Photograph courtesy DeSoto Public Library.)

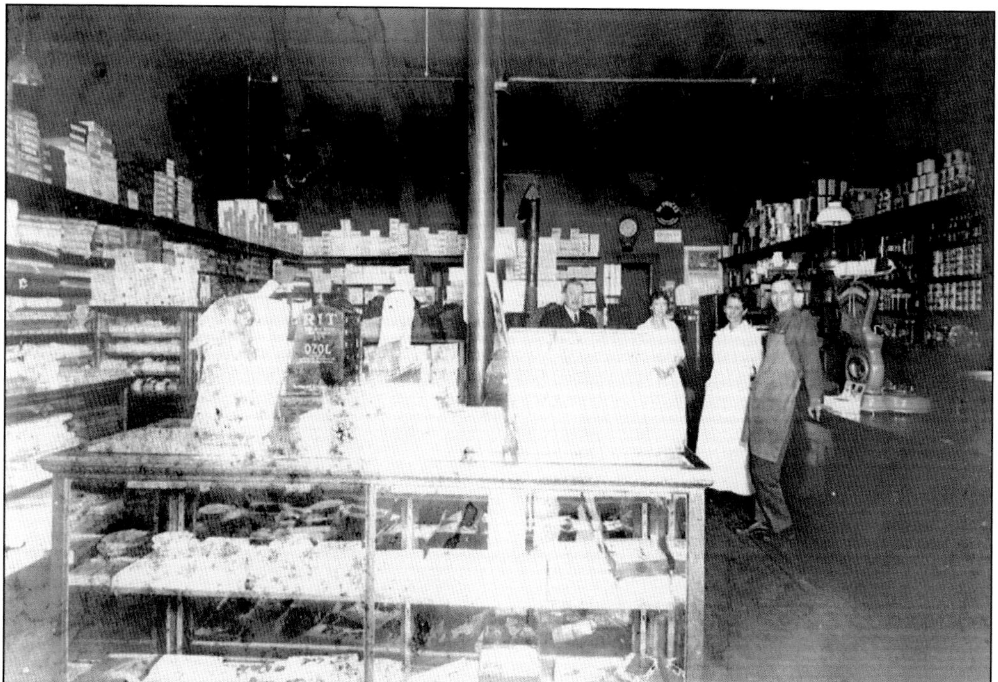

SCHMITZ GROCERY STORE, MAIN STREET. Among those pictured here are Frances Schmitz Eaton, Lillian Schmitz Sr., and Ferd Schmitz. (Photograph courtesy DeSoto Public Library.)

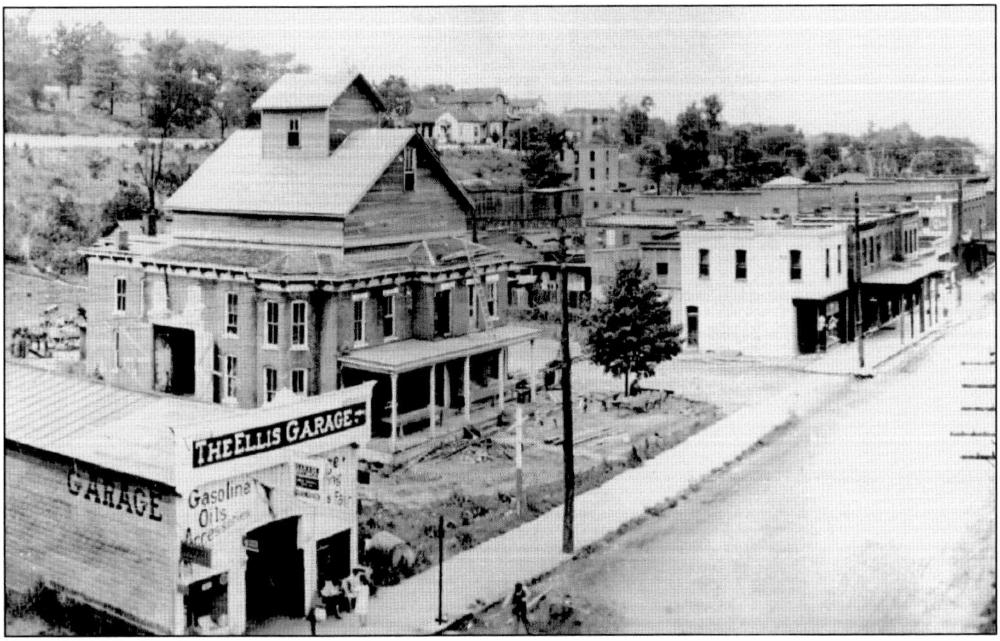

Ellis Garage, Main Street. Here is the Ellis Garage as it appeared in 1919, when it was located next to the Dietrich-Mothershead Funeral Home on Main Street. (Photograph courtesy DeSoto Public Library.)

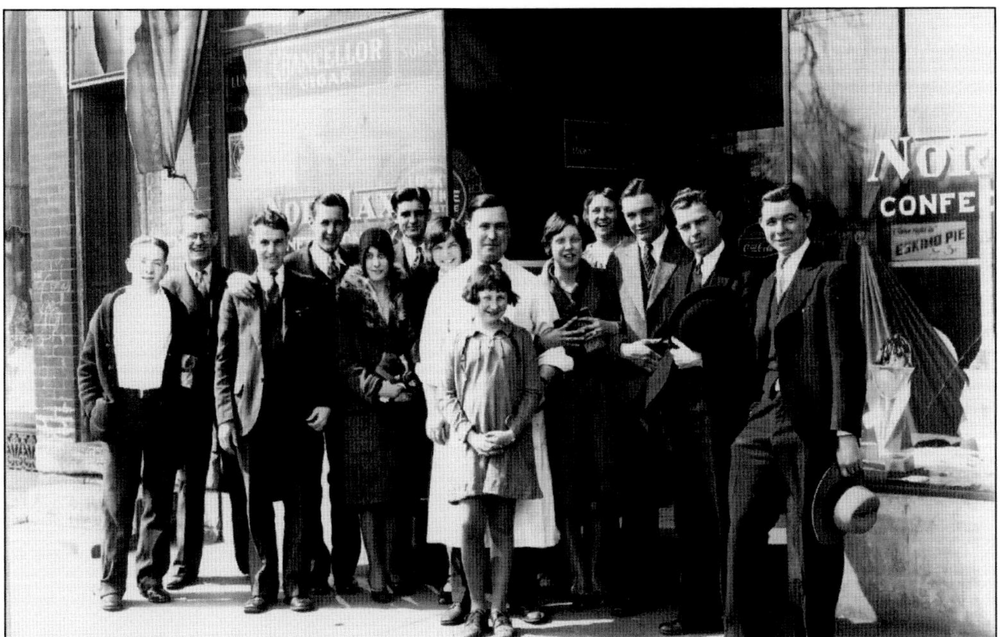

Group in Front of Nor-Max Confectionary, Main Street. Those pictured in this photo include Russell Goodnight, Vincent Carter, Eileen Stahl, unidentified, Max Schwaegerle, Doris Green (child), Dorothy Stahl, Jim Stroupe, Alfred Kaufman, Eddie Williams, James Rehm, Theodore Shell, Andy Agers, and Clara Tibbits. (Photograph courtesy DeSoto Public Library.)

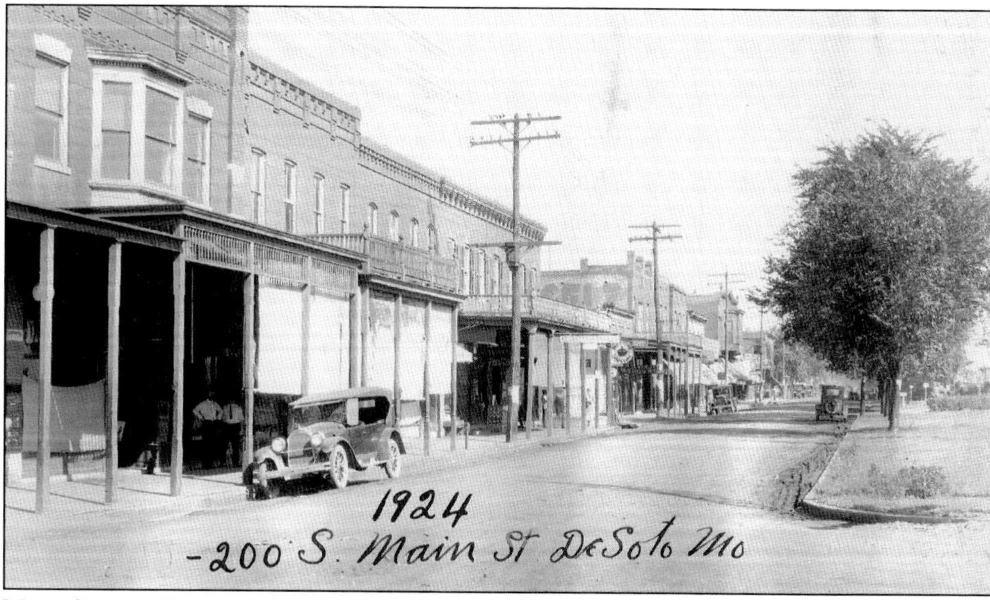

MAIN STREET, LOOKING SOUTH. This photograph, taken in 1924, shows only a few automobiles on Main Street. (Photograph courtesy DeSoto Public Library.)

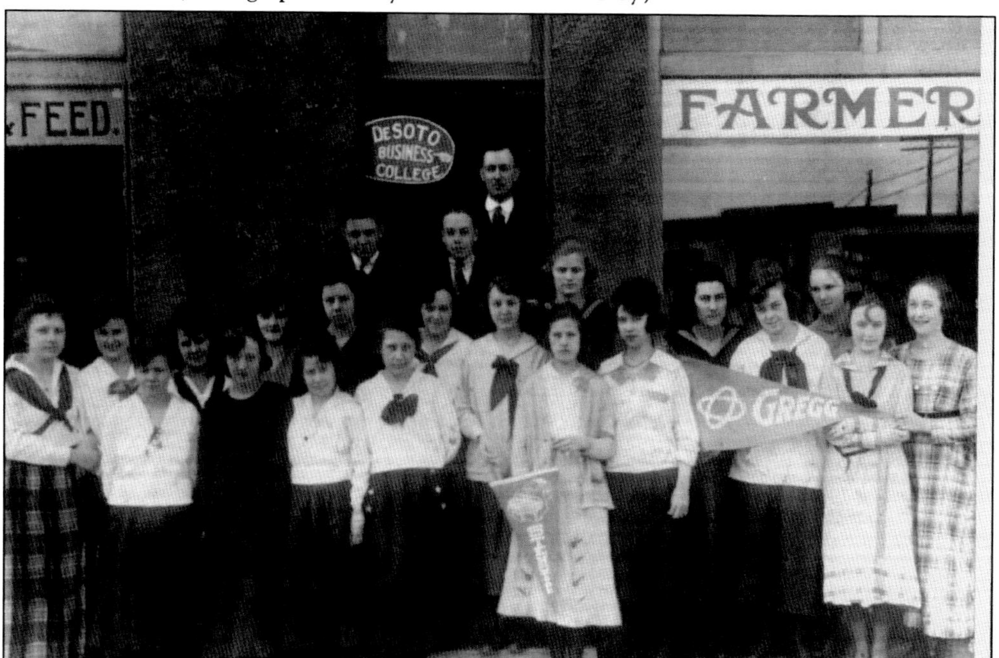

DESOTO BUSINESS COLLEGE, 11 BOYD STREET. Pictured in this photo are Hazel Haverstick Dorsey, Hazel Dodson, Edith Guinther, Leota Dover Hulsey, Carrie Pease, Nellie Forshee, Elida Johnson Kent, Gertrude Penley Hiffman, Helen Wilson Byington, Julia Kennedy Frazier, Zella Strother, Kathleen McBride Rozier, Adele Franey Muller, Julia Parmely Mary Staton Franey, Edith Pierce Maness, Gertrude Ingalls, Aurora Judicy, Easthel Hornsey, Creighton Turner, and William Staton. In the back is Harry Thomas, administrator. (Photograph courtesy DeSoto Public Library.)

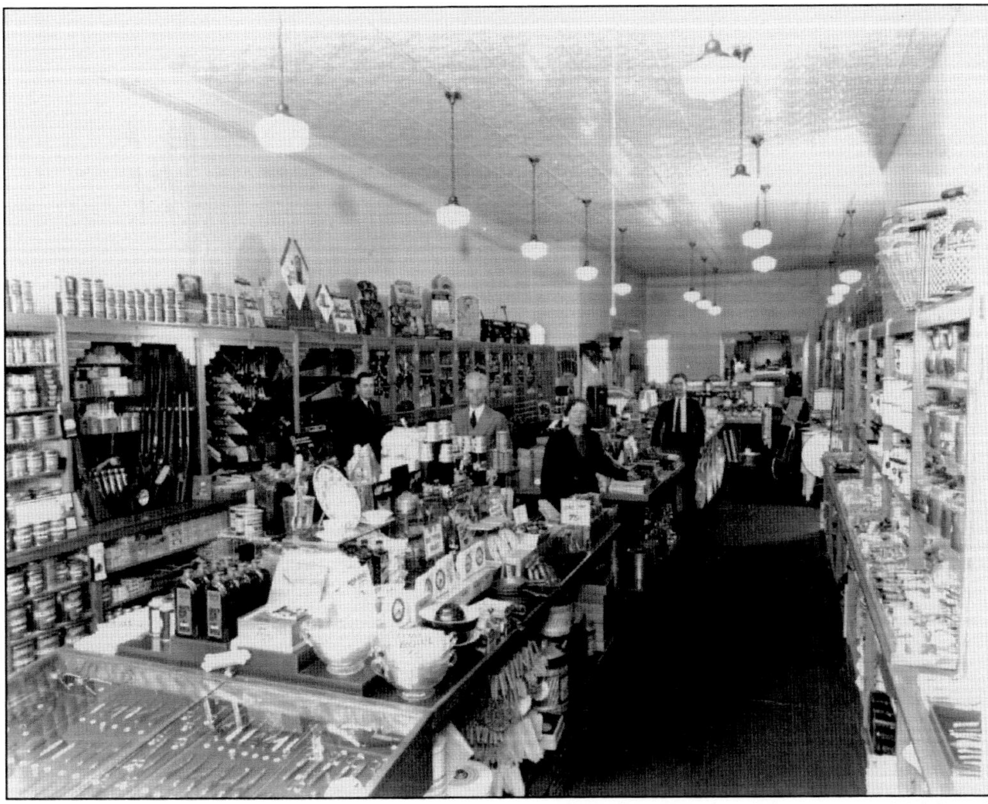

HAMEL AND ROWE STORE, INTERIOR. Included in this photograph of the store at 206 South Main Street, from left to right, are Lindell Rowe, Ward Hamel, Florence Hamel, and the housekeeper (name unknown). (Photograph courtesy DeSoto Public Library.)

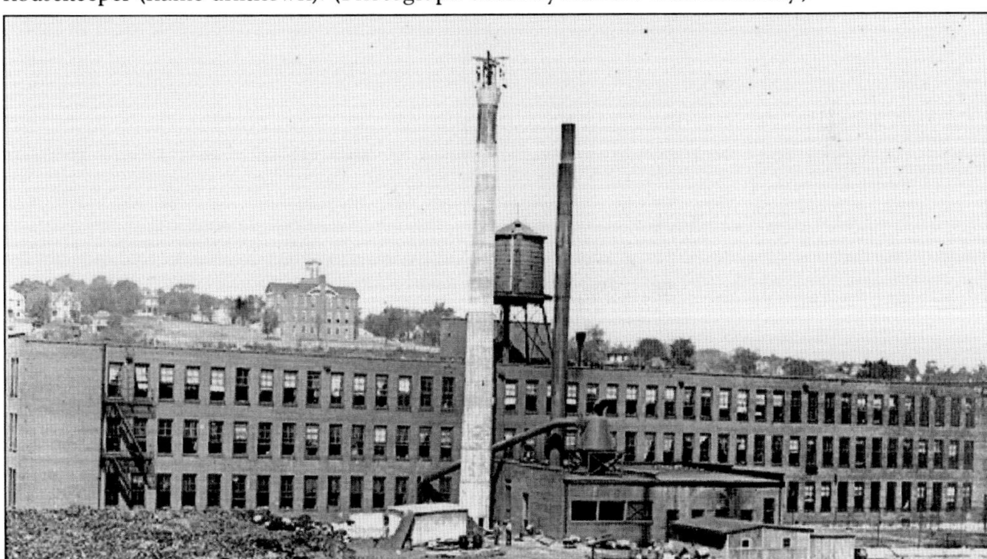

DESOTO INTERNATIONAL SHOE FACTORY, 1924. This photograph of the Shoe Factory, located on the East side, was taken shortly after the factory was opened in 1924. (Photograph courtesy DeSoto Public Library.)

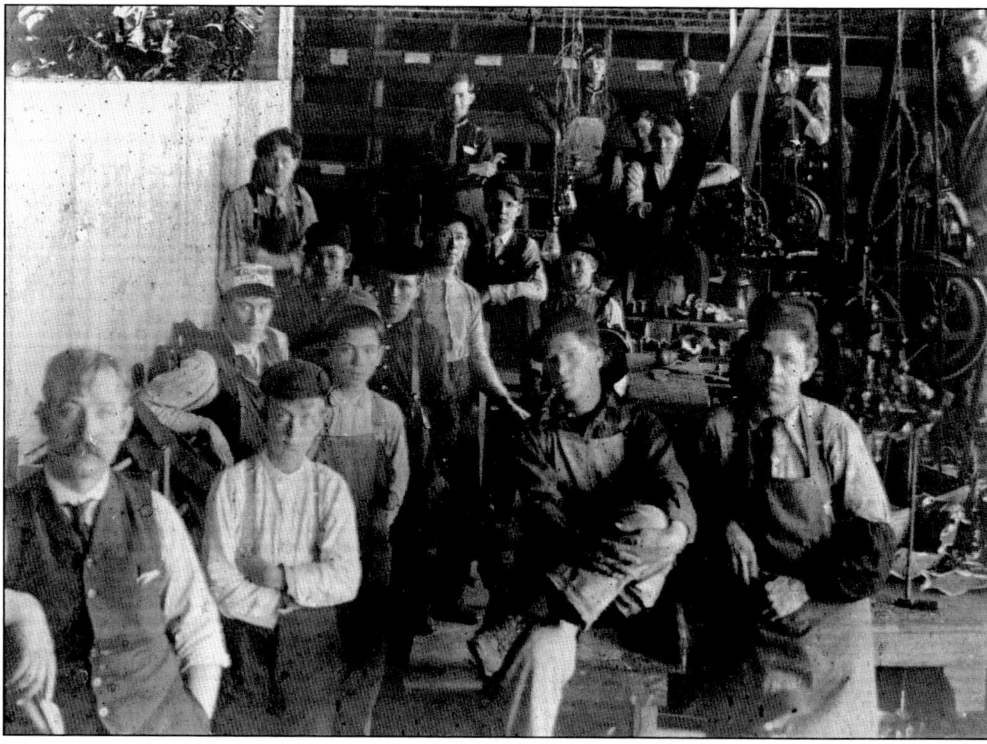

Workers at the Shoe Factory. Included in this photograph are Harry Becker Sr. and E. S. Fauth (factory superintendent). (Photograph courtesy DeSoto Public Library.)

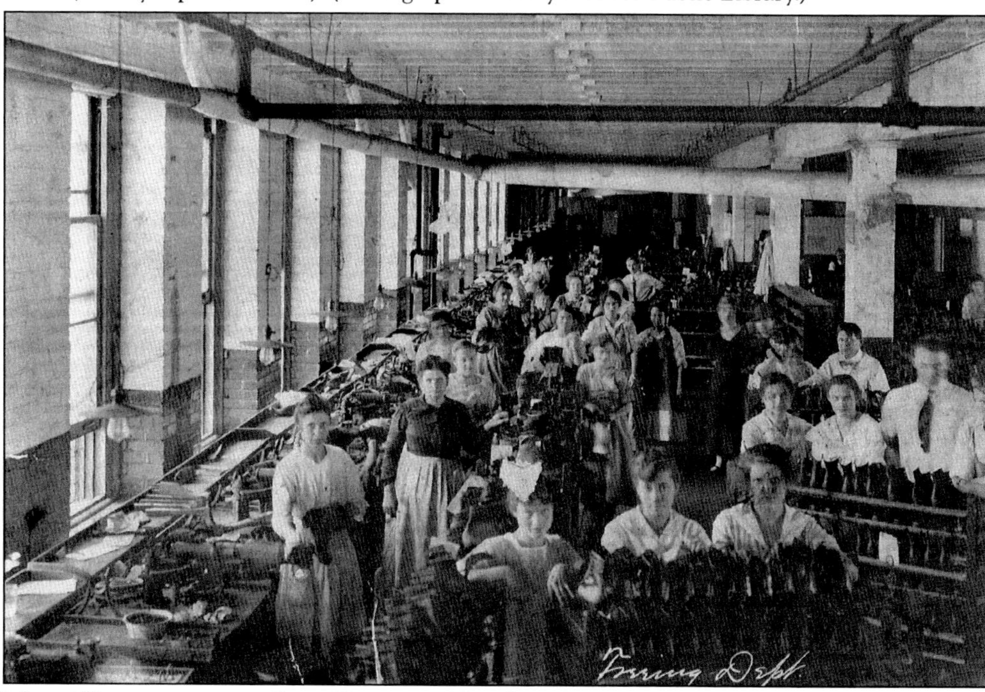

More Workers in the Shoe Factory. The shoe factory was the source of employment for many people in DeSoto. (Photograph courtesy DeSoto Public Library.)

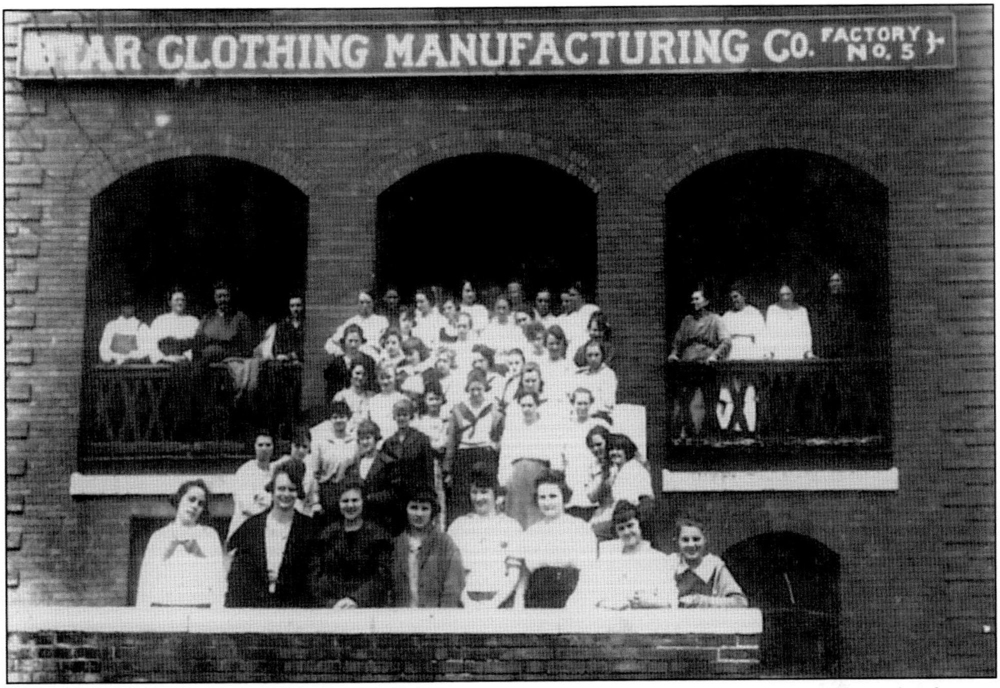

STAR GARMENT FACTORY, 1920–1921. The Star Garment Factory was located in the former YMCA/Booster Hall building located between the tracks and Main Street. (Photograph courtesy DeSoto Public Library.)

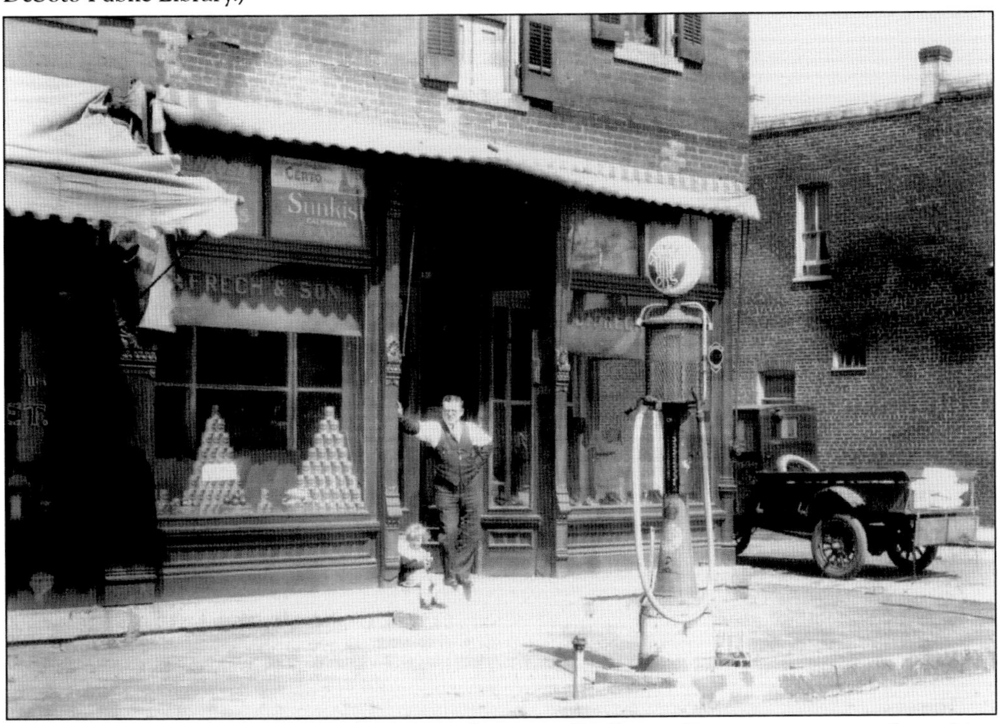

MAIN AND JEFFERSON STREETS. This area of Main and Jefferson Streets is now part of a parking lot by Queen's Store. (Photograph courtesy DeSoto Public Library.)

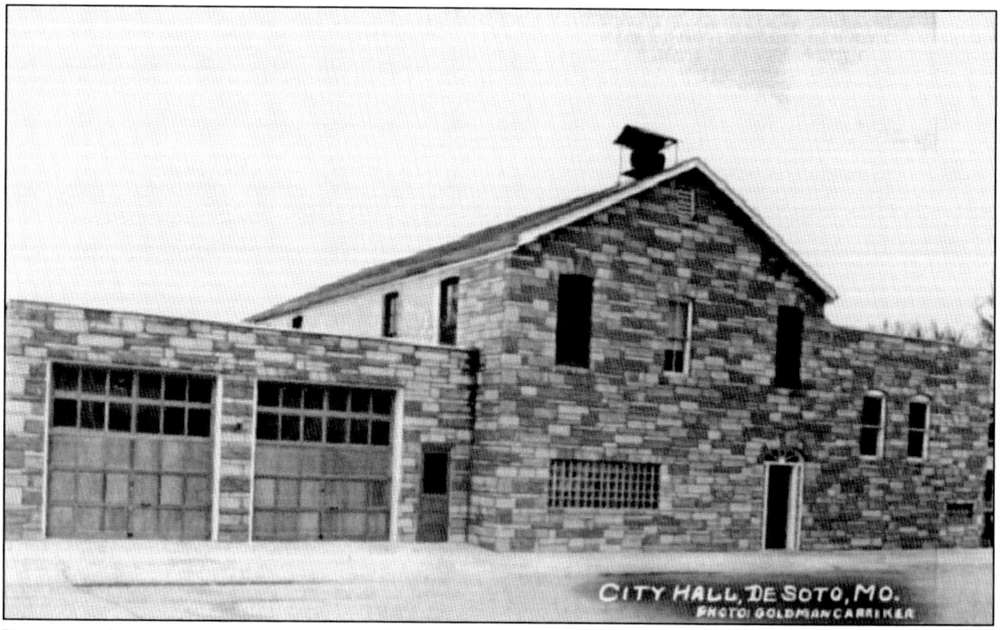

FORMER CITY HALL, 413 SOUTH SECOND STREET. This building, which no longer exists, included the DeSoto Public Library, the fire department, the police department, and the council room. (Photograph courtesy DeSoto Public Library.)

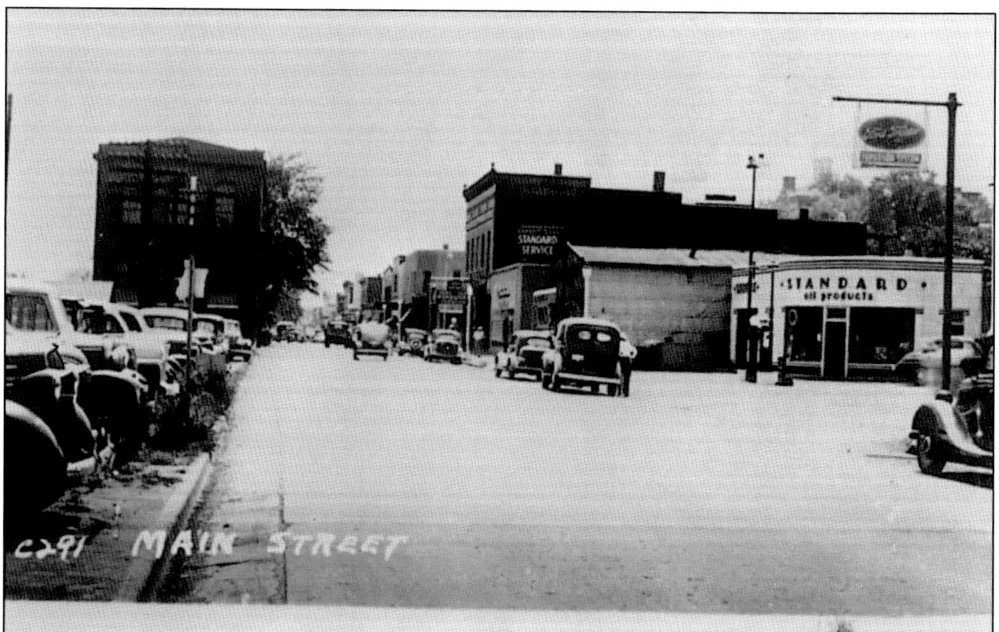

SOUTH MAIN STREET. This view of the 100 block of South Main Street was taken in the 1930s. (Photograph courtesy DeSoto Public Library.)

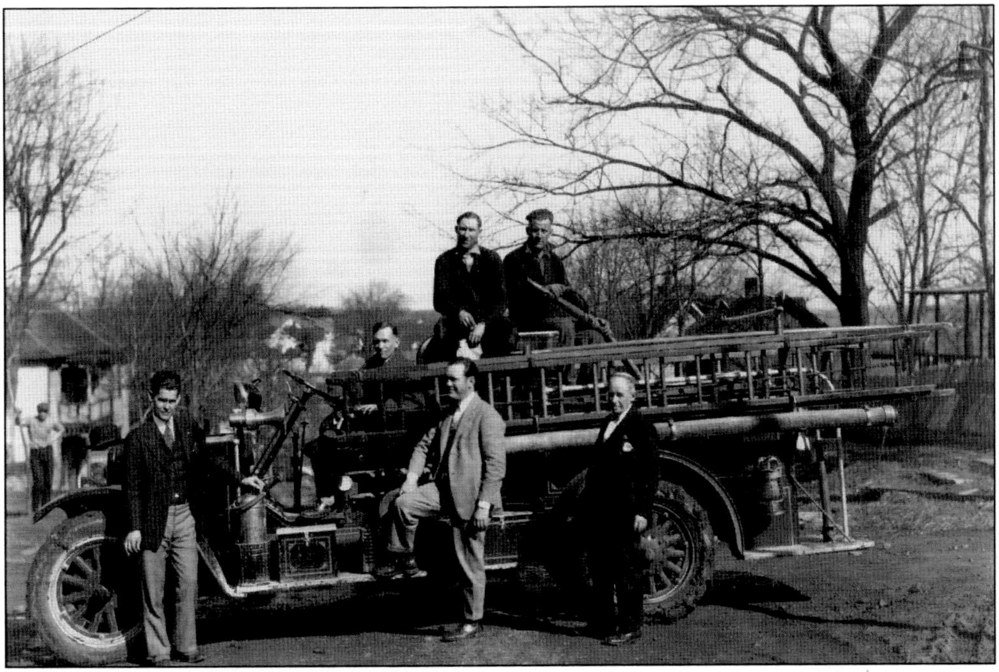

VOLUNTEER FIRE DEPARTMENT, 1925 OR 1926. Included in this photograph are Frank Wall (mayor), San Dore (city marshall), Ferd Schmitz, Richard Hale, and Carl Young. (Photograph courtesy DeSoto Public Library.)

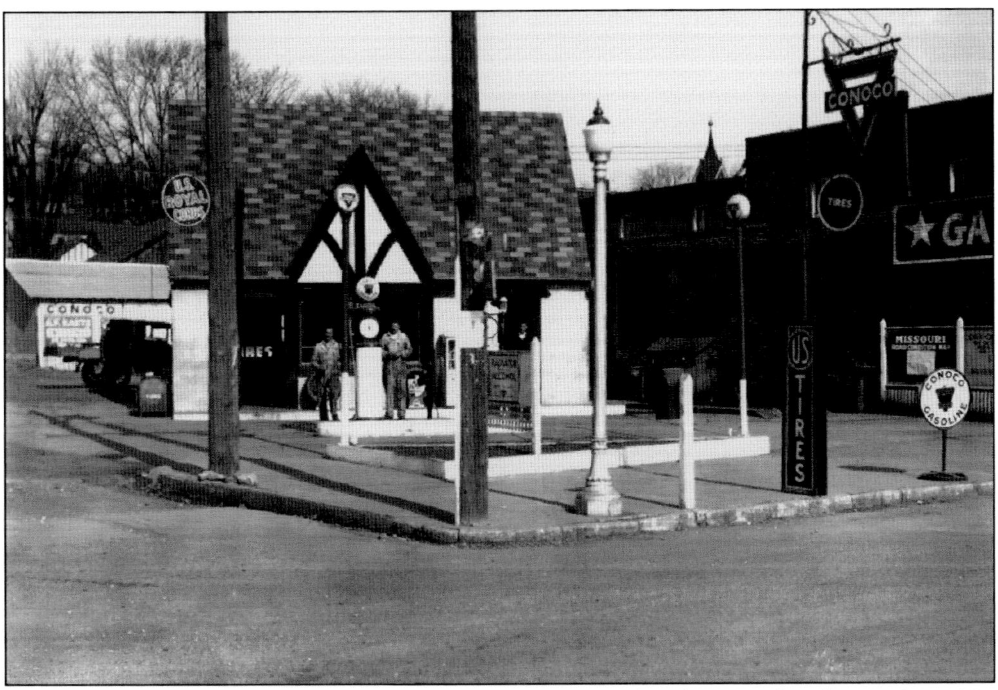

CONOCO SERVICE STATION, MAIN AND MILLER STREETS. This photograph, taken in the 1930s, shows Walter Wilson and Frank Scott standing in front of the station. (Photograph courtesy DeSoto Public Library.)

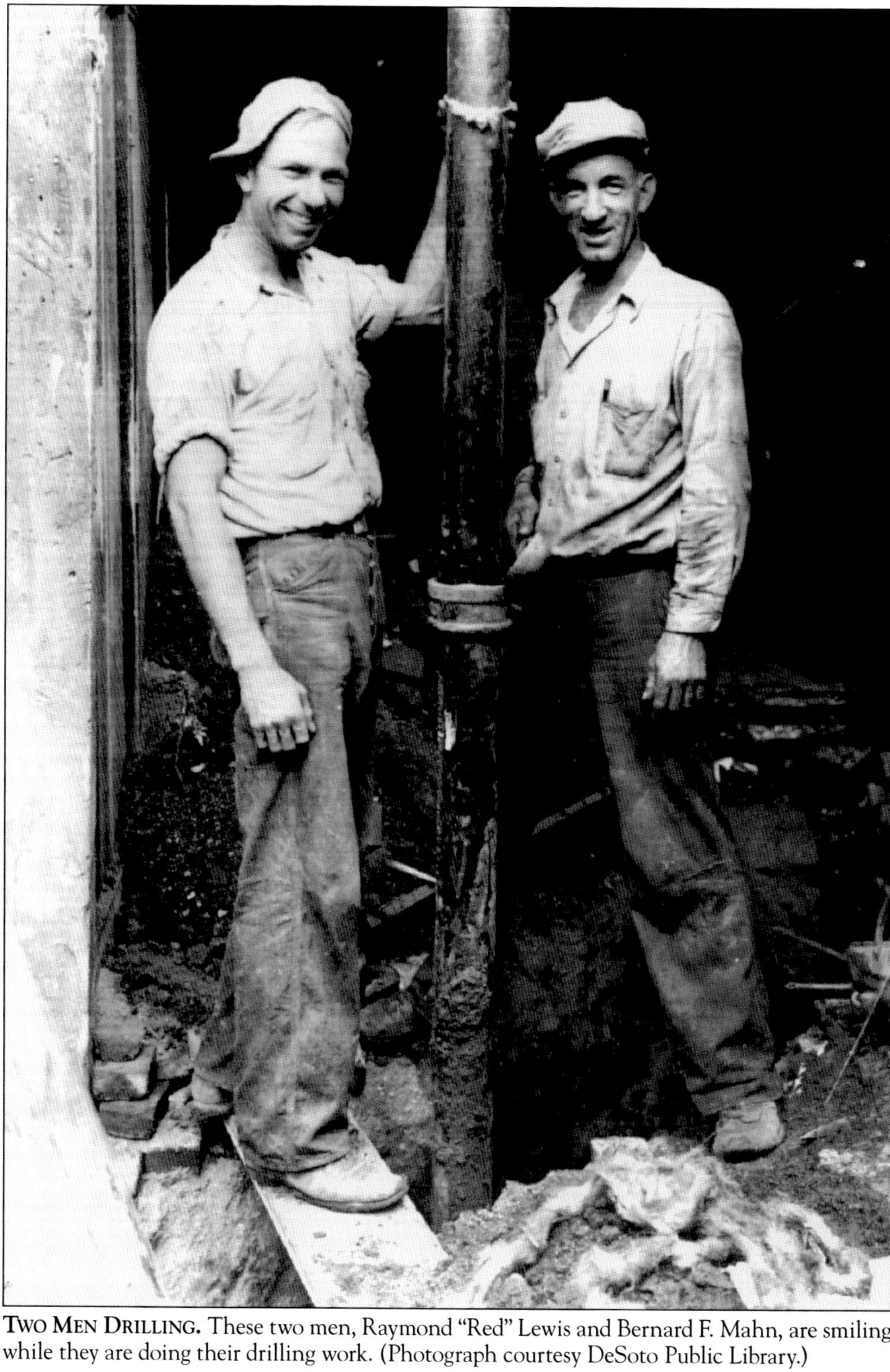

Two Men Drilling. These two men, Raymond "Red" Lewis and Bernard F. Mahn, are smiling while they are doing their drilling work. (Photograph courtesy DeSoto Public Library.)

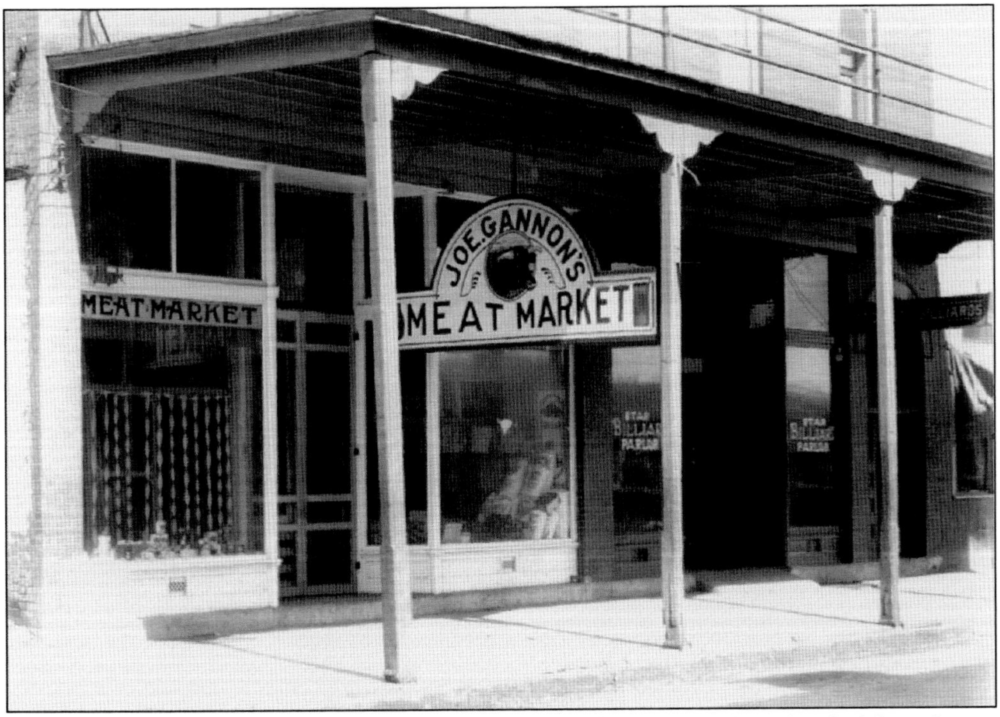

GANNON'S MEAT MARKET. Joe Gannon's Meat Market was at 308 South Main Street. (Photograph courtesy DeSoto Public Library.)

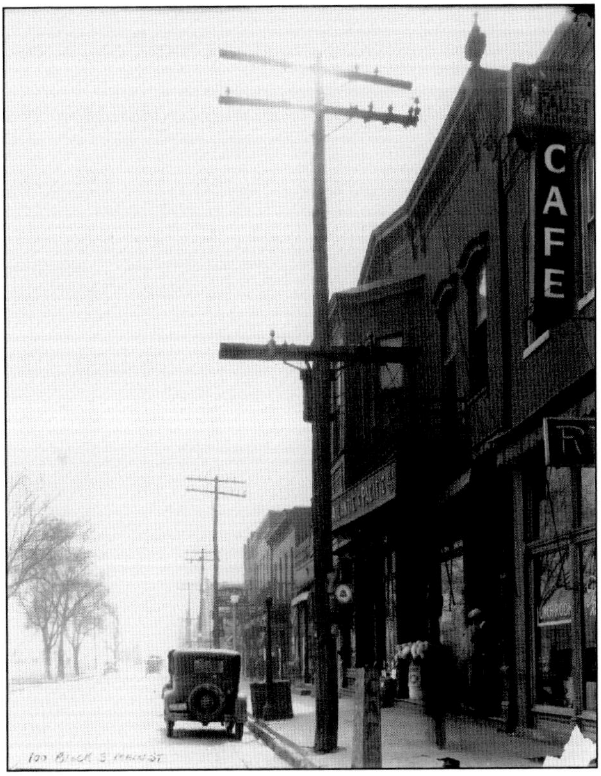

NORTH MAIN STREET, 1930S. DeSoto has been considered the "Gateway to the Ozarks." This photograph of Main Street was taken in the 1930s. (Photograph courtesy DeSoto Public Library.)

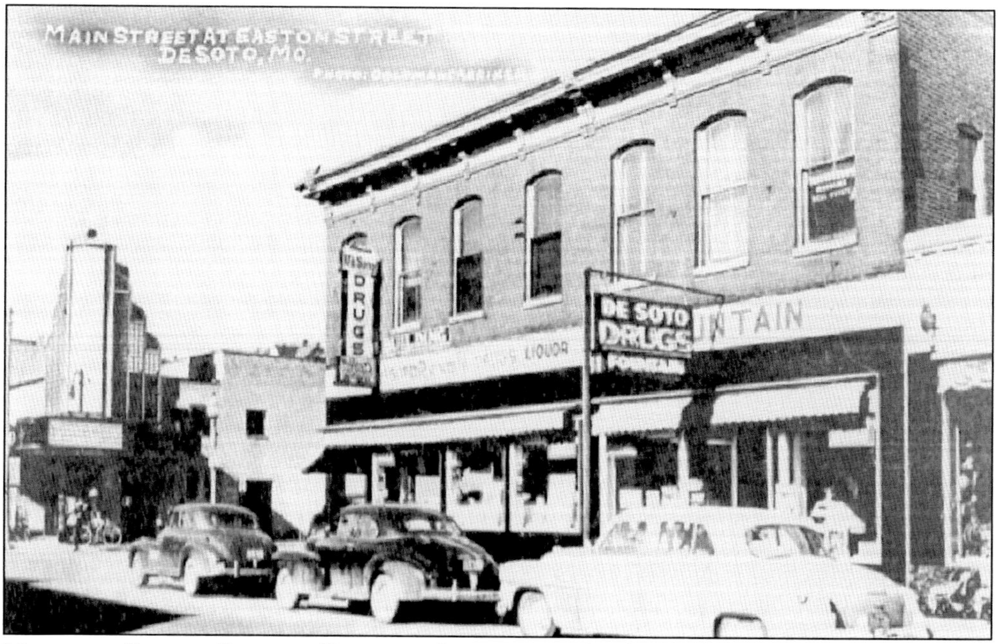

MAIN AND EASTON STREETS. Prominent businesses and a theater dotted the west side of Main Street as shown in this photograph. (Photograph courtesy DeSoto Public Library.)

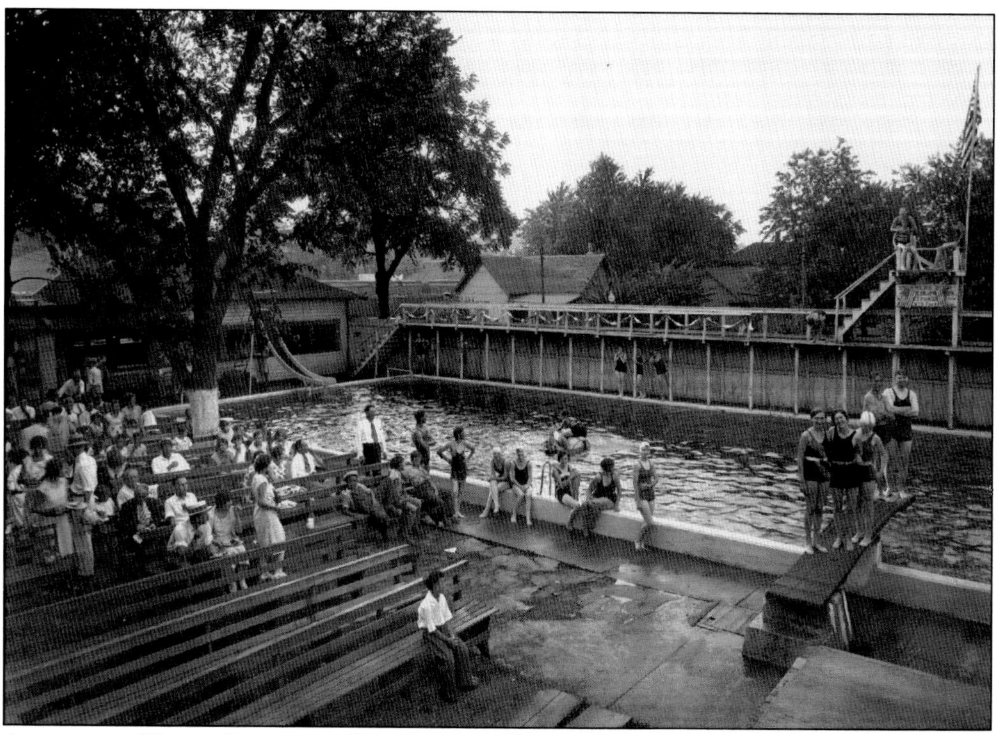

ARLINGTON HOTEL SWIMMING POOL, 1930S. The swimming pool at the Arlington was the first public swimming pool in DeSoto and it was always a popular spot in the hot weather. (Photograph courtesy DeSoto Public Library.)

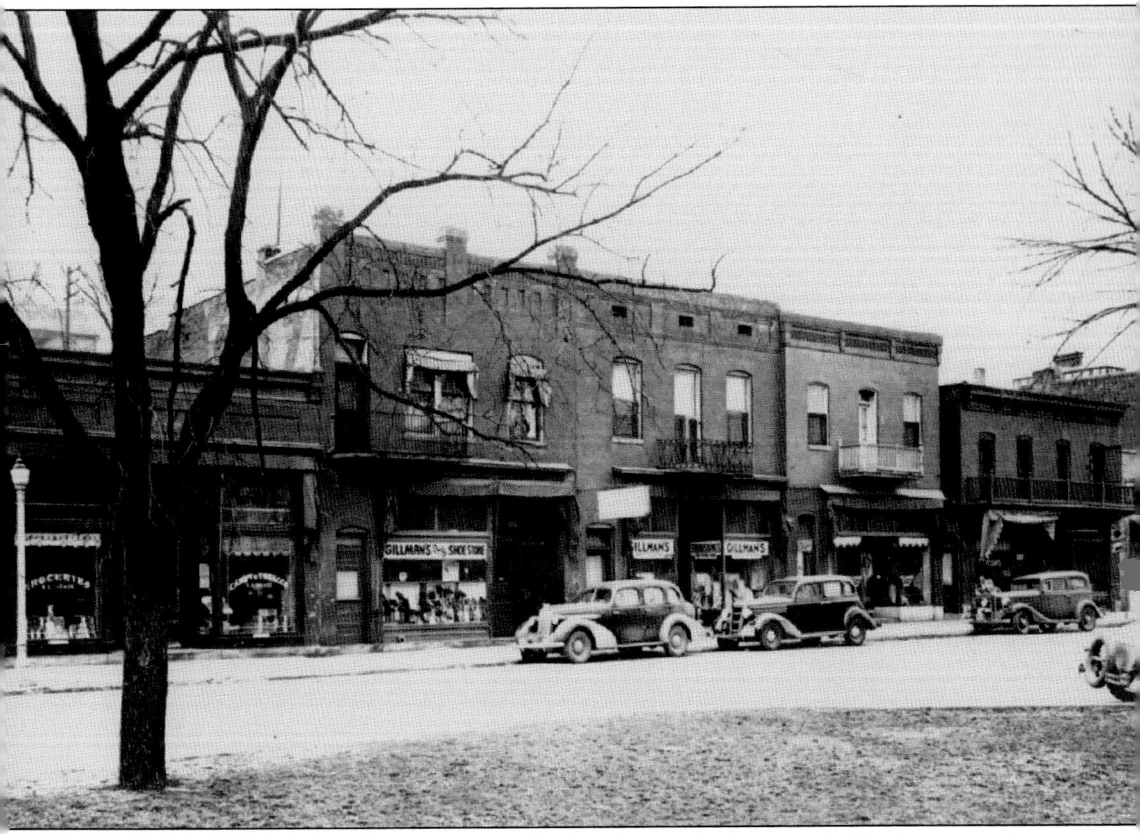

SOUTH MAIN STREET, 1930S. This view of South Main Street is looking south. The license on the car pictured in this photograph is from Ohio, 1932. (Photograph courtesy DeSoto Public Library.)

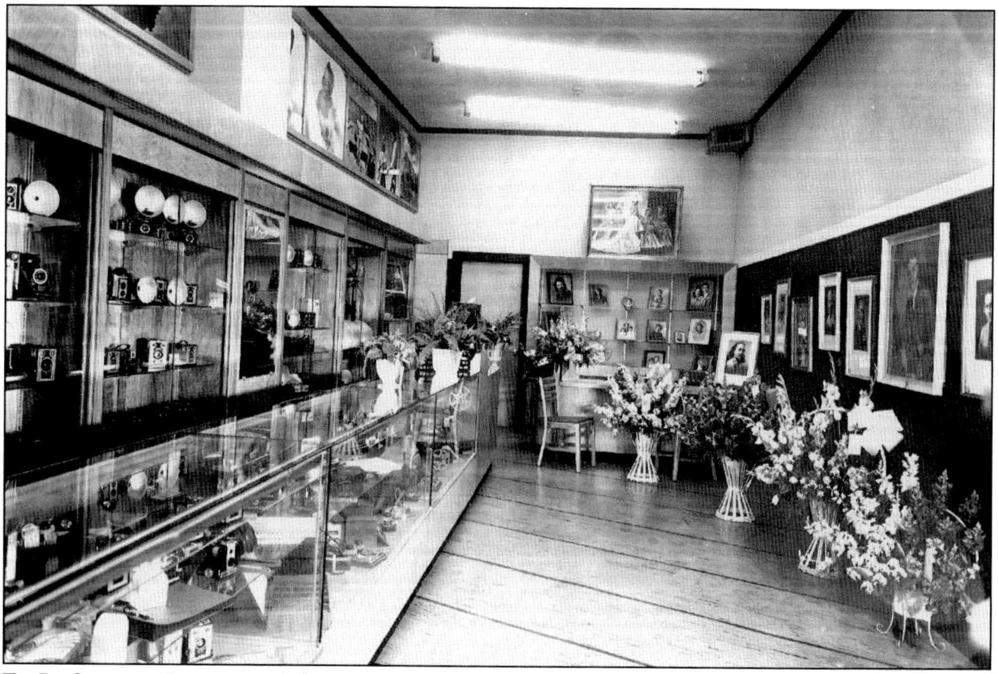

FO-JO STUDIO, INTERIOR. This view is of the interior of the Fo-Jo Studio on Main Street. The Fo-Jo company got its name from a customer who saw a message in the show window from F. J. Milfeld. Thinking that the sign in the window indicated Fo-Jo rather than F. J. (because his periods were more like "o's" rather than periods) she asked to speak to "Fo-Jo." Thus began the use of the name Fo-Jo, which endures to this day. (Photograph courtesy Fo-Jo Studio.)

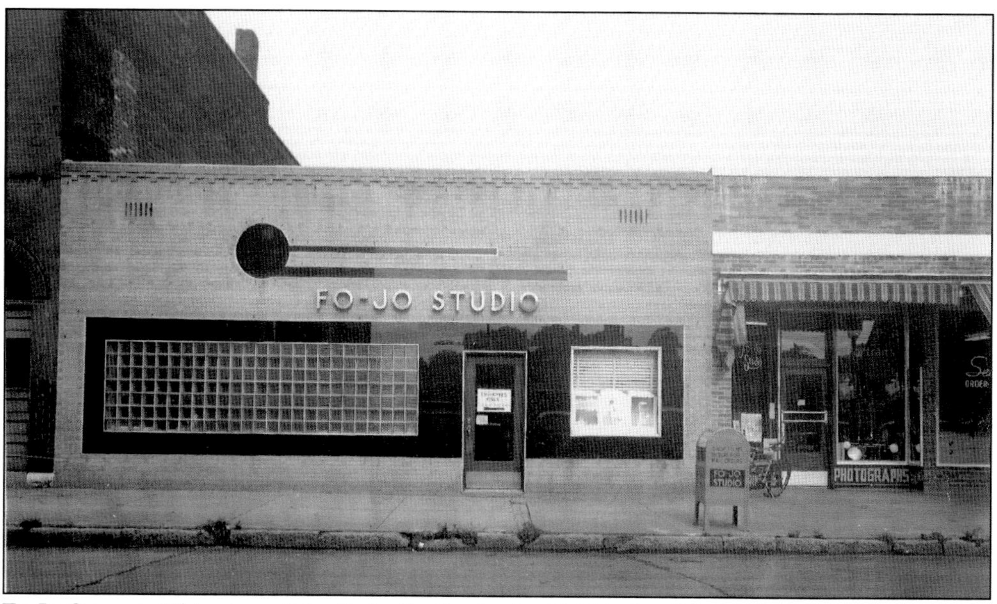

FO-JO STUDIO. This view of the Fo-Jo Studio, in the 200 block of North Main Street, was taken in the mid-1950s. For many years the outdoor advertising of Fo-Jo Studio and their development of photographs was prominent throughout the United States. (Photograph courtesy Fo-Jo Studio.)

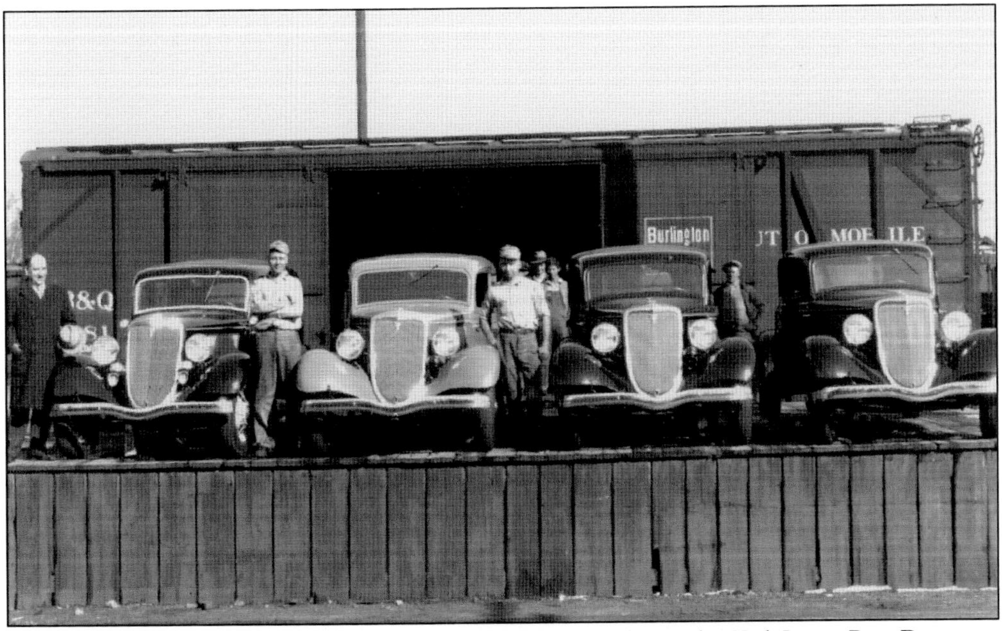

FOUR CARS. These 1933 Ford cars are pictured with, from left to right, Kirk Jones, Burt Drennen, Charley Wilson, and Pat Vivrett. (Photograph courtesy DeSoto Public Library.)

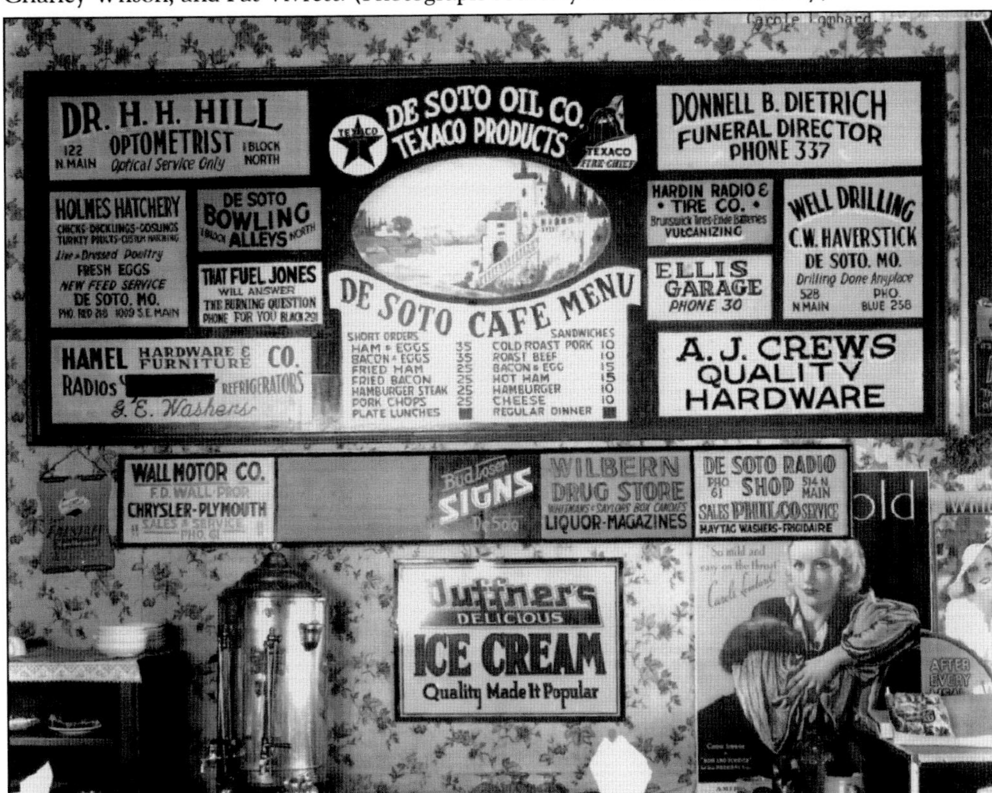

DESOTO CAFÉ. In 1934, the DeSoto Café on Main Street looked like this. (Photograph courtesy DeSoto Public Library.)

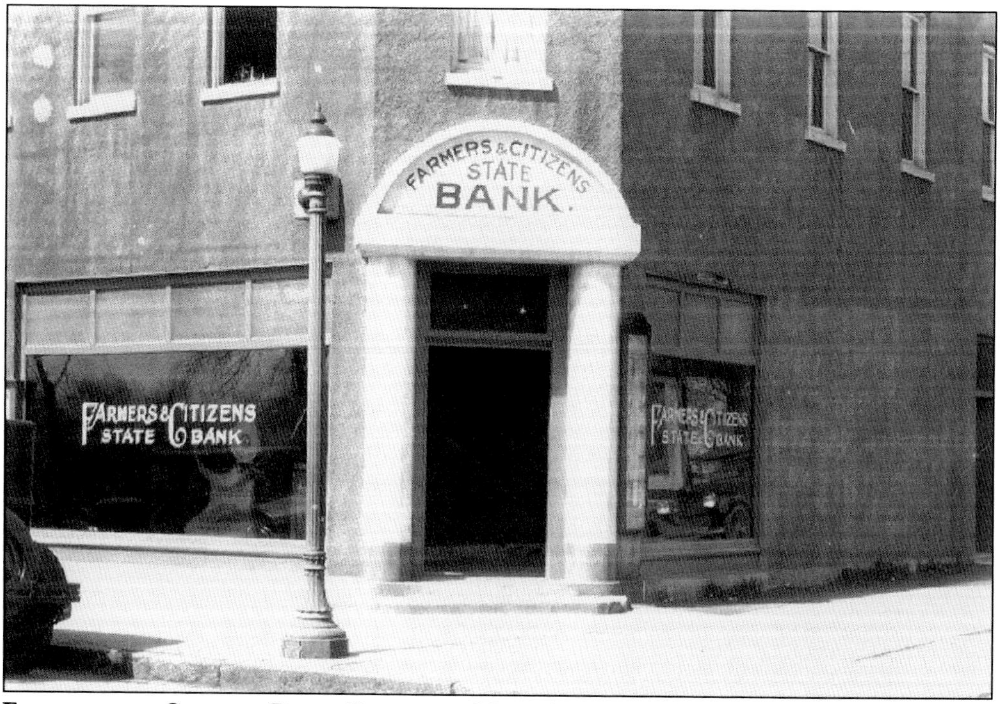

FARMERS AND CITIZENS BANK, BOYD AND MAIN STREETS. The Farmers and Citizens Bank occupied the prominent corner of Boyd and Main Streets. (Photograph courtesy DeSoto Public Library.)

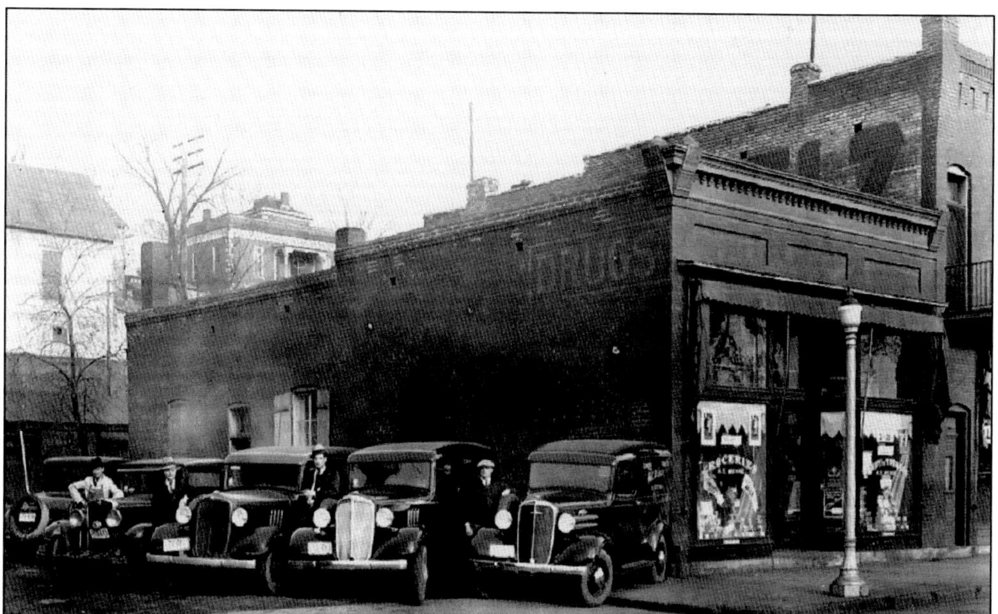

MORE CARS, 1930S. These cars are identified as a 1935 Ford (third from left), 1935 or 1936 Buick or Pontiac (fourth), and 1933 Chevrolet (fifth). (Photograph courtesy DeSoto Public Library.)

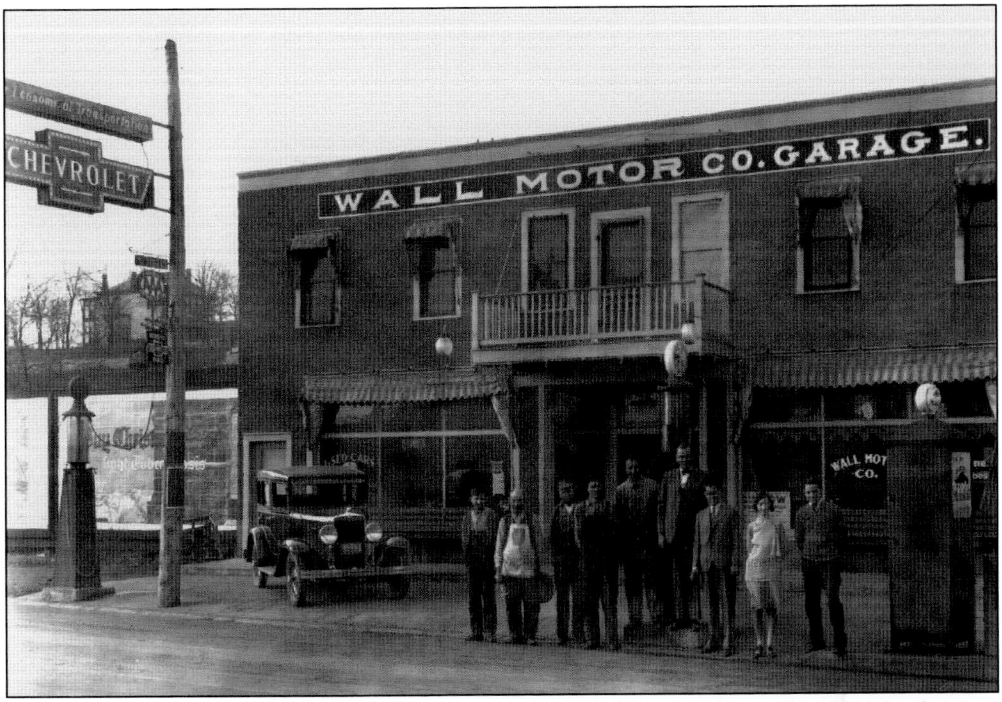

WALL AUTOMOBILE DEALERSHIP. This automobile dealership was located at 514 North Main Street. (Photograph courtesy DeSoto Public Library.)

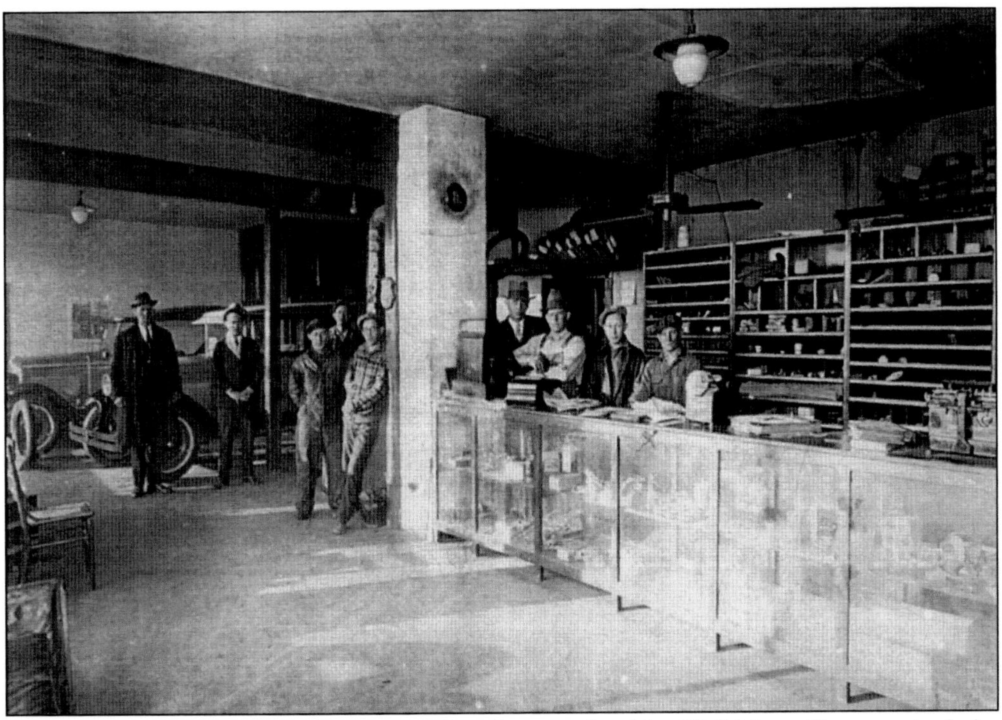

INTERIOR OF WALL MOTOR COMPANY. This photograph of the Wall Motor Company includes Frank and Evelyn Wall. (Photograph courtesy DeSoto Public Library.)

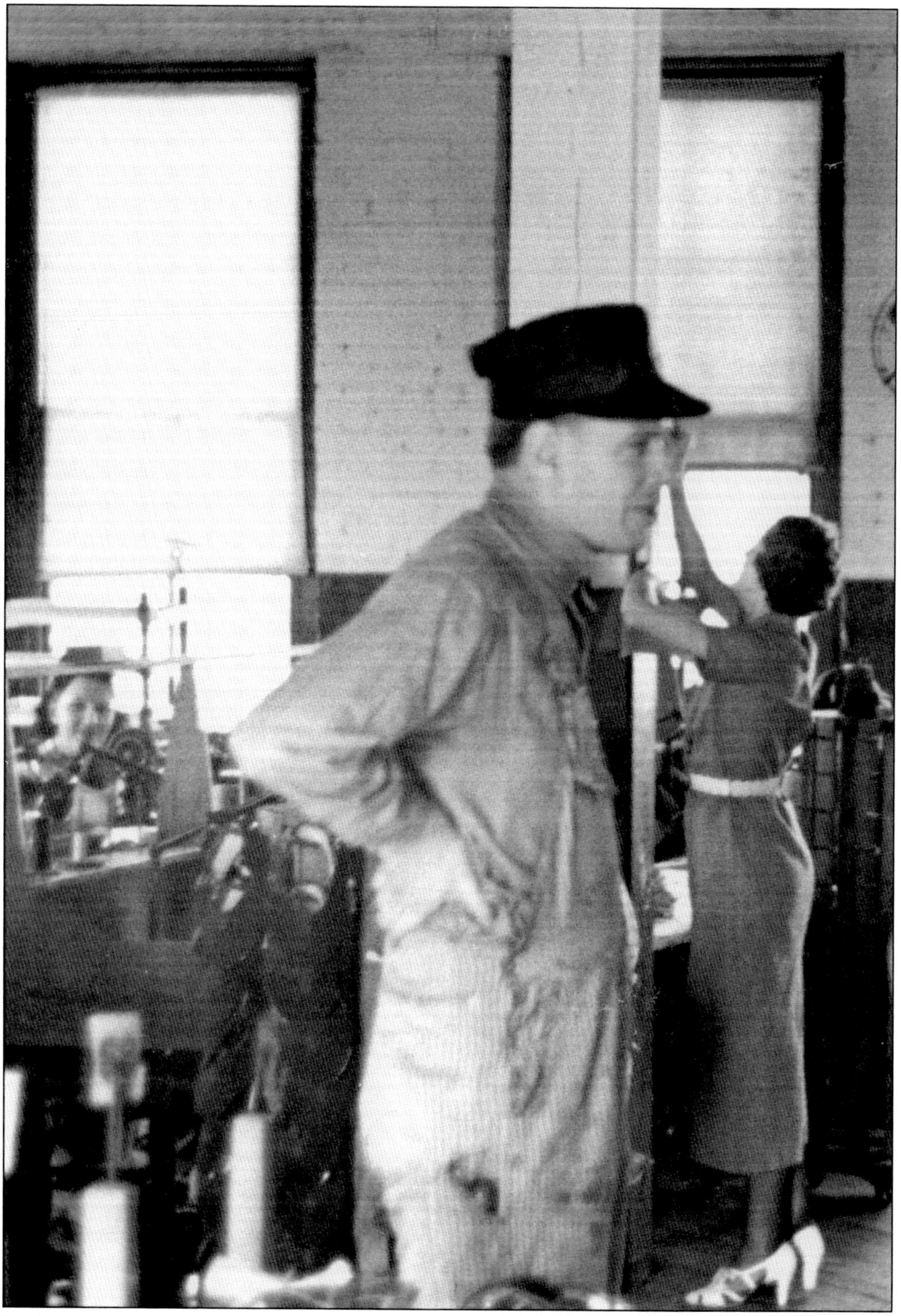

Theodore "Slim" Mueller. This photograph of Slim Mueller was taken when he was working at the International Shoe Factory in DeSoto. (Photograph courtesy DeSoto Public Library.)

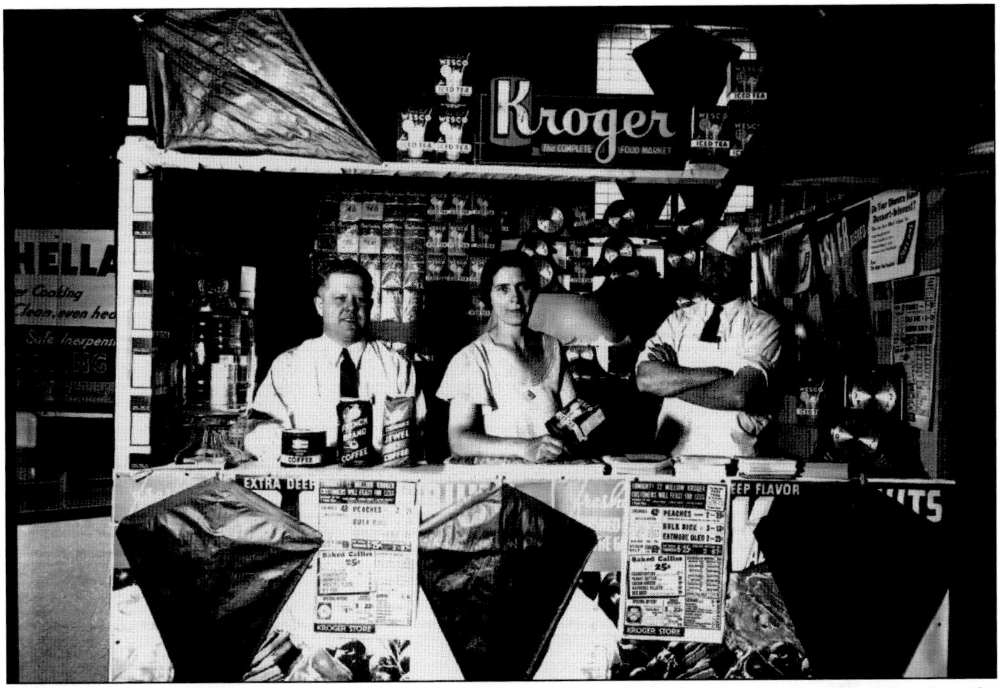

KROGER FOOD BOOTH, 1935. The Home Show in DeSoto included the Kroger Food Fair booth. Identified here are I. Barnhart, Fern Spence, and Dana Kirk (Kroger manager). (Photograph courtesy DeSoto Public Library.)

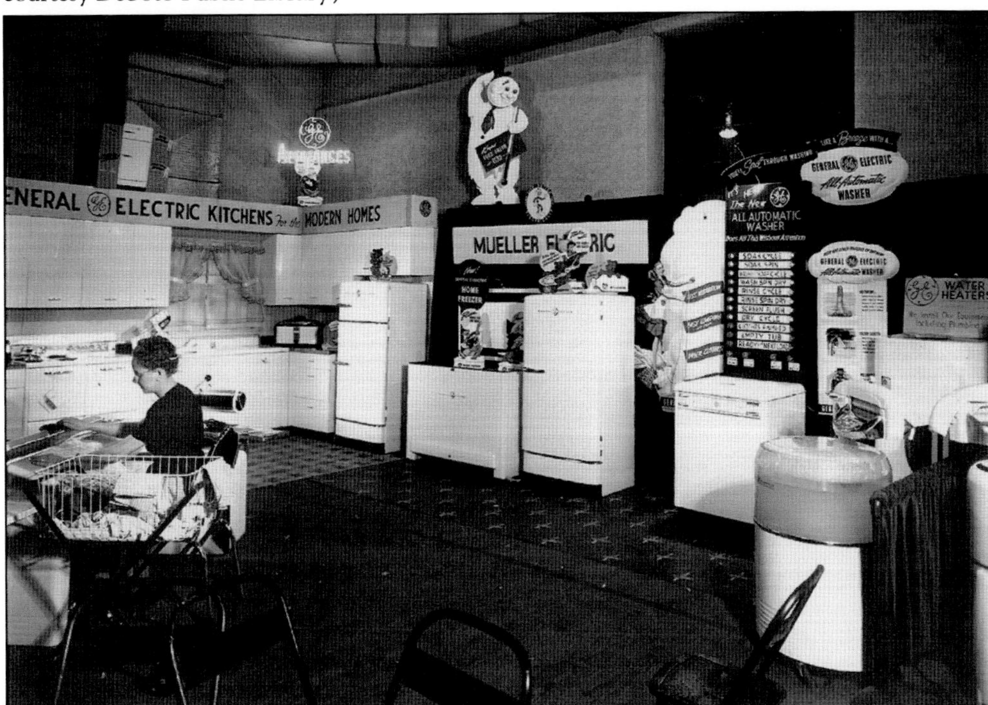

MUELLER ELECTRIC DISPLAY. The Mueller Electric Company displayed its latest products at the Home Show. (Photograph courtesy DeSoto Public Library.)

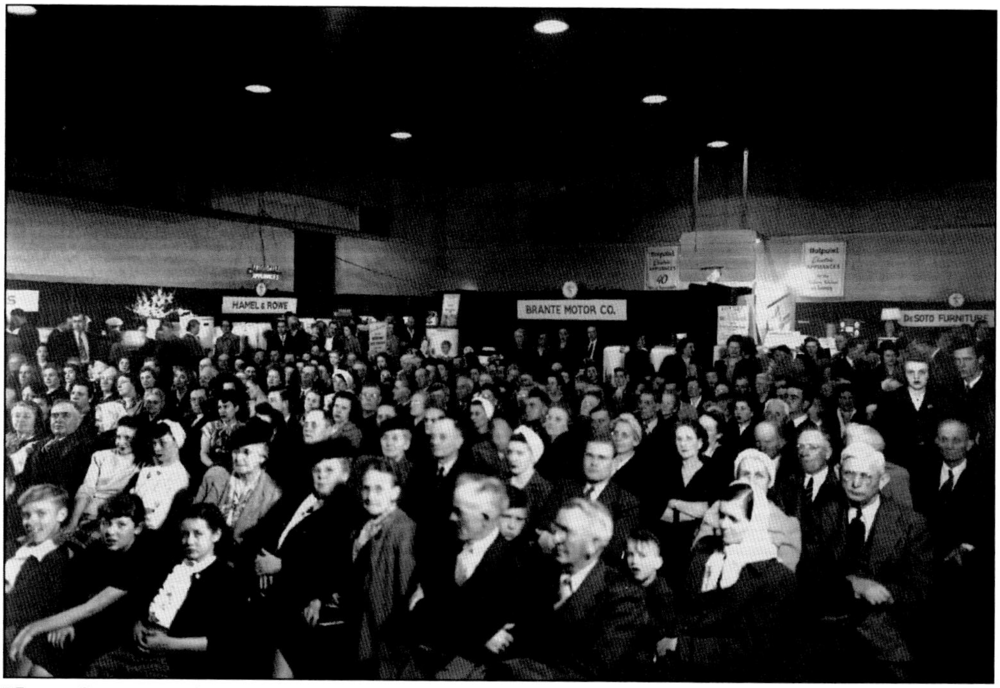

HOME SHOW AT ARMORY ON SECOND STREET. The Home Show had entertainment for the public every evening. This photograph shows a large audience at the show. (Photograph courtesy DeSoto Public Library.)

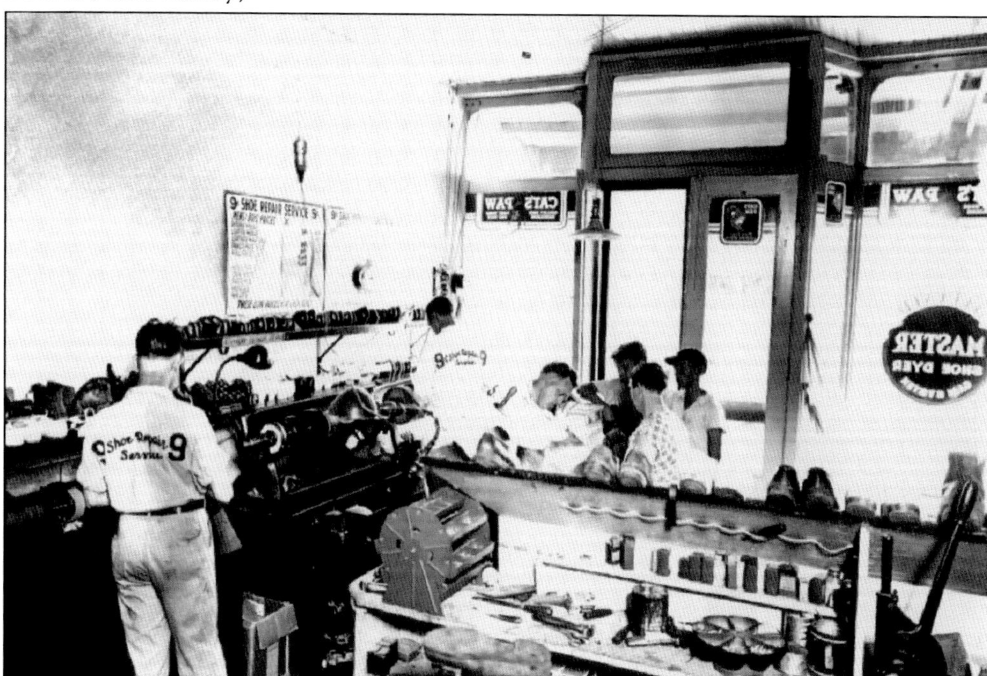

KITE'S SHOE SHOP. This shoe shop was an important place of business for the local clientele. Pictured in the shop are Ila Kite, Gordon Redfield Sr., and Vernon Kite. (Photograph courtesy DeSoto Public Library.)

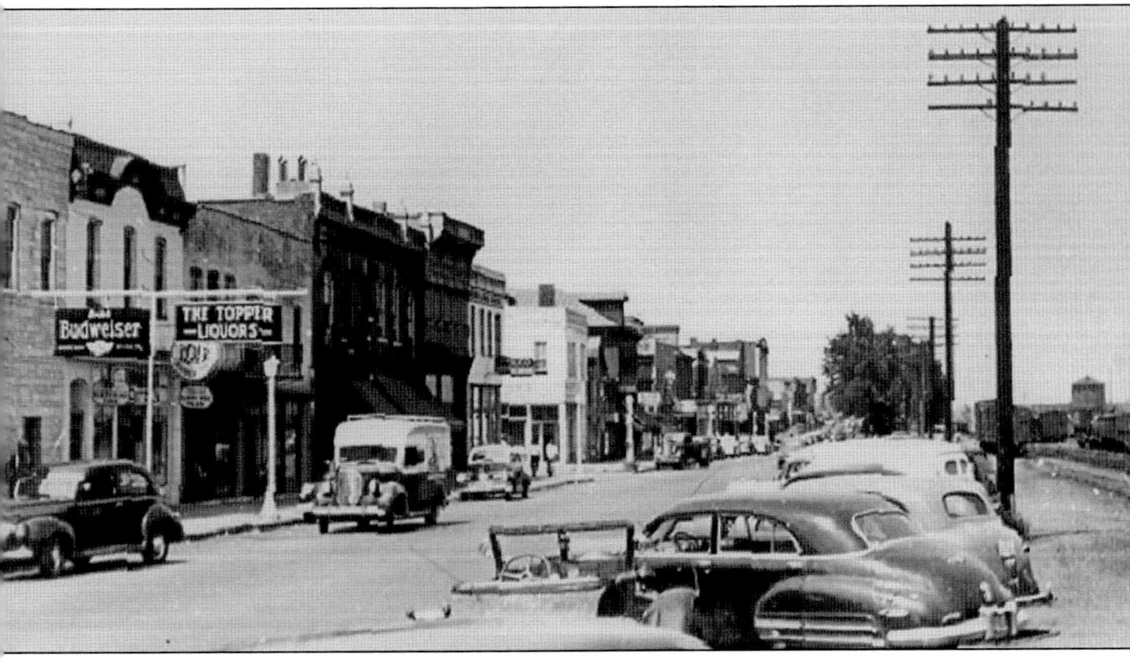

South Main Street. This photograph was made from a postcard that was once available for sale in various DeSoto stores. (Photograph courtesy DeSoto Public Library.)

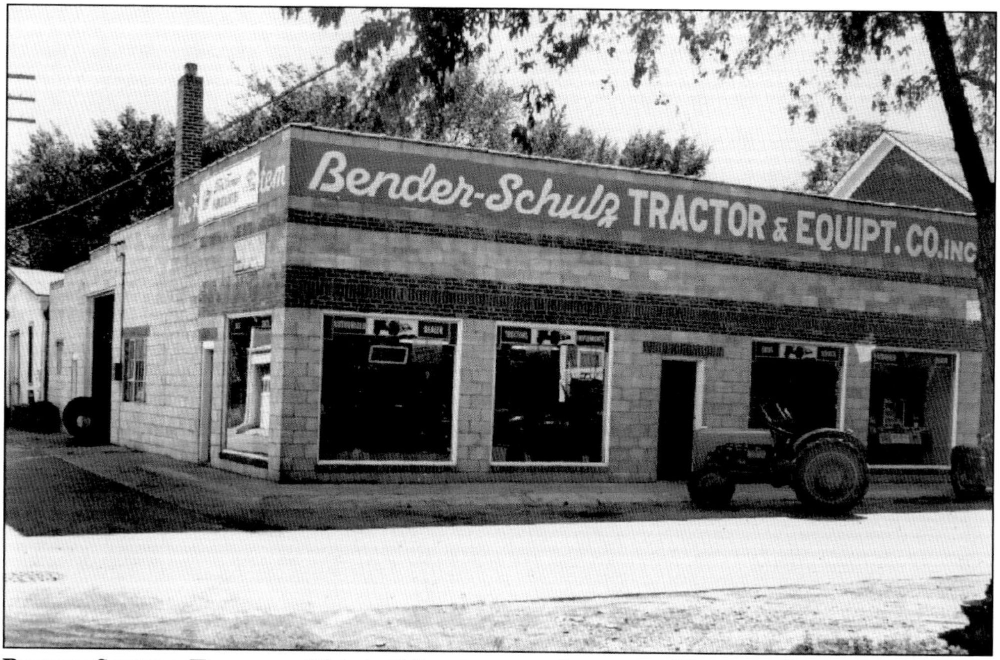

BENDER-SCHULZ TRACTOR. This building is presently occupied by Purcell Tire Company on Main Street. (Photograph courtesy DeSoto Public Library.)

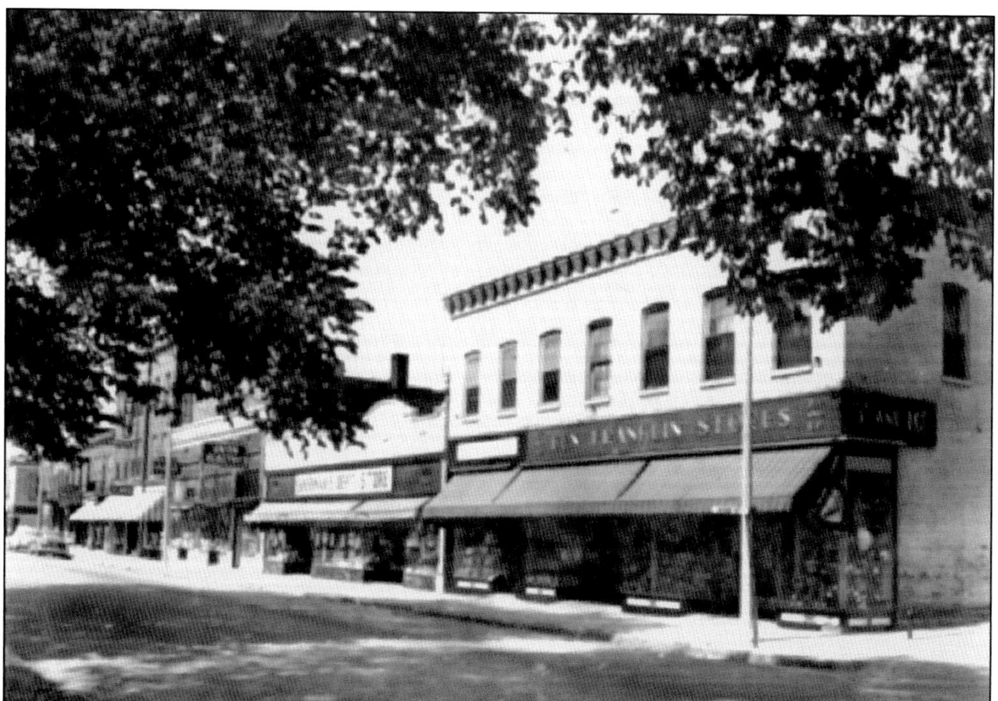

WOOLWORTH STORE ON MAIN STREET. For many years this dime store was a prominent feature on DeSoto's Main Street. (Photograph courtesy DeSoto Public Library.)

Five

People and Civic Affairs

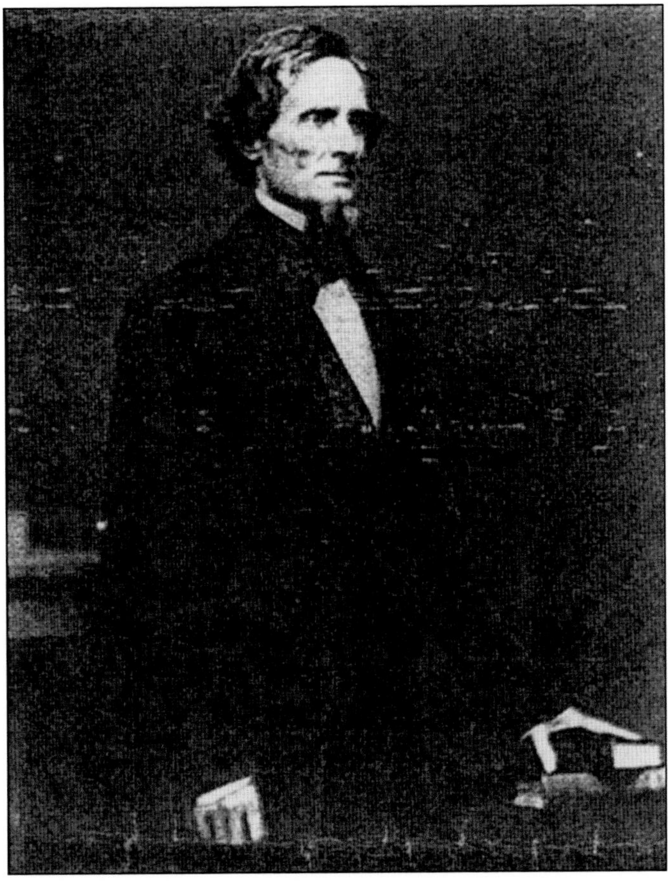

Jefferson Davis, President of the Confederate States. Jefferson Davis received an invitation to speak at the Jefferson County Agricultural Society in DeSoto in 1875. His visit was solely to exchange views on how best to advance agriculture in our area as well as to help in healing some of the psychological wounds left by the Civil War. While he was in DeSoto, Jefferson Davis stayed at the Arlington Hotel where he was entertained and dined by the town's leaders. After speaking at the fair, he was given a gala reception at the Alta Vista Mansion, home of Louis J. Rankin. (Photograph courtesy DeSoto Historical Society.)

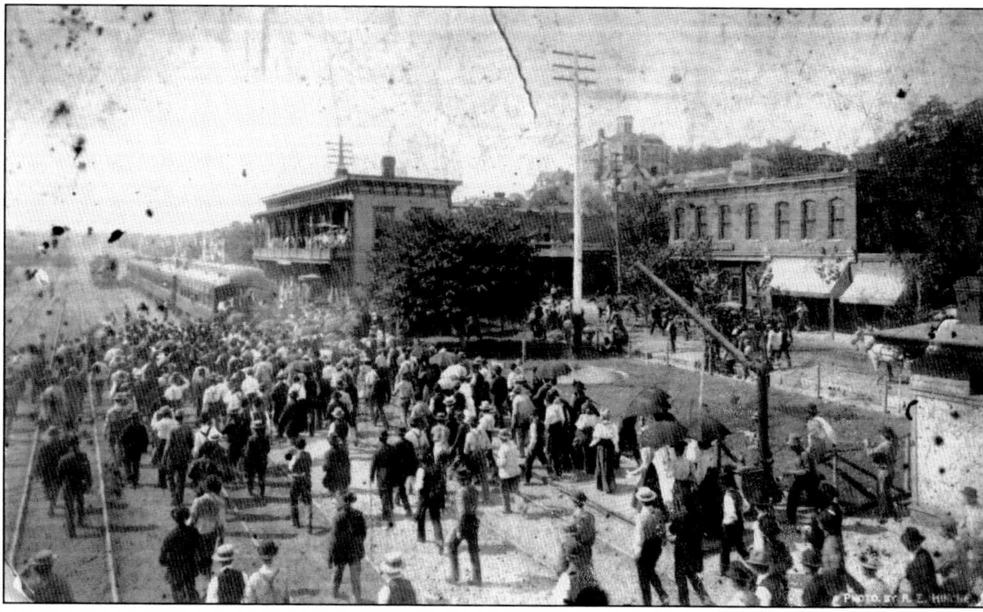

WILLIAM JENNINGS BRYAN, PRESIDENTIAL CANDIDATE. In 1891, William Jennings Bryan, a presidential candidate, came to DeSoto and spoke from the rear of an Iron Mountain Railroad train. (Photograph courtesy DeSoto Public Library.)

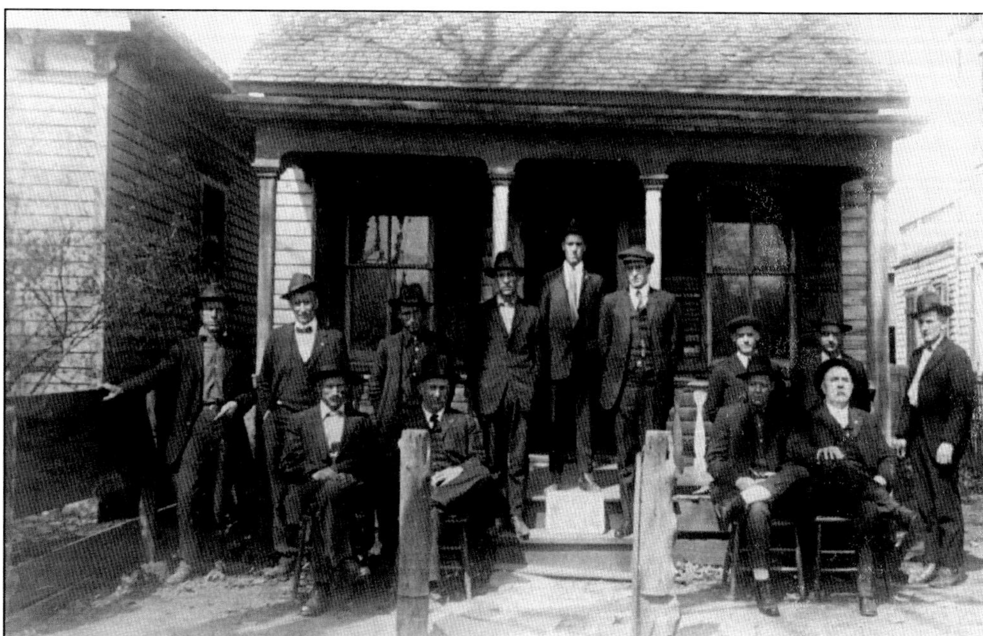

MEN'S CLUB OF DESOTO. This photograph of the men's club was taken in front of a house on South Main Street in 1902. Included in this photograph are Jack Hague, Dick Hopkins, John Hamel, Leon Ames, George Hamel, John Hopson, and the Fry brothers. (Photograph courtesy DeSoto Public Library.)

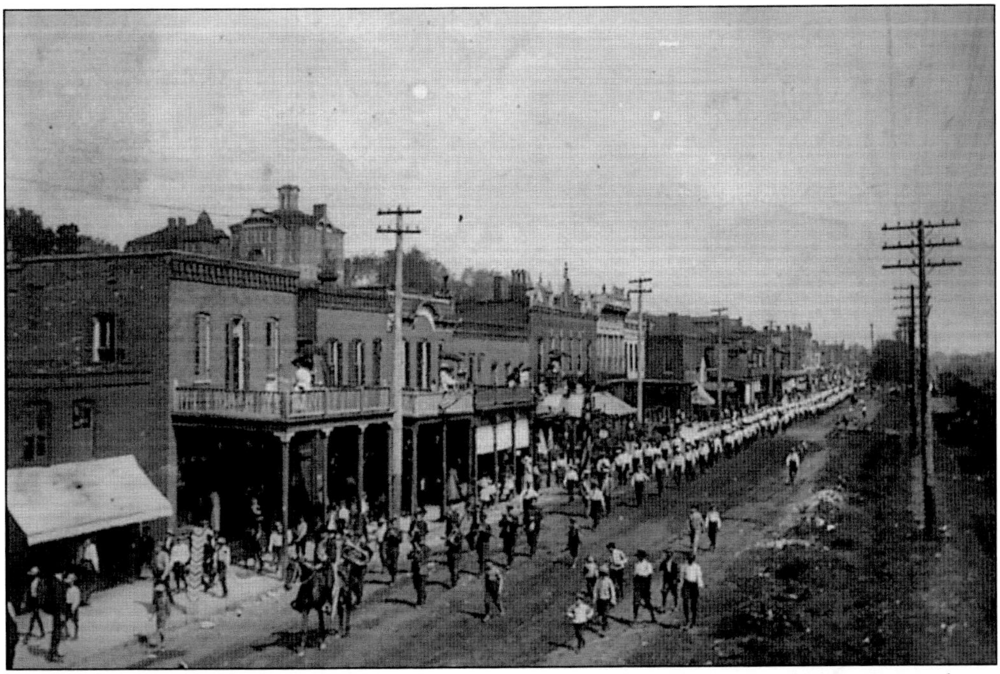

AN EARLY PARADE. DeSoto has been famous for its parades. This view of Main Street shows the parade, the buildings along Main Street, and the persons viewing the parades from the upper balconies. (Photograph courtesy DeSoto Public Library.)

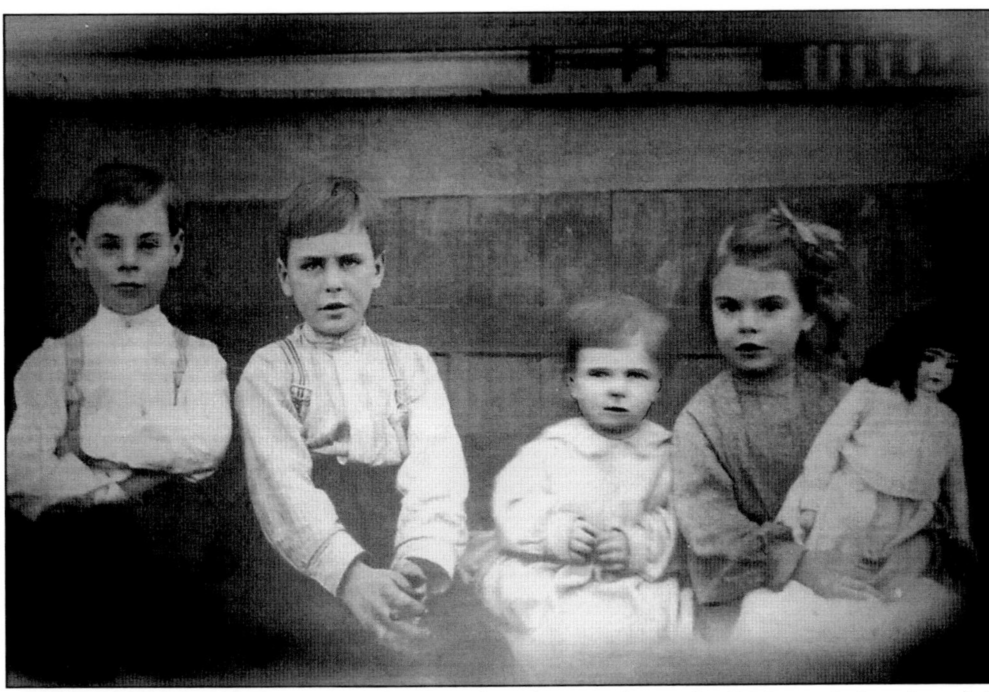

MCMULLIN PHOTOGRAPH. This photograph, taken in the early 1900s, includes, from left to right, Woodie McMullin, Hugh P. Shannon, Pete Shannon, and Lillian Shannon Yaeger. (Photograph courtesy Loretta Shannon Goehring.)

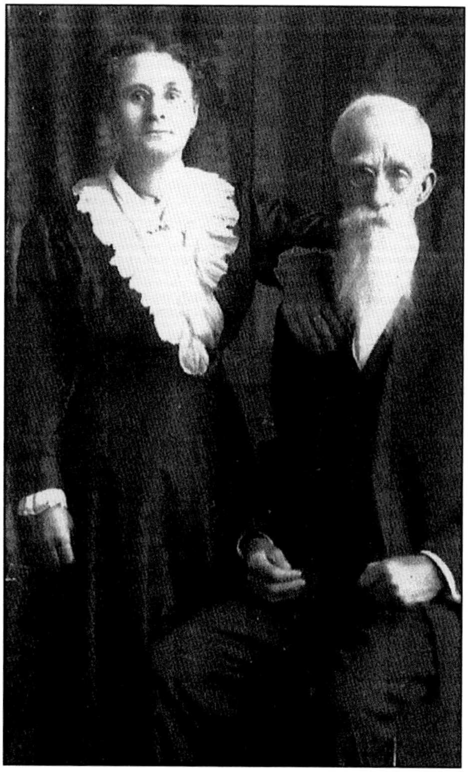

SAMUEL PIPKIN MCMULLIN AND LEATHA ANN MCMULLIN. This photograph was taken in the couple's later years. (Photograph courtesy Loretta Shannon Goehring.)

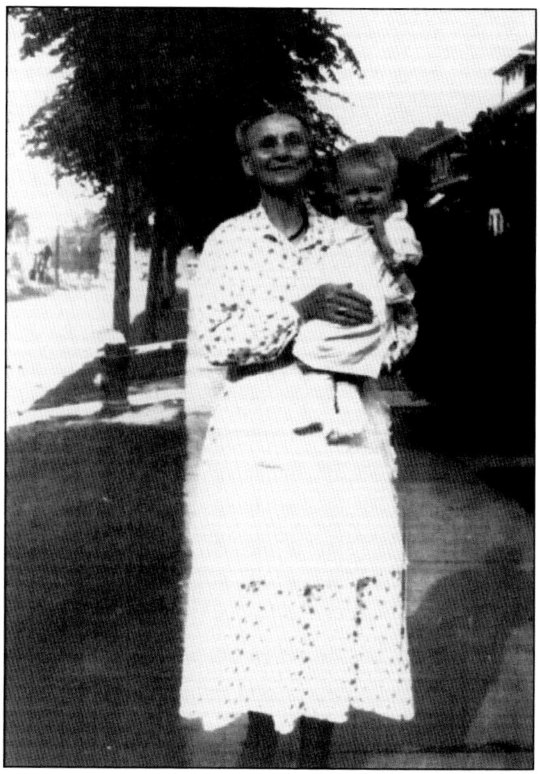

LEATHA ANN MCMULLIN AND GRANDDAUGHTER. The grandmother in this photograph, Leatha Ann Josephine McMullin, is holding her granddaughter Patsy Shannon, child of Hugh Pipkin Shannon. (Photograph courtesy Loretta Shannon Goehring.)

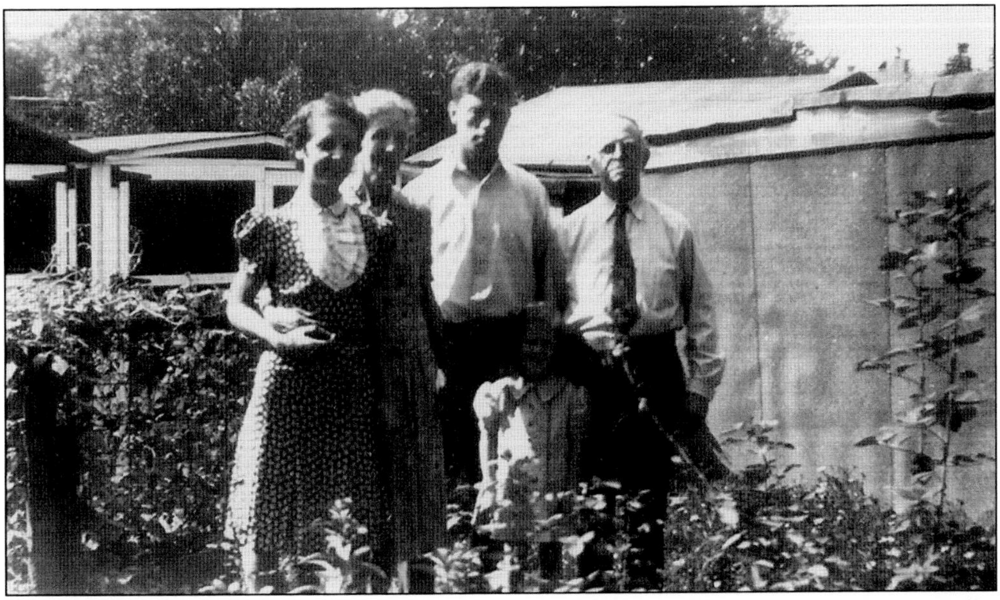

SISSY SHANNON YEAGER AND FAMILY, 1940. Pictured here are Sissy Shannon Yeager, Hallie Lura McMullin Shannon, Stanley Ross Shannon, and Lewis Ross Shannon. The child is Loretta Shannon, about age five or six. (Photograph courtesy Loretta Shannon Goehring.)

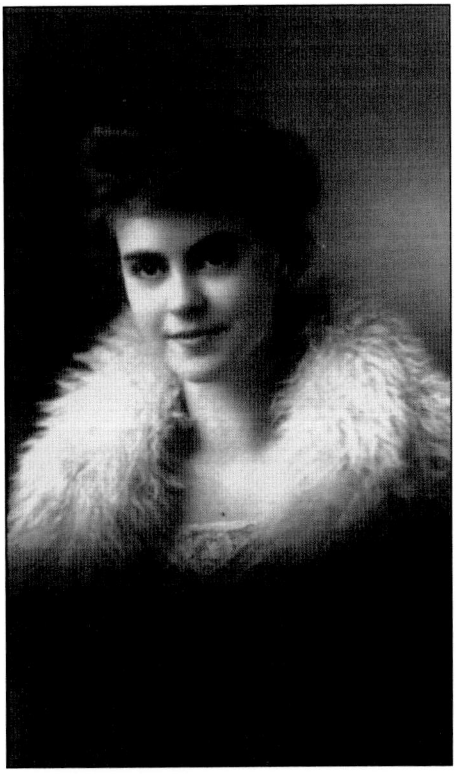

LILLIAN SHANNON YEAGER. Lillian Shannon Yeager, born 1899, was in her twenties when this photograph was taken. (Photograph courtesy Loretta Shannon Goehring.)

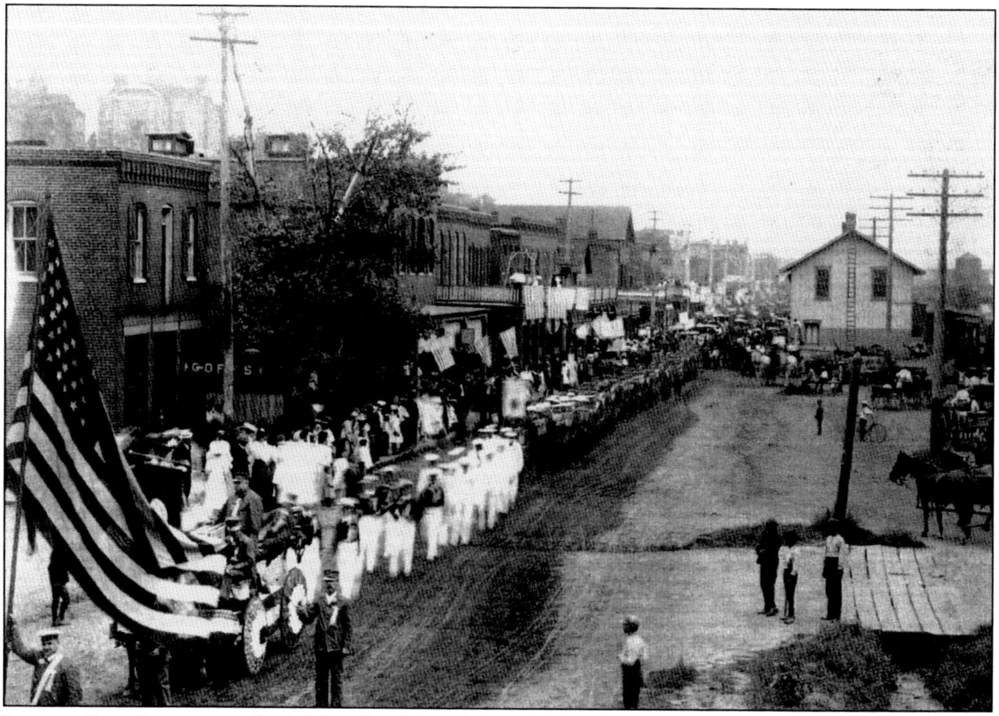

Labor Day Parade, 1907. The Blacksmiths and Helpers participated in the 1907 Labor Day parade. (Photograph courtesy DeSoto Public Library.)

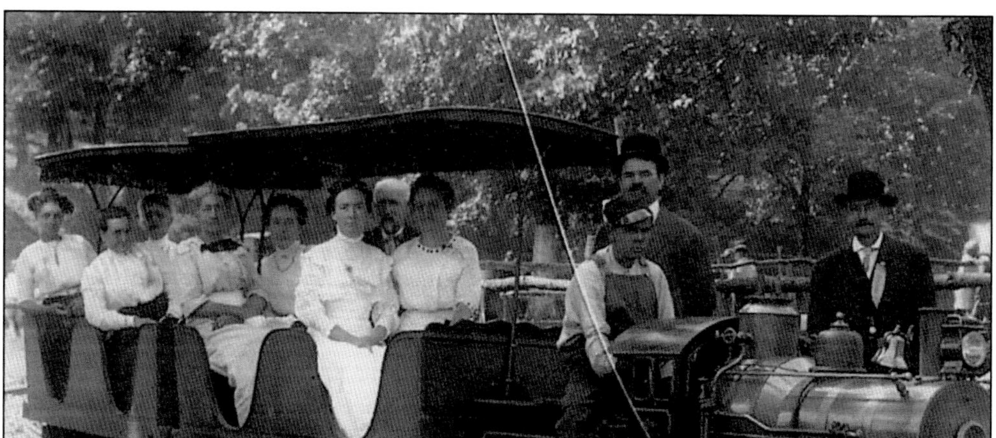

Women's Committee for 1911 DeSoto Fair. The DeSoto Fair was a very popular event in the town. This photograph shows the women's committee for the 1911 fair. (Photograph courtesy DeSoto Public Library.)

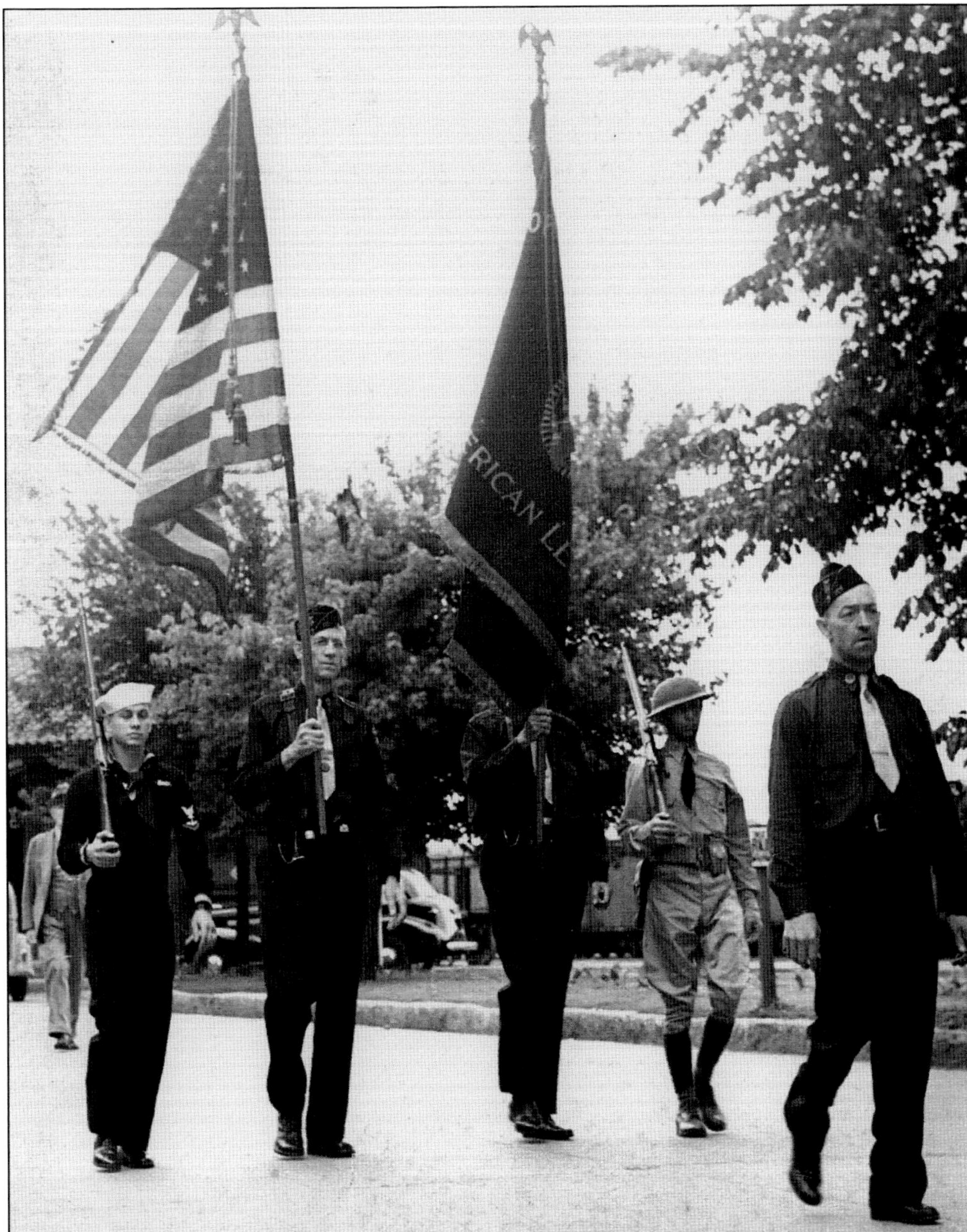

COLOR GUARD. The Color Guard proudly leads the parade down Main Street in DeSoto. (Photograph courtesy DeSoto Public Library.)

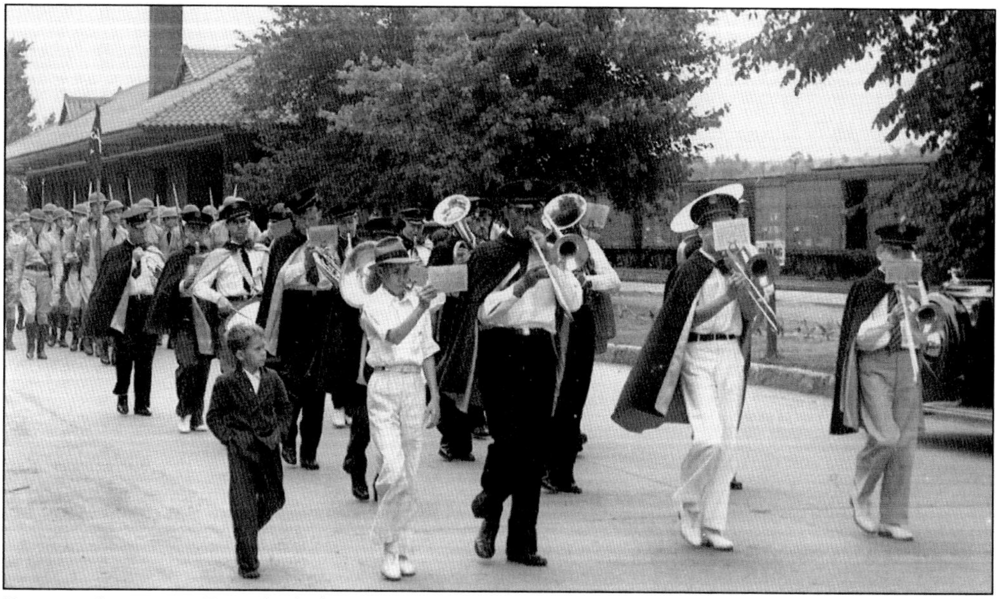

PARADE LEADERS. Everybody loves a parade, especially those who walk next to the musicians. (Photograph courtesy DeSoto Public Library.)

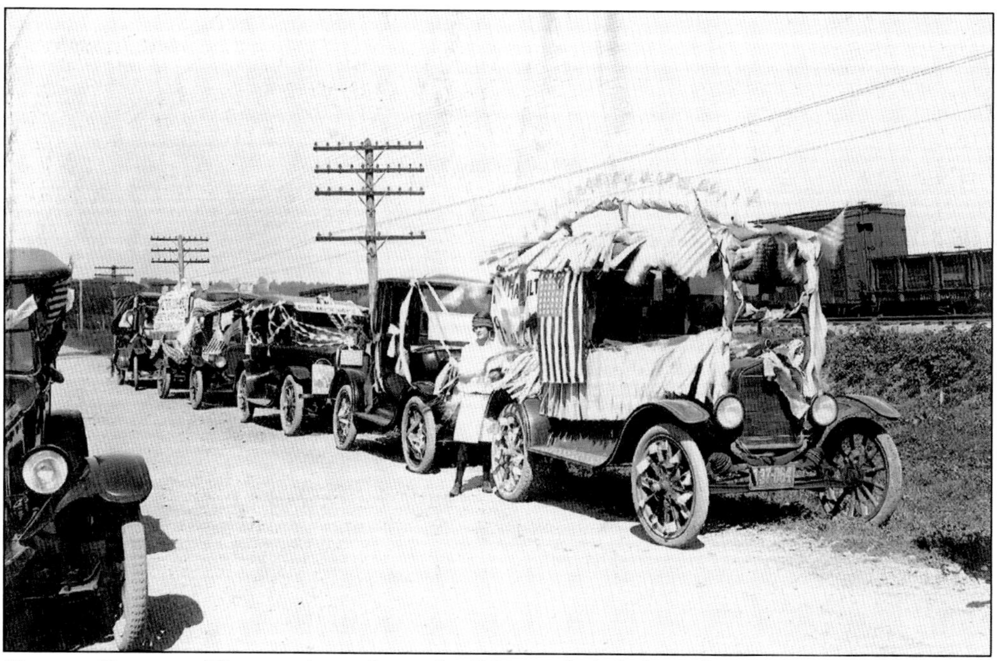

CARS IN PARADE. The parade in the early 1900s included these decorated cars. Perhaps cars were used in the parade because they were relatively few in number in those days. (Photograph courtesy Fo-Jo Studio.)

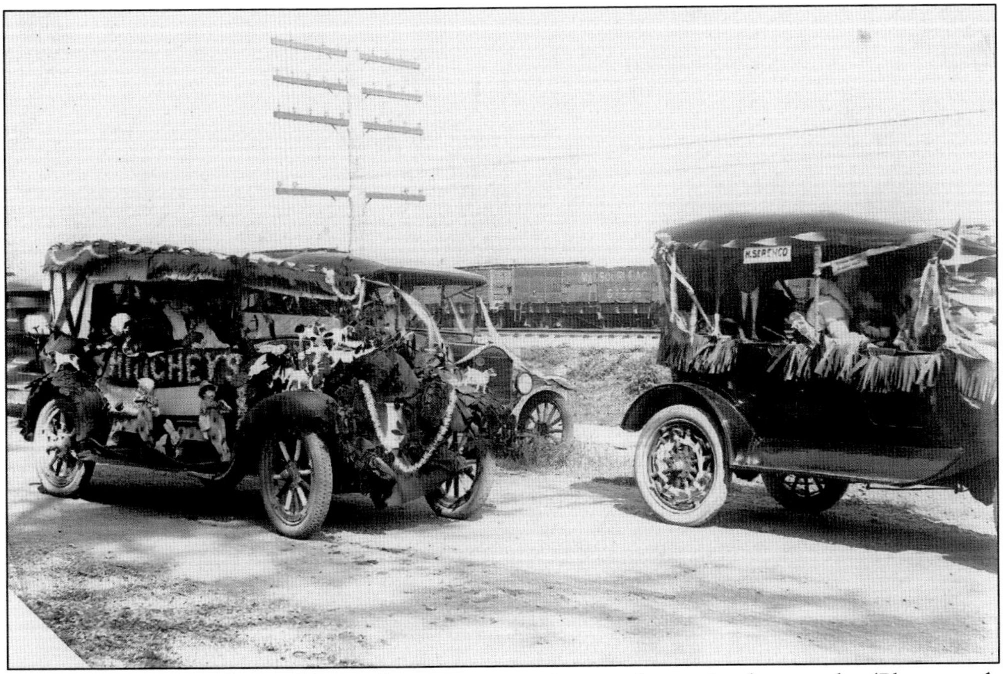

MORE DECORATED CARS. Shown here are more decorated cars in the parade. (Photograph courtesy Fo-Jo Studio.)

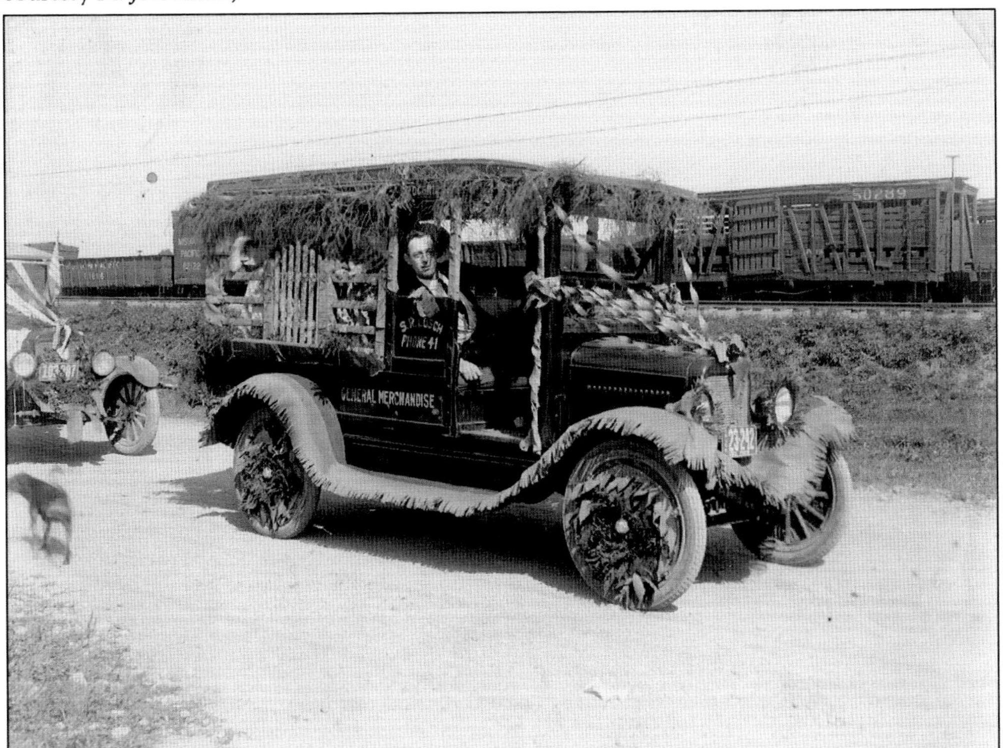

MR. HINCHEY'S CAR. Hinchey, a well-known business man in DeSoto, took great pride in his decorated car. (Photograph courtesy Fo-Jo Studio.)

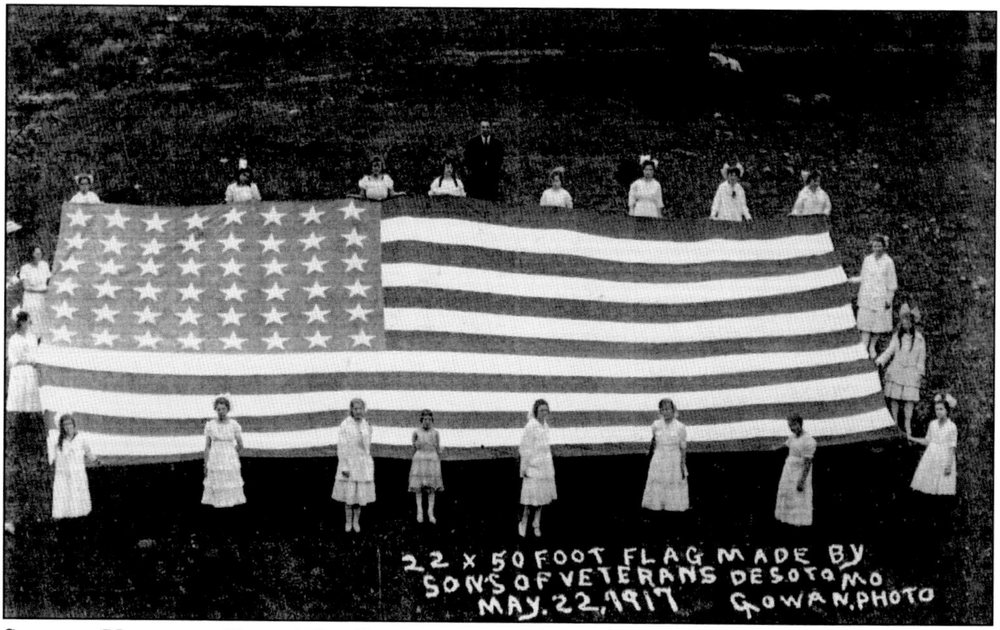

SONS OF VETERANS FLAG. This flag, measuring 22 feet by 50 feet, was made by the Sons of Veterans, May 22, 1917. (Photograph courtesy DeSoto Public Library.)

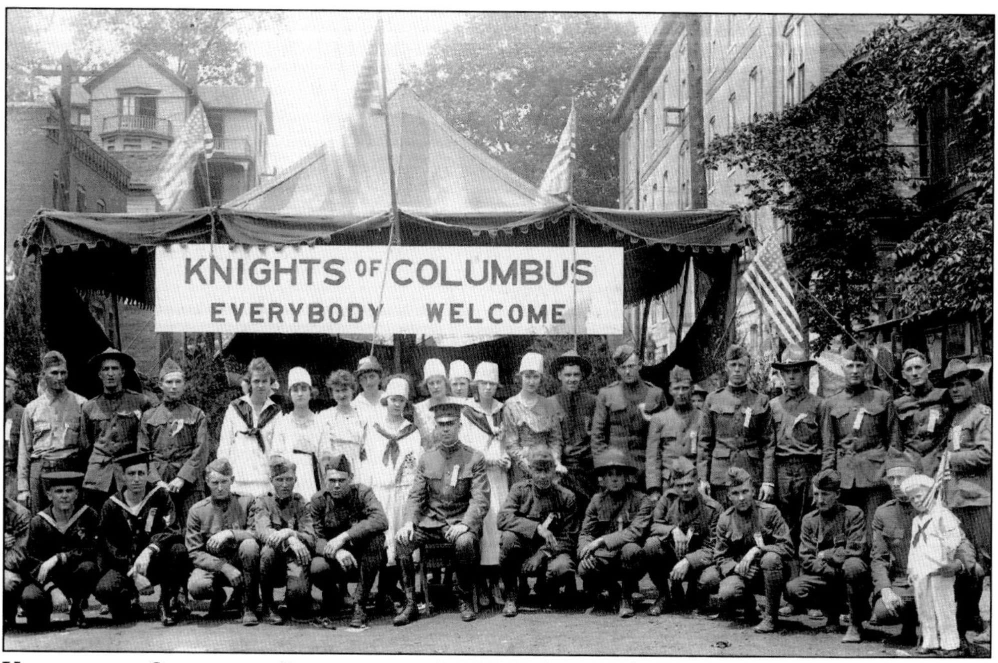

KNIGHTS OF COLUMBUS CONVENTION. In 1919, the Knights of Columbus (K.C.'s) had this booth for the servicemen of World War I. The booth was located on Easton Street, next to the old post office. (Photograph courtesy DeSoto Public Library.)

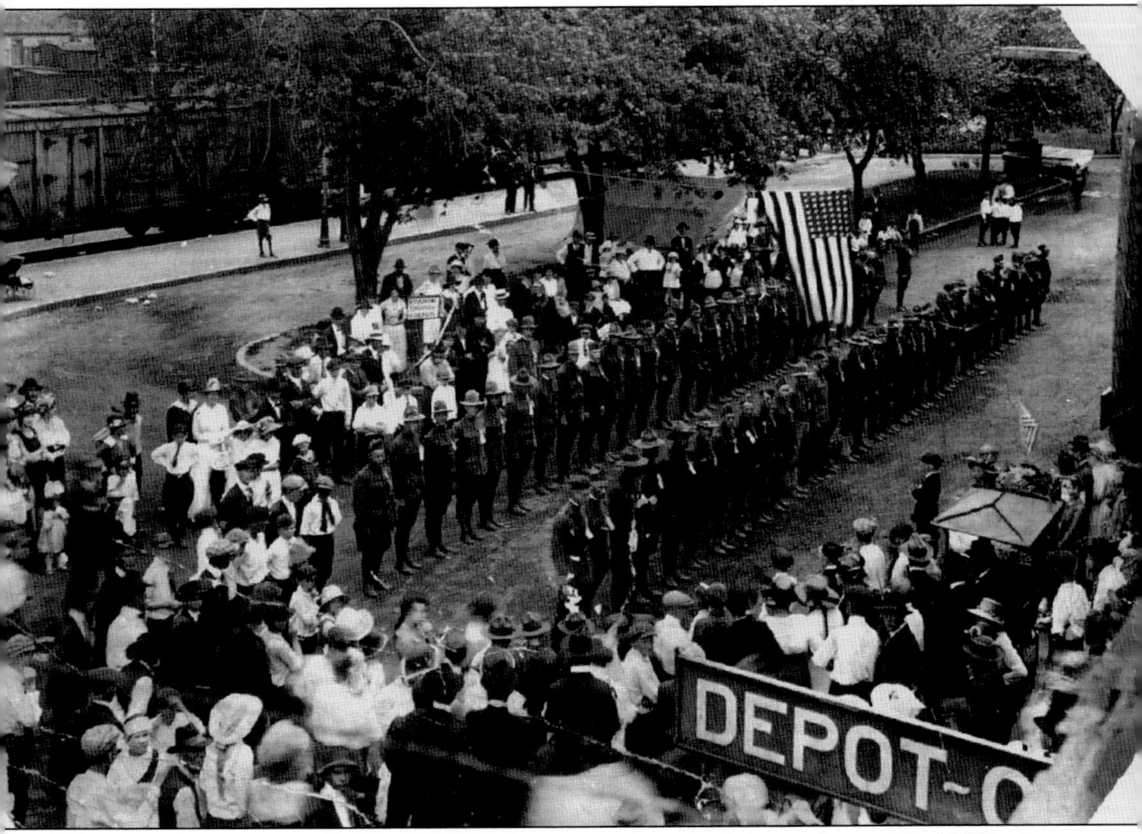

ARMED FORCES. Many of DeSoto's citizens were in the armed forces during World War I. Pictured here are some soldiers preparing to leave for war in 1917. (Photograph courtesy DeSoto Public Library.)

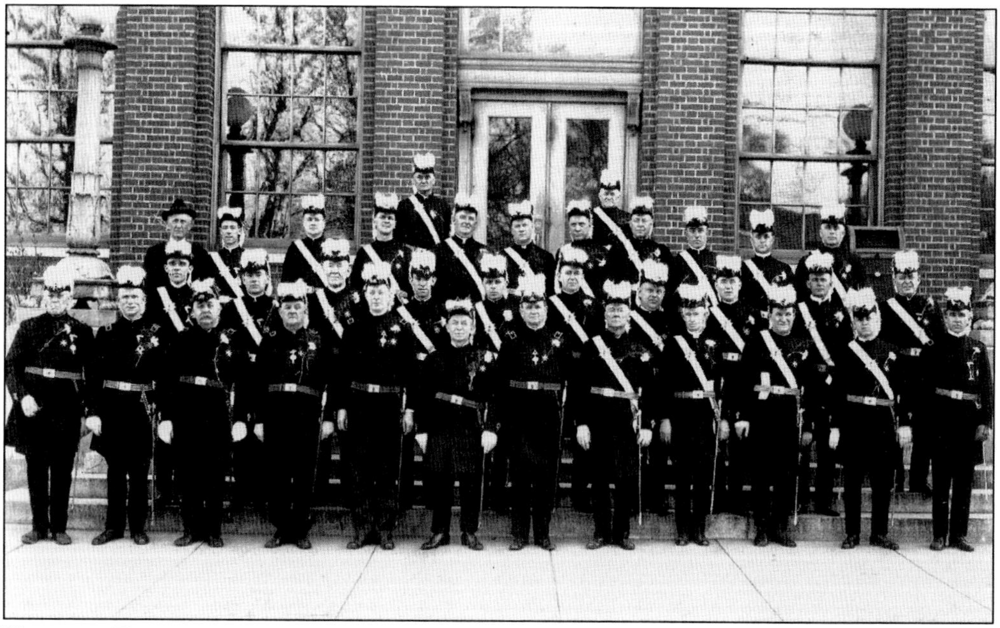

KNIGHTS TEMPLAR OF THE MASONIC LODGE, DESOTO. Partial identification includes, (first row) Bill Mallicoat, and Otto Kitinsky; (second row) Harry Crow, Joe Withington, Dr. W. W. Wieman, Frank Boyd, and Gus Freech; (third row) Dr. Auerswald, and a Mr. Green; (fourth row) D. A. Mallicoat, and T. H. Donnell. (Photograph courtesy DeSoto Historical Society and Dava Lee England.)

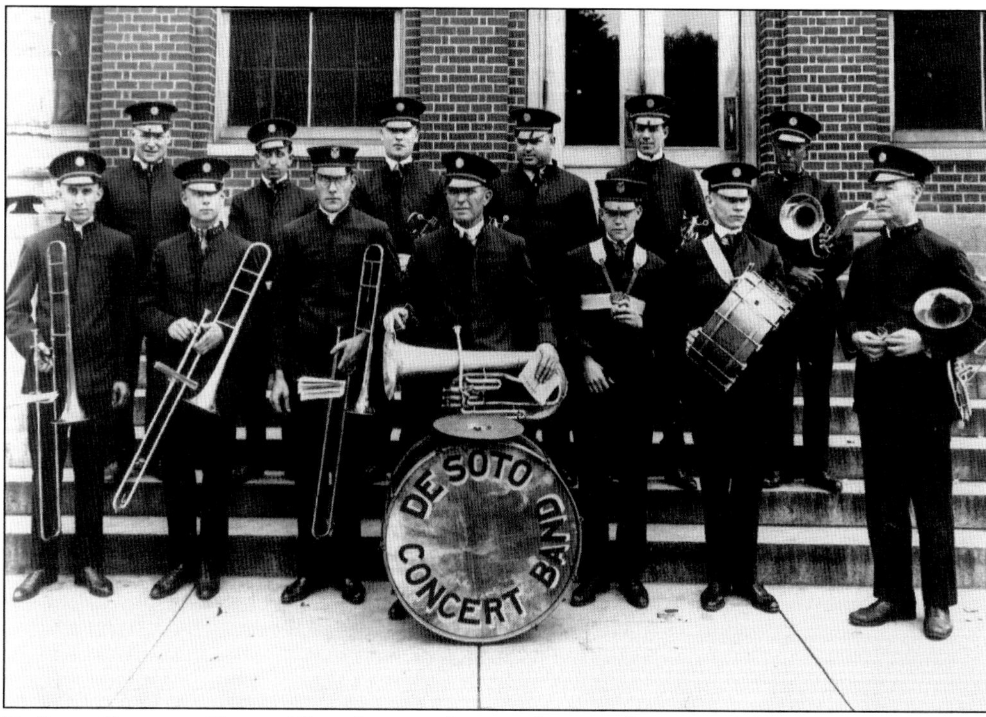

DESOTO CONCERT BAND. This photograph was taken on the steps of the former DeSoto Post Office, now city hall. (Photograph courtesy DeSoto Historical Society.)

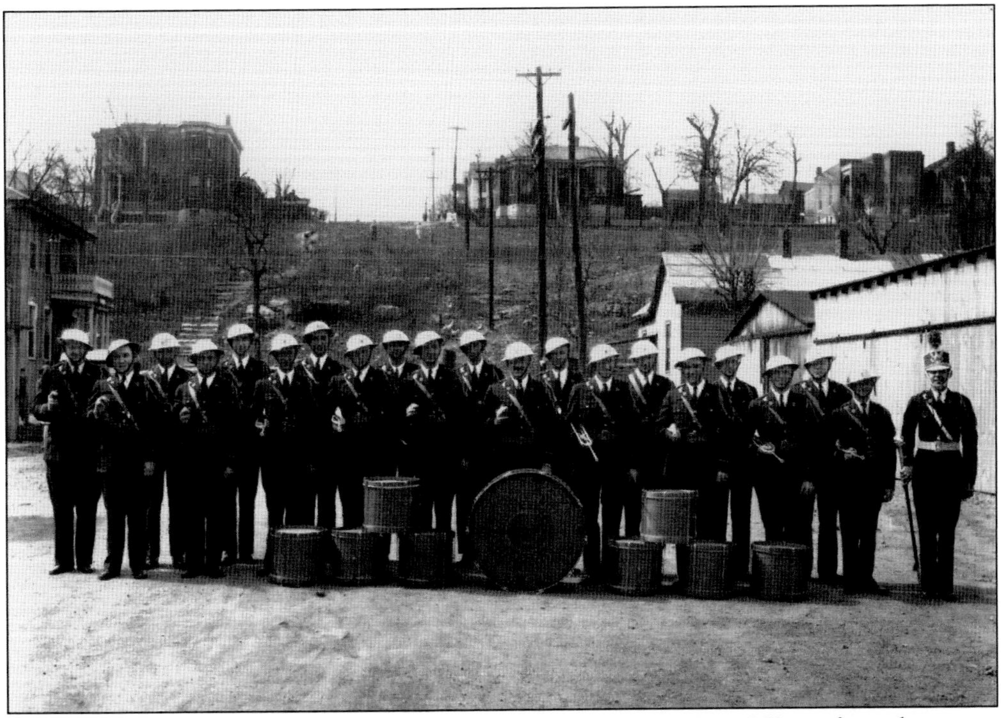

American Legion Band. The Band of the American Legion, Post 253, performed at many civic functions. (Photograph courtesy DeSoto Historical Society.)

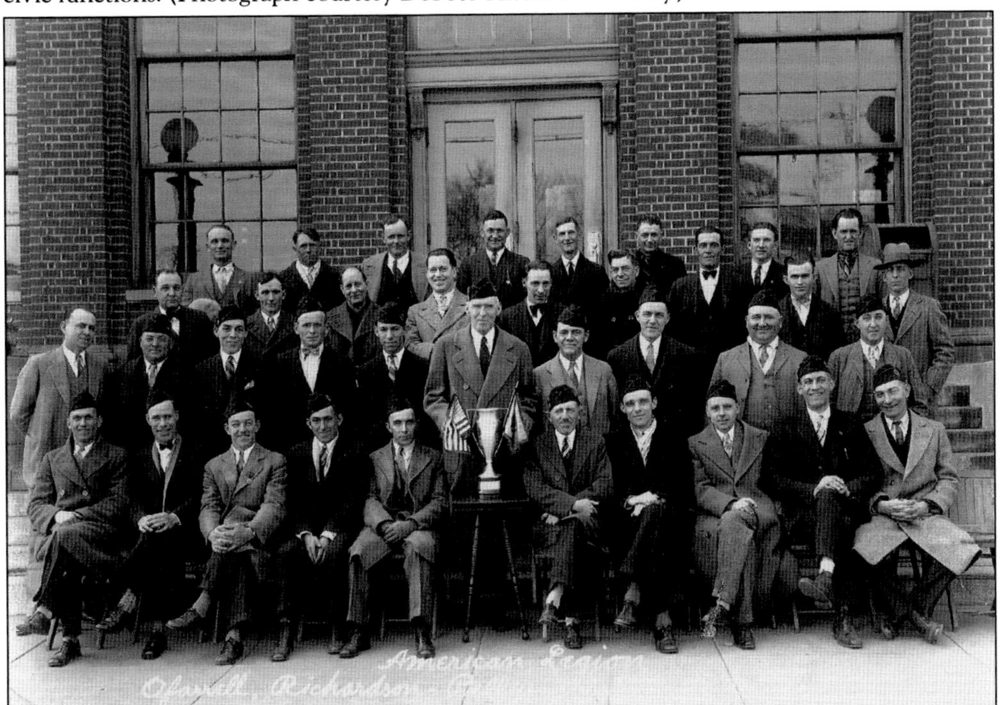

American Legion. The American Legion is just one of the many service organizations that have been established in DeSoto over the years. (Photograph courtesy Fo-Jo Studio.)

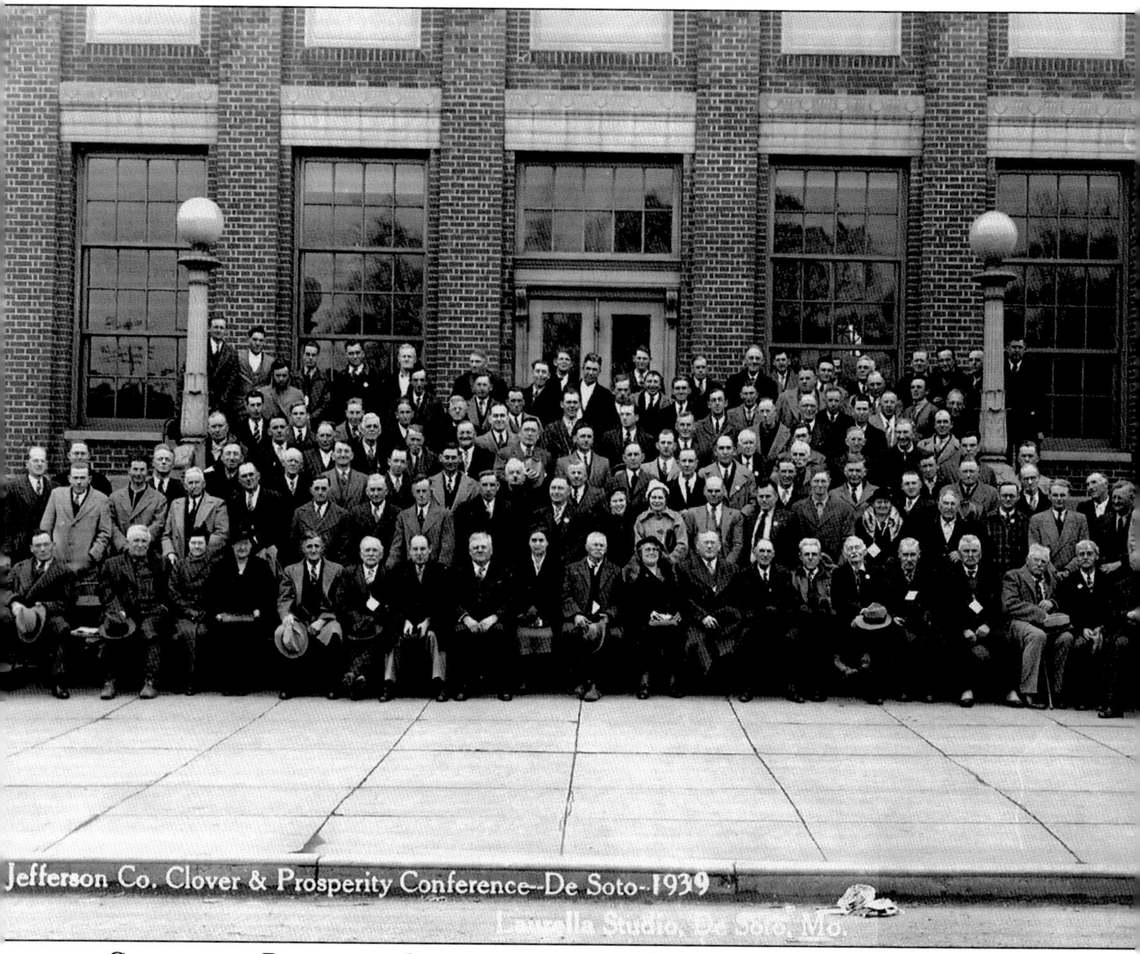

CLOVER AND PROSPERITY CONFERENCE, 1939. This organization of prominent persons in Jefferson County flourished throughout the 1930s. (Photograph courtesy Fo-Jo Studio.)

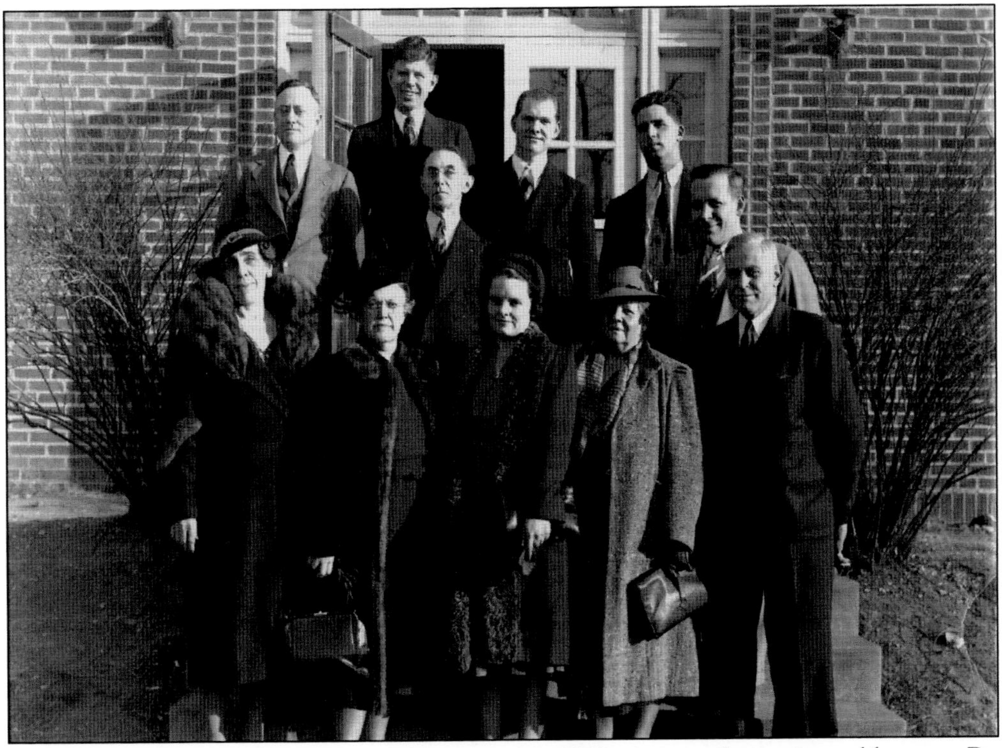

CHRISTMAS CAROL ASSOCIATION, DECEMBER 20, 1939. Among those pictured here are Dr. Mary Ann McMillen, Floyd Wilson, Florence Donnelly, Dr. T. B. Turnbaugh, George Burgess, John Boles, Dudley Milton, and Walker Ames. The original founder of this group was Geraldine Fauth. Caroling groups from various churches sang throughout the town and collected funds to be used for various charitable purposes. (Photograph courtesy DeSoto Public Library.)

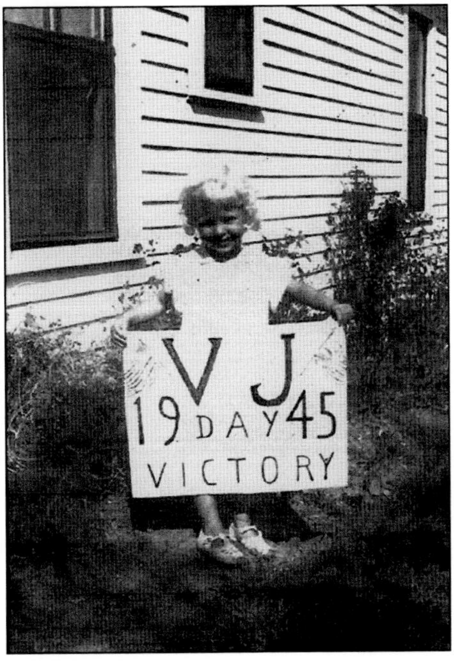

J SIGN. This 1945 photograph shows Leatha Ann Watt at 1018 South Third Street holding the sign indicating "VJ Day." (Photograph courtesy Leatha Watt Combs.)

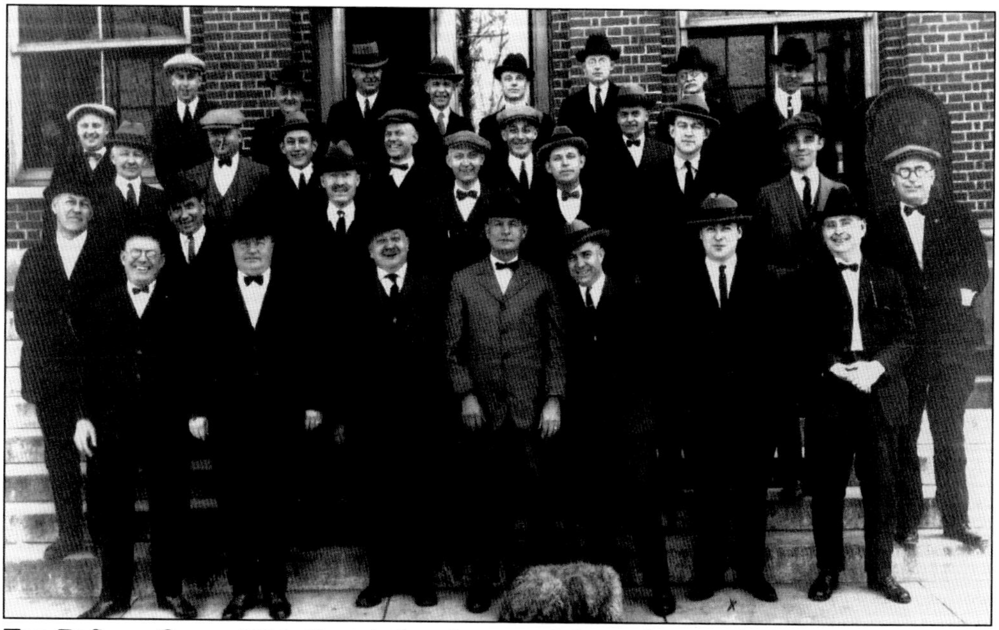

THE DESOTO CLUB, 1924. Partial identification of those photographed are, (first row) Bert Ewing, Dr. Chamberlin, Charles Davidson, and Max Schwaegerle; (second row) Kirk Jones, Gene Edgar, Bern Duffner, E. S. Fauth, and Harry Crow; (third row) Lee Mothershead, Joe Pieschel, and Ward Hamel; (fourth row) Bob Coxwell, A. F. Slawson, and Lucas Duffner. (Photograph courtesy DeSoto Historical Society and Marguerite Schwaegerle.)

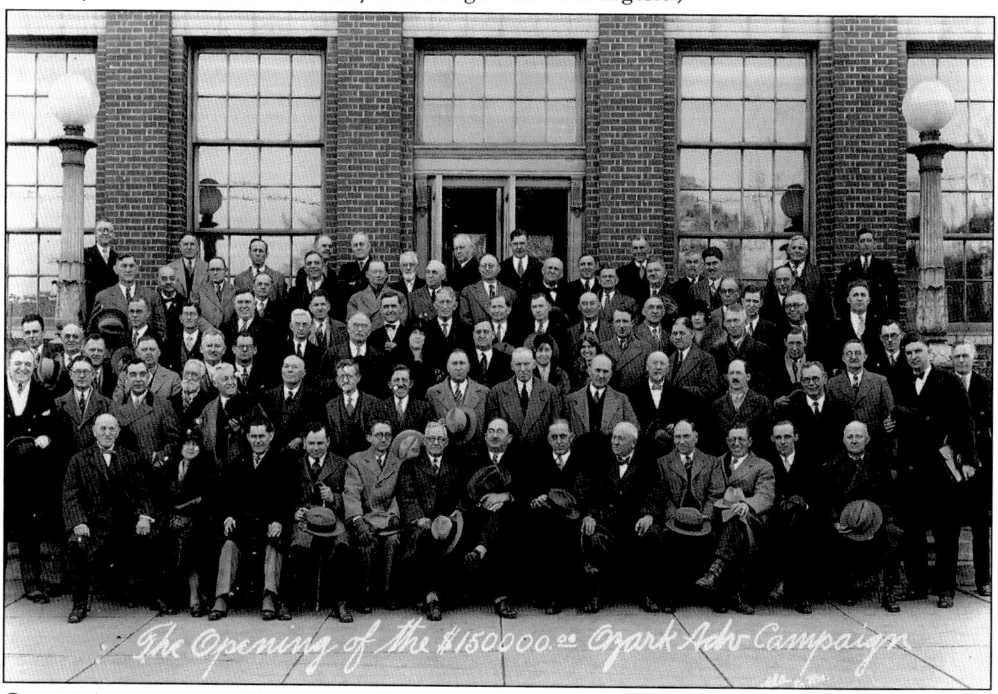

OZARK ADVERTISING CAMPAIGN. Prominent business leaders gather in front of the DeSoto Post Office (presently city hall) for the opening of the $150,000 Ozark Advertising Campaign. (Photograph courtesy Fo-Jo Studio.)

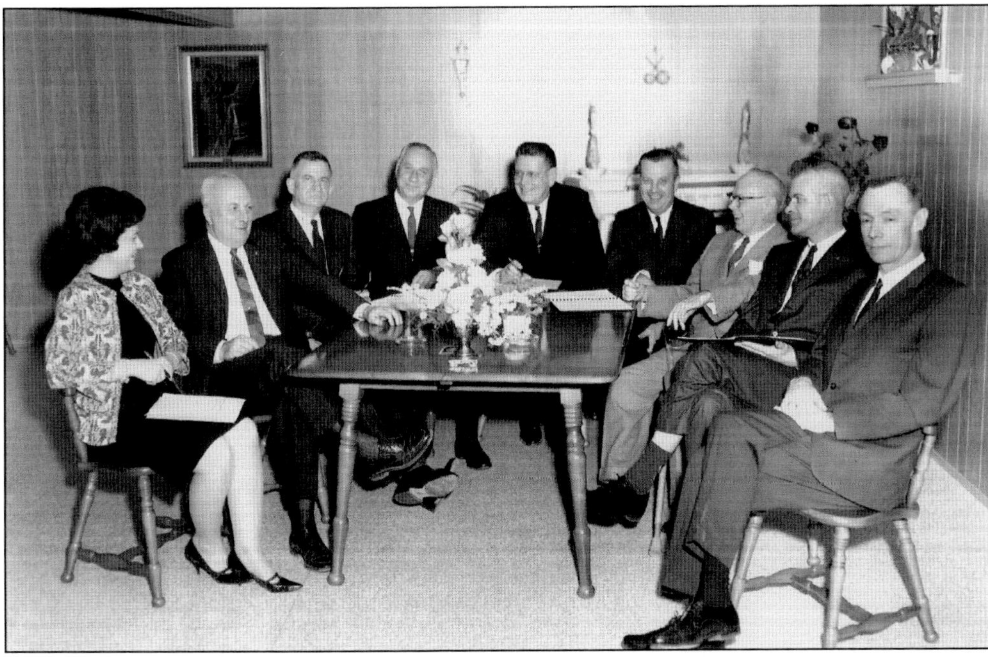

DIRECTORS OF STATE BANK OF DESOTO. The directors of the newly chartered State Bank of DeSoto are, from left to right, Mary Lee Doyen, Gilbert J. Long, Dr. Thomas A. Donnell, Claude J. Cook, Theo P. Mueller Sr., Alfred E. DeRousse, Felix J. Milfeld, Dr. Harold E. Donnell, and Charles Baker. (Photograph courtesy DeSoto Historical Society.)

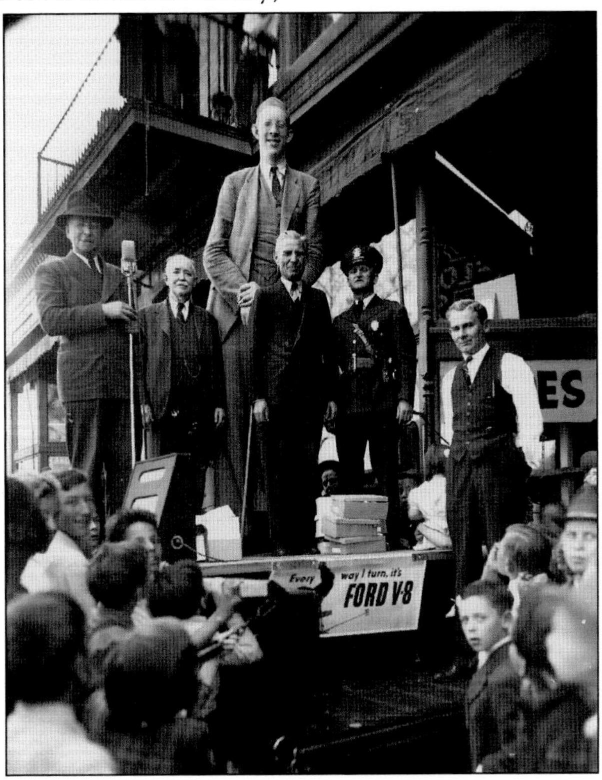

ROBERT WADLOW. Robert Wadlow visited DeSoto in 1939 to advertise Peter's Shoes, which were sold at Gillman's Department Store. Wadlow was nine feet tall and was known as the "Gentle Giant of Alton, Illinois." Also included in this photo are Dr. Gibson (mayor of DeSoto), Dave Lewis, Ray Williams (police chief), and J. R. Marshall. (Photograph courtesy DeSoto Public Library.)

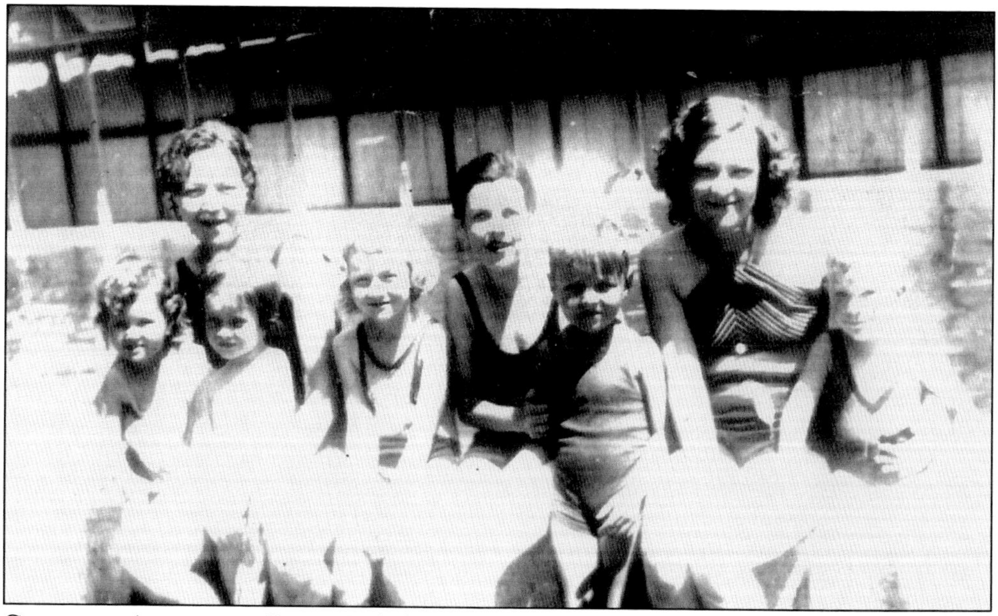

GROUP AT ARLINGTON POOL. Included in this group at the pool are Jeri Schrum LaBratt, Katherine Schrum Page, Opal Salisbury Schrum, Barbara Salisbury Stapes, Charles Salisbury, Billy Olster, and Helen Ditch Salisbury. (Photograph courtesy Arlington Bed and Breakfast and Diana Johnson.)

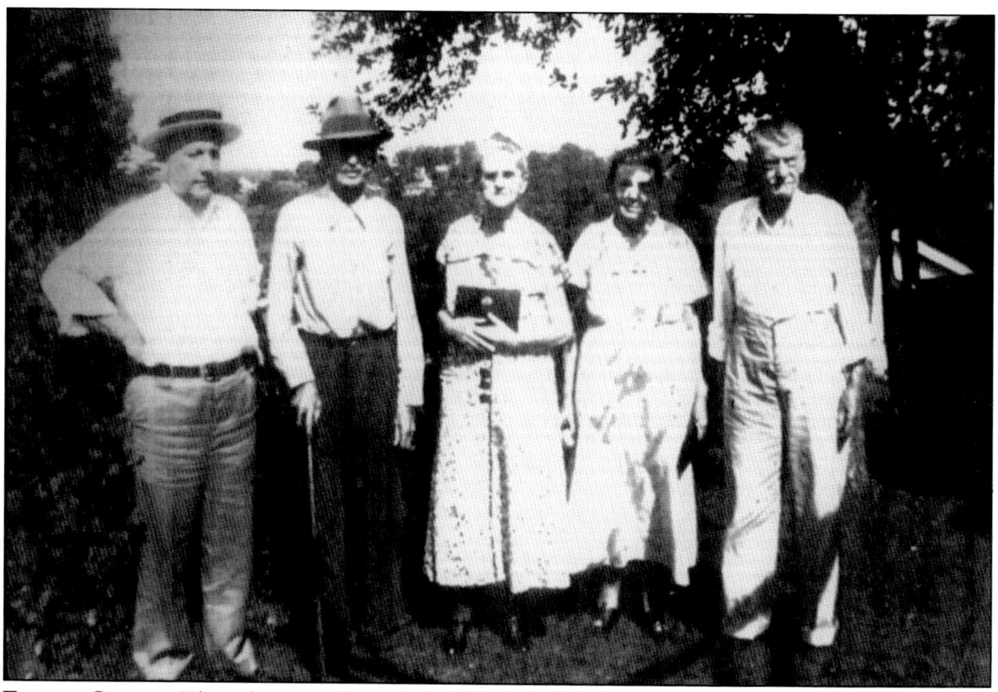

FAMILY GROUP. This photograph includes James Edgar Hopson, Newton West Frazier, Alice McMullin Butler, Elizabeth Watt Frazier, and James Latimer Watt. (Photograph courtesy Loretta Shannon Goehring.)

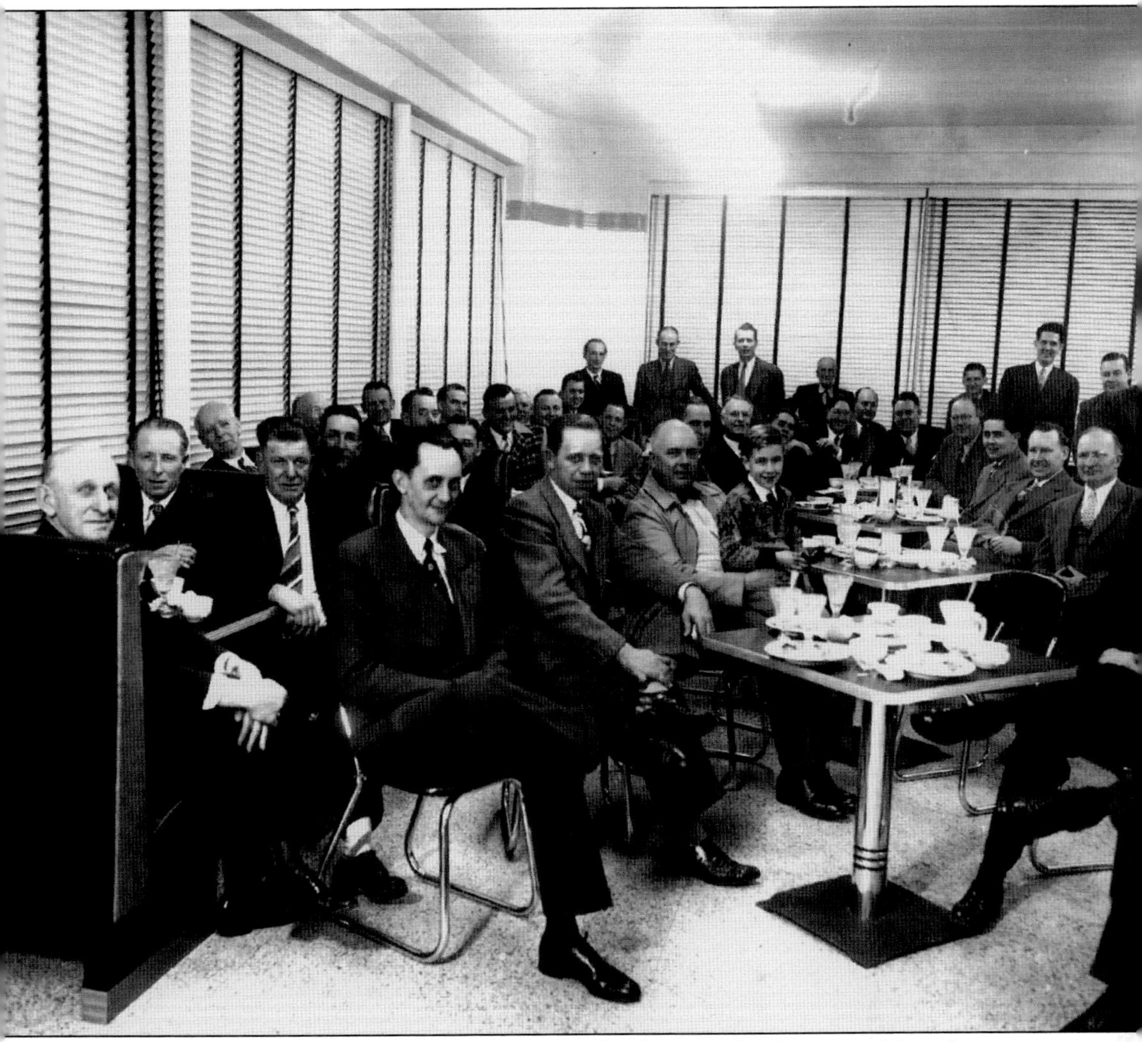

Rotary Club Meeting. This rotary meeting was held in People's Dairy on Main Street in 1944. Included in this photograph are Bob Browning, Frank Arnote, Ed Underwood, Harold Holmes, Richard Semple, Vernie Page, Dr. I. P. Ingels, M. A. Bay, Harold Ellas, Oscar Klaus, Bill Ehreaberg, Edwin Mathes, Earl Kisler, Raymond Gasche, Ralph Poole, Edward Wiggen, Dr. S. M. Hoffee, Marvin Oakes, R. J. Windsor, Fred Couch, Roy Reel (mayor), Byron Munson, Walter Finnical, Lindell Rowe, Nich Karthen of Bonne Terre, Dr. M. P. McDonoght, Larry Higdon, Harold Loomis, Clarence Preiss, Don Dietrich, Mickey Vaughn, Rev. Liston Johnson, Cecil Cross, Walker Ames, Dr. George Hopson, Dr. C. A. Rehm, Al Gilmore, "Spud" Allers (past district governor for Rotary), Ward Tierney, Lewis Roop, A. E. Vaughn (host), and Claude Cook. (Photograph courtesy DeSoto Public Library.)

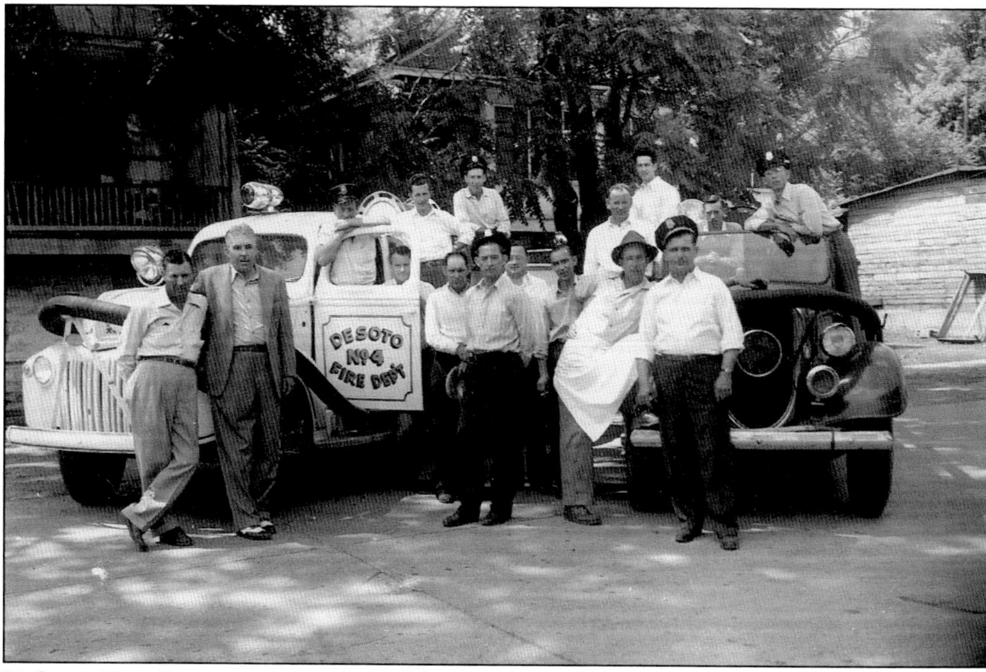

DESOTO FIRE DEPARTMENT, 1940S. The members of the DeSoto Fire Department pose for their official photograph. (Photograph courtesy DeSoto Historical Society.)

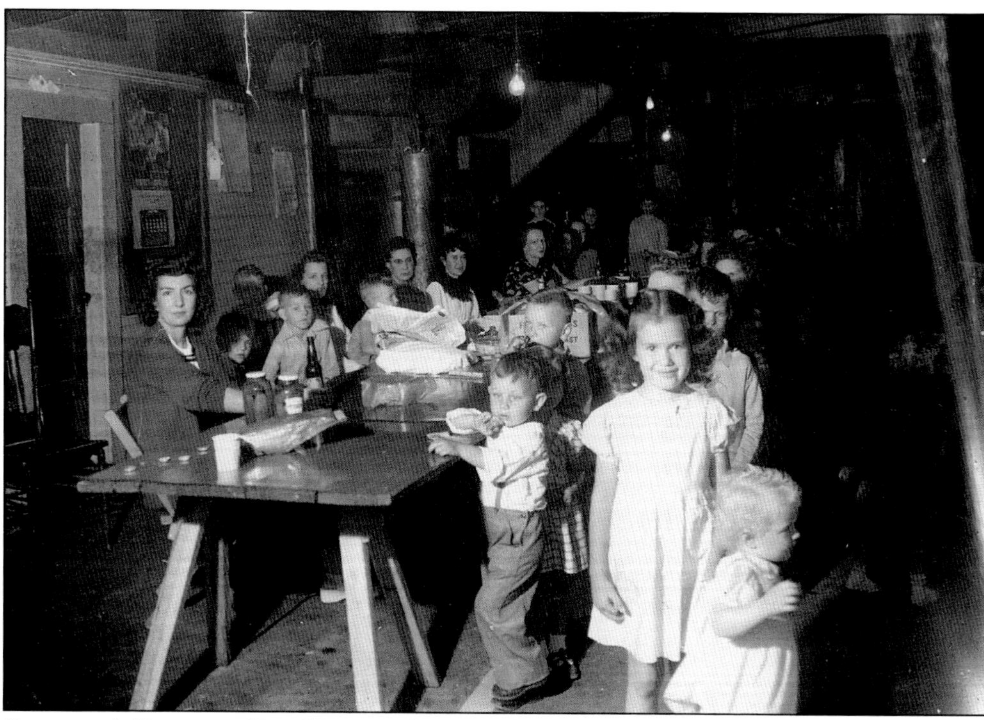

CHILDREN'S PARTY AT FIRE HOUSE. This party for the children of DeSoto was held in the old fire house in the 1940s. (Photograph courtesy DeSoto Historical Society.)

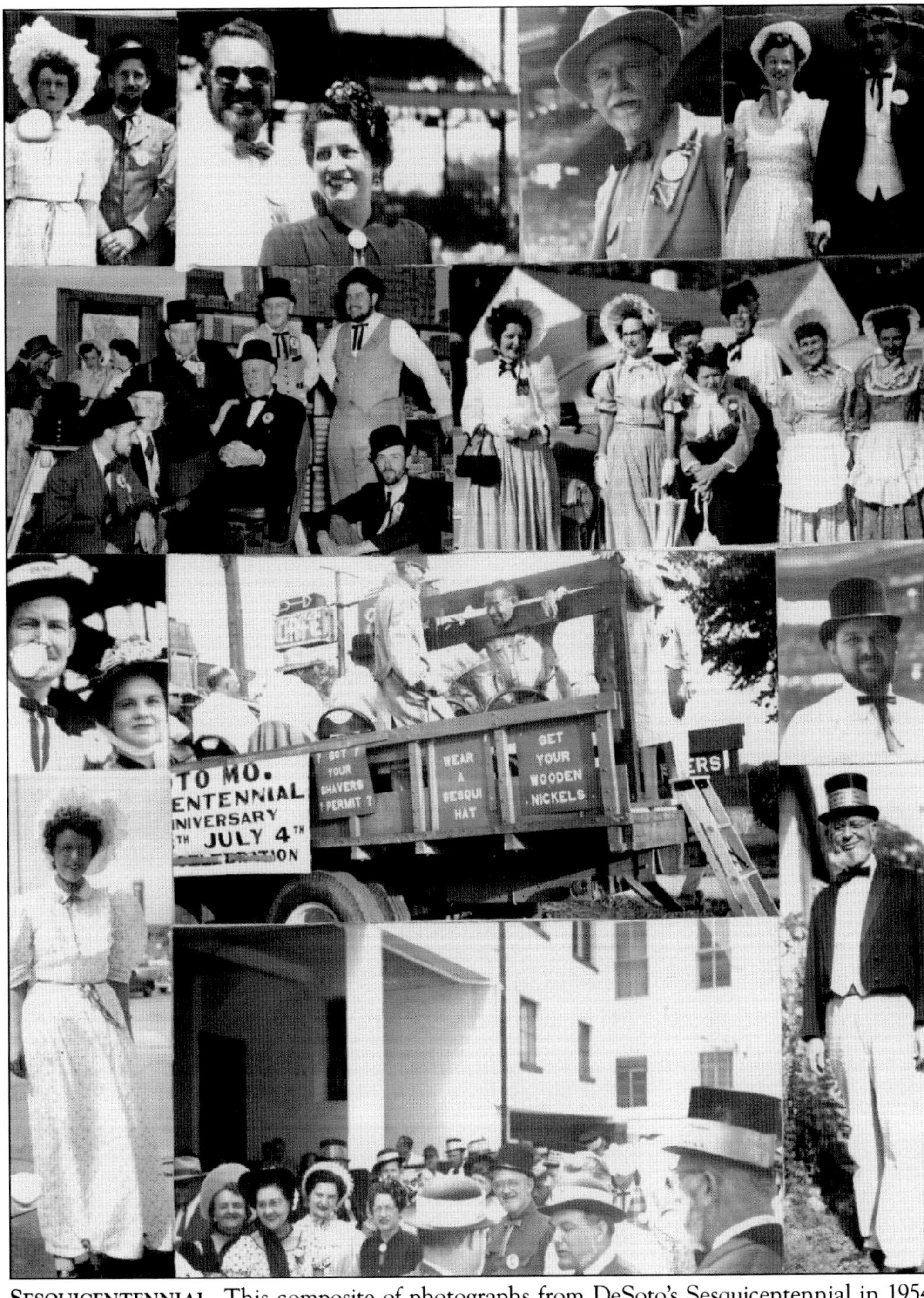

SESQUICENTENNIAL. This composite of photographs from DeSoto's Sesquicentennial in 1954 depict the many activities that took place during that celebration. (Photograph courtesy DeSoto Public Library.)

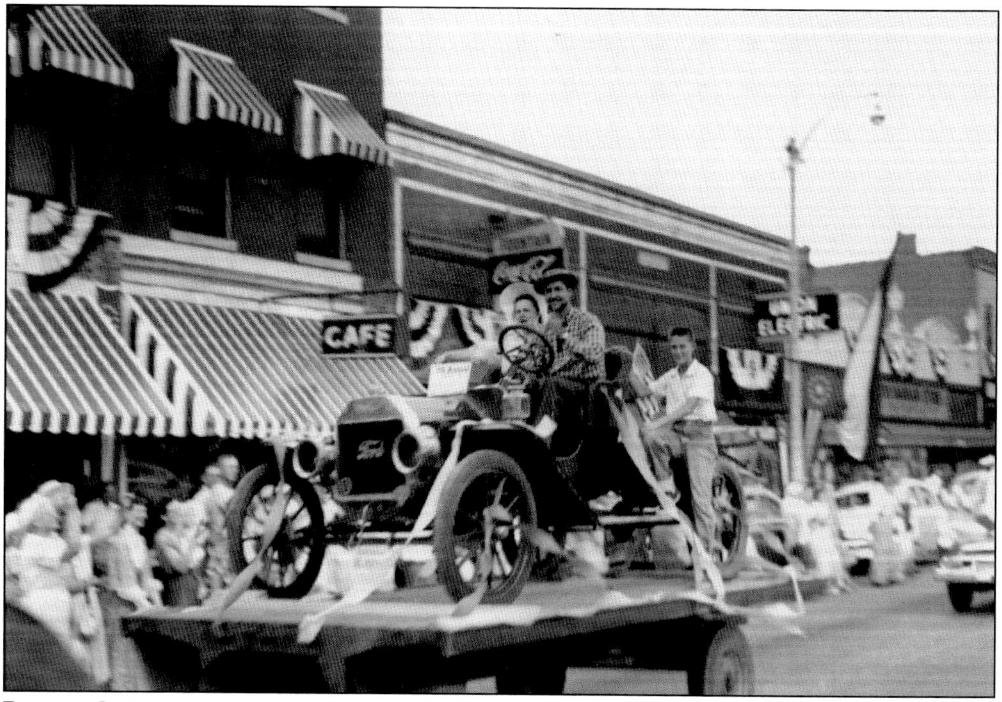

PARADE CARS, 1954. Antique cars were the focus during the parade on Main Street. (Photograph courtesy DeSoto Public Library.)

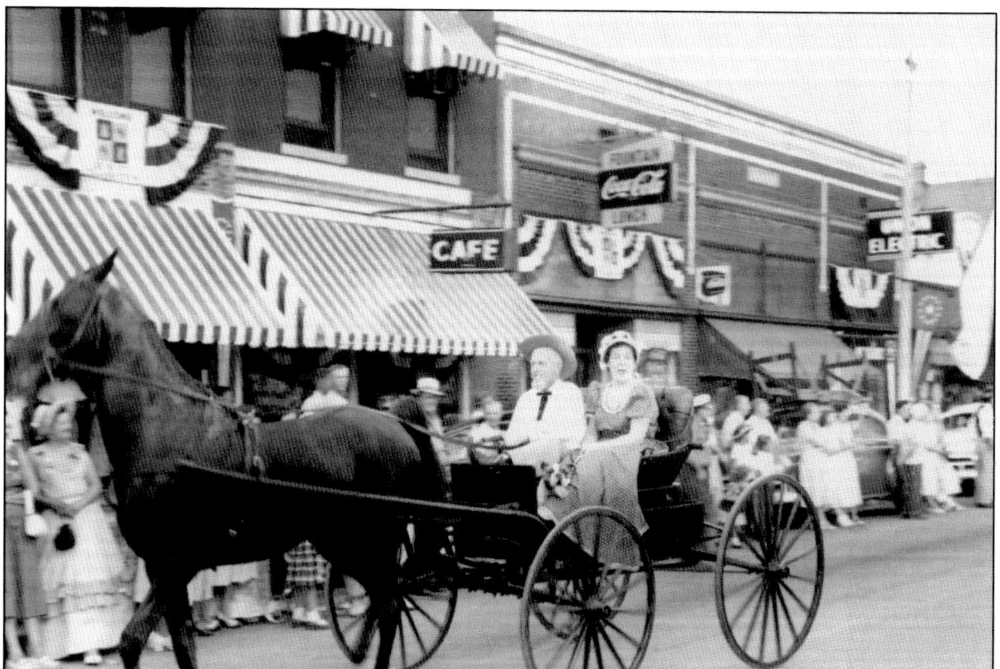

MAIN STREET PARADE, 1954. Another view of the historical parade on Main Street. (Photograph courtesy DeSoto Public Library.)

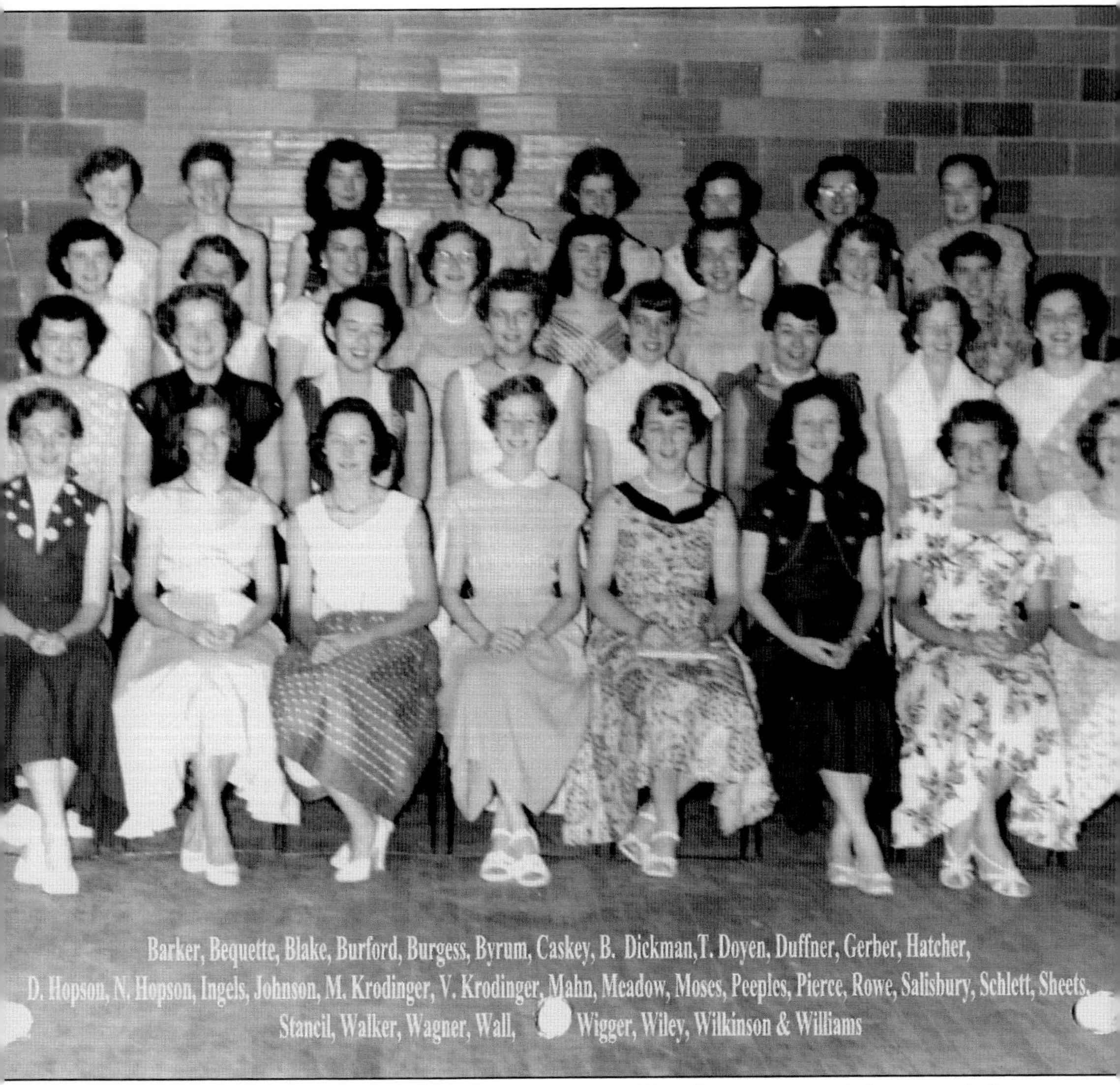

QUEEN CONTESTANTS DURING THE SESQUICENTENNIAL. The family names of the young ladies pictured here are, Barker, Bequette, Blake, Burford, Burgess, Byrum, Caskey, B. Dickman, Doyen, Duffner, Gerber, Hatcher, D. Hopson, N. Hopson, Ingels, Johnson, M. Krodinger, V. Krodinger, Mahn, Meadow, Moses, Peeples, Peirce, Rowe, Salisbury, Schlett, Sheets, Stancil, Walker, Wall, Wigger, Wiley, Wilkinson, and Williams. (Photograph courtesy DeSoto Public Library.)

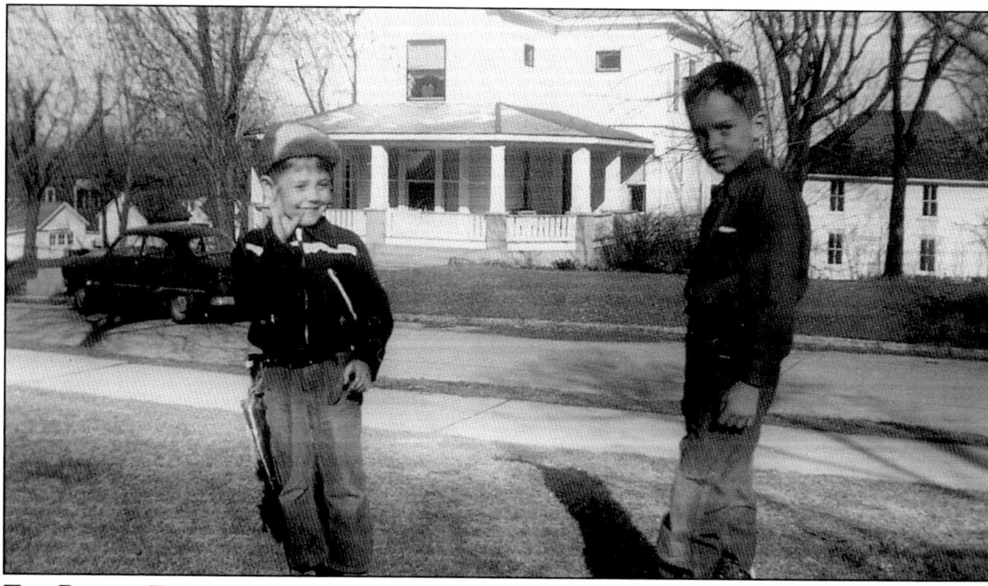

TWO BOYS IN FRONT OF HOUSE AT 401 SOUTH FIFTH STREET, 1953. This home, built in 1871 by Charles Hemme, was part of the Rathbun and Donaldson addition to DeSoto. The house was first purchased by Frank Smith, a postmaster of DeSoto between 1871 and 1889, and his wife Mattie. John E. Putnam, a railroad night weigher for the Iron Mountain and Southern Railroad, and his wife Sarah were the next owners of the house. When John died in 1904, the house was sold to Dr. and Mrs. Walter Easton Gibson. The home was used for many years as a residence and doctor's office. Dr. Gibson was also a mayor of DeSoto in the late 1930s and early 1940s. (Photograph courtesy Stephen Pipitone.)

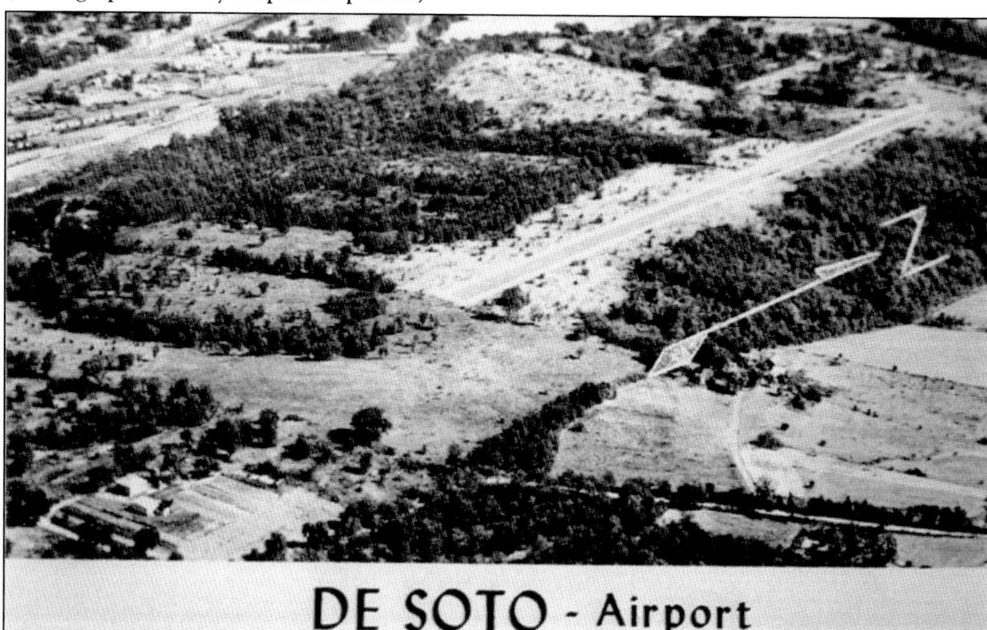

DESOTO AIRPORT. Seen here is an aerial view of the DeSoto Airport that was located one-half mile east of the city in the area of Harmony Hills Road. (Photograph courtesy DeSoto Historical Society.)

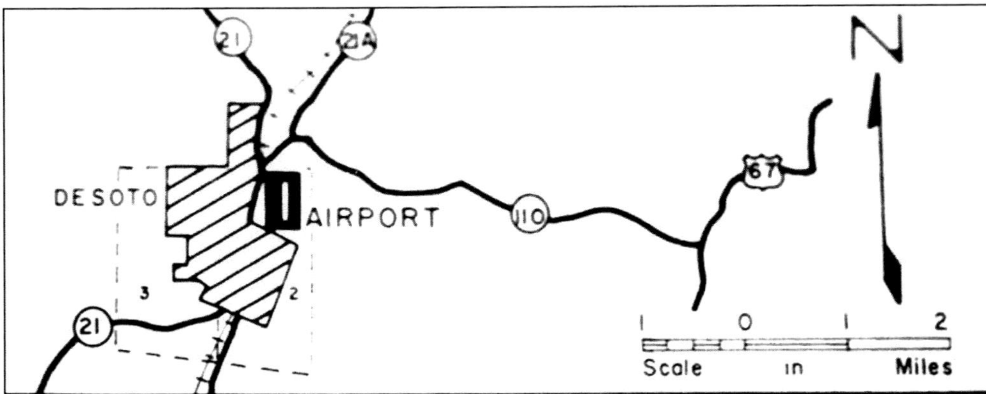

Elevation: 675' | Lights: None
From City: ½ mi. E | Telephone: 9656
Latitude: 38° 08' | Transportation: Taxi
Longitude: 90° 33' | Meals & Lodging: In town
Runways: 1-19 2000'x75' Turf | Services: 80 oct., hangar, tie-down
Communications: None | Remarks: Attended by request

STATISTICS ON THE DESOTO AIRPORT. This small airport, operational in the 1950s, is no longer in existence. (Photograph courtesy DeSoto Historical Society.)

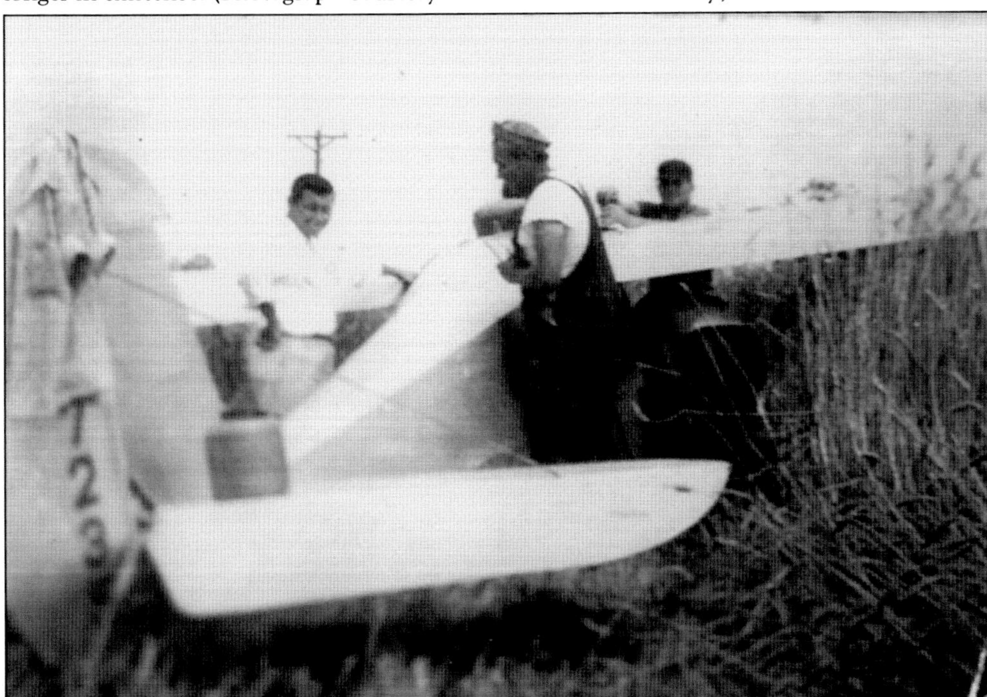

PLANE CRASH. This small airplane was downed in a minor crash on land near Olson's. (Photograph courtesy DeSoto Historical Society.)

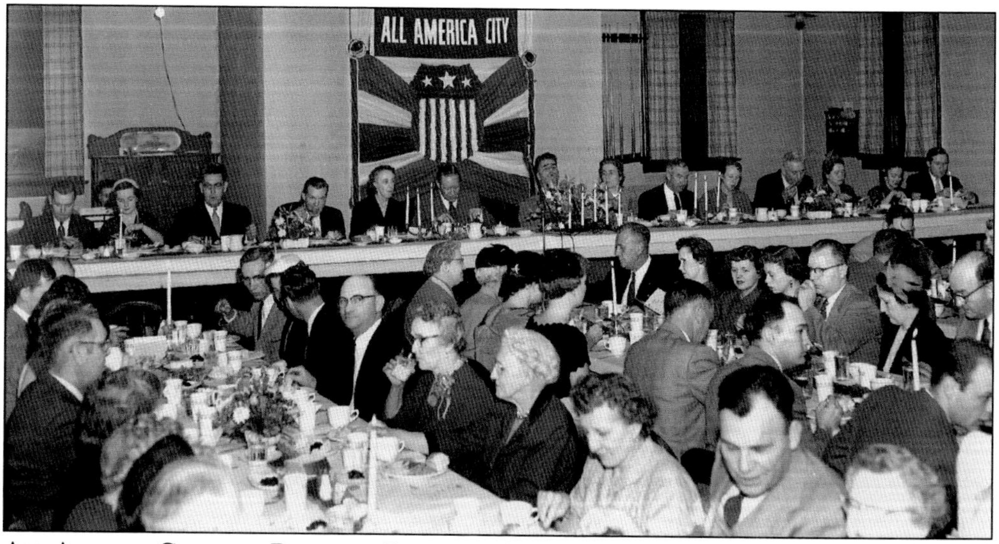

ALL AMERICA CITY AND PLANNED PROGRESS AWARDS DINNER, FEBRUARY 20, 1954. Seated at the head table are, from left to right, Colbert Lais (Jefferson district sales manager for Union Electric), Mary Lais, Walter Finnical (chairman of Planned Progress Council), Harry R. Scott (regional manager of Union Electric), Olive Fitch (DHS faculty advisor), Merrill Skinner (Union Electric vice president), Walker Ames (toastmaster), Edith Ames, Thomas "Coke" Brickey (Jefferson district manager of Union Electric), Margaret Brickey, E. G. McCreary (mayor of DeSoto), Rosalie McCreary, Mrs. Robert McNamara, and Rev. Robert McNamara. (Photograph courtesy DeSoto Historical Society.)

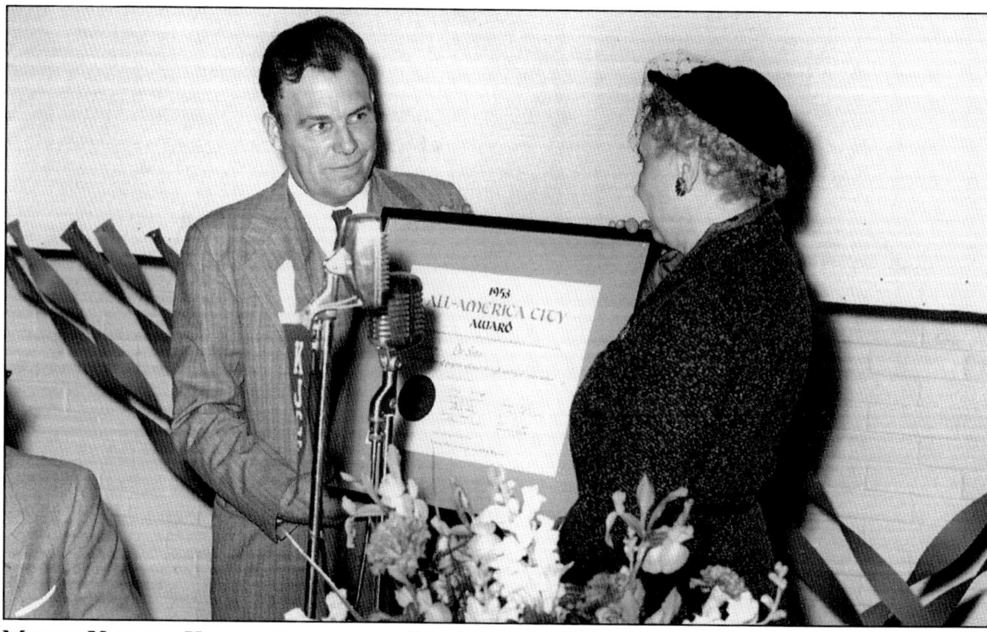

MAYOR VERNON YOUNG ACCEPTING ALL AMERICA CITY AWARD. Mayor Young accepted the All America City Award for 1953 from Mrs. Virgil Loeb, director of the National Municipal League. The award was given for noteworthy citizen action directed toward improvement in government, schools, housing, welfare, and other important areas of civic activity. (Photograph courtesy DeSoto Historical Society.)

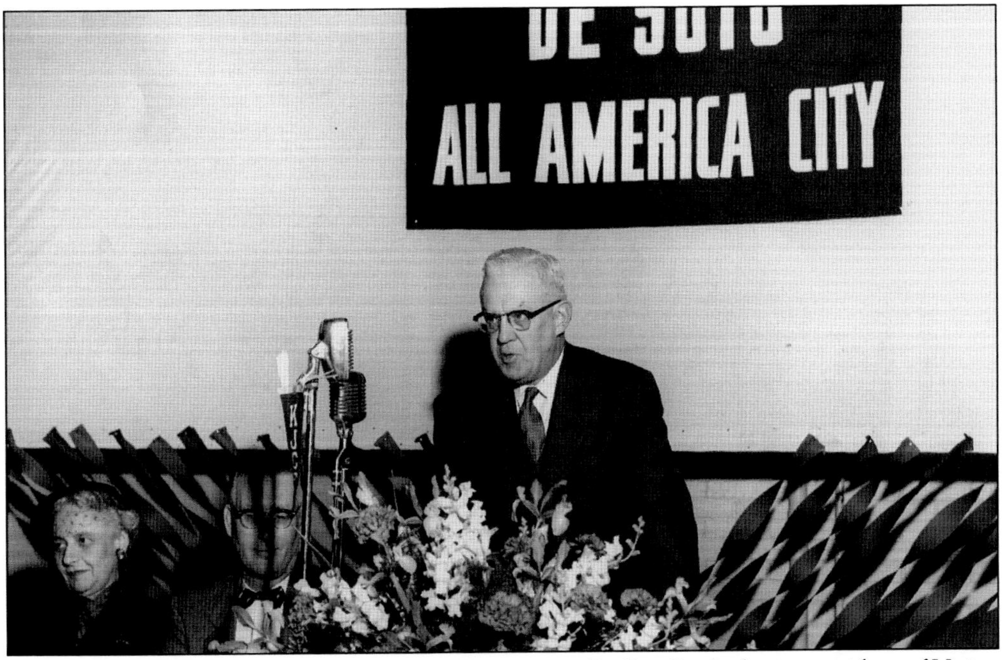

DUDLEY SANFORD, SPEAKING AT AWARDS CEREMONY. Dudley Sanford, vice-president of Union Electric, spoke at the 1953 All America City and Planned Progress Awards Banquet on February 20, 1954 in the DeSoto High School Auditorium. (Photograph courtesy DeSoto Historical Society.)

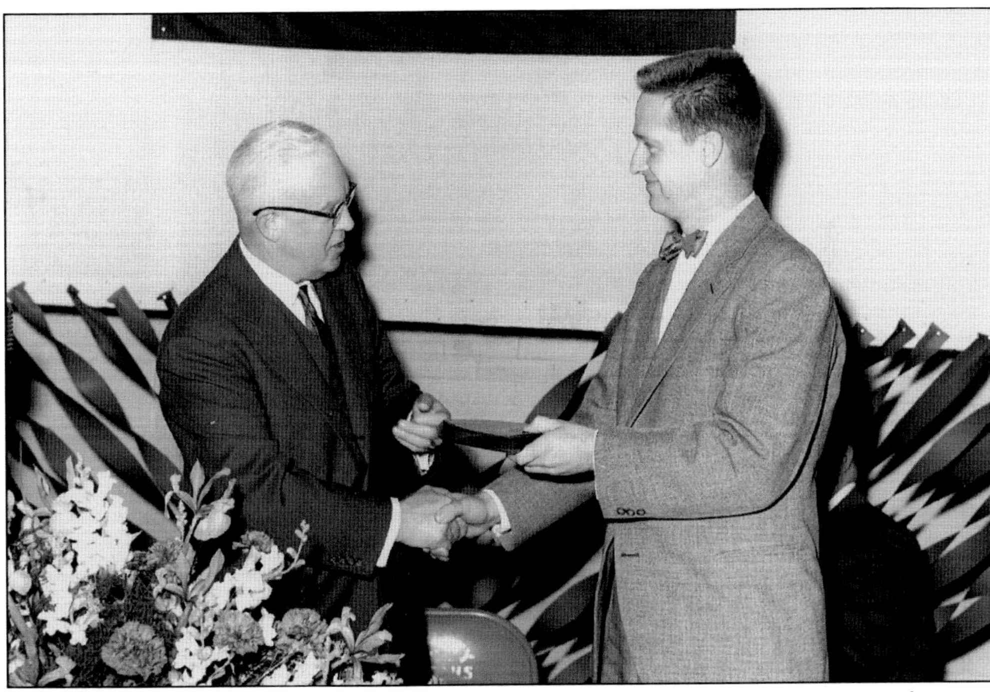

DUDLEY SANFORD PRESENTING PLAQUE TO JEREMIAH NIXON. Jeremiah Nixon was chairman of the 1953 Adult Council that worked on recommendations made by the school survey in 1952. (Photograph courtesy DeSoto Historical Society.)

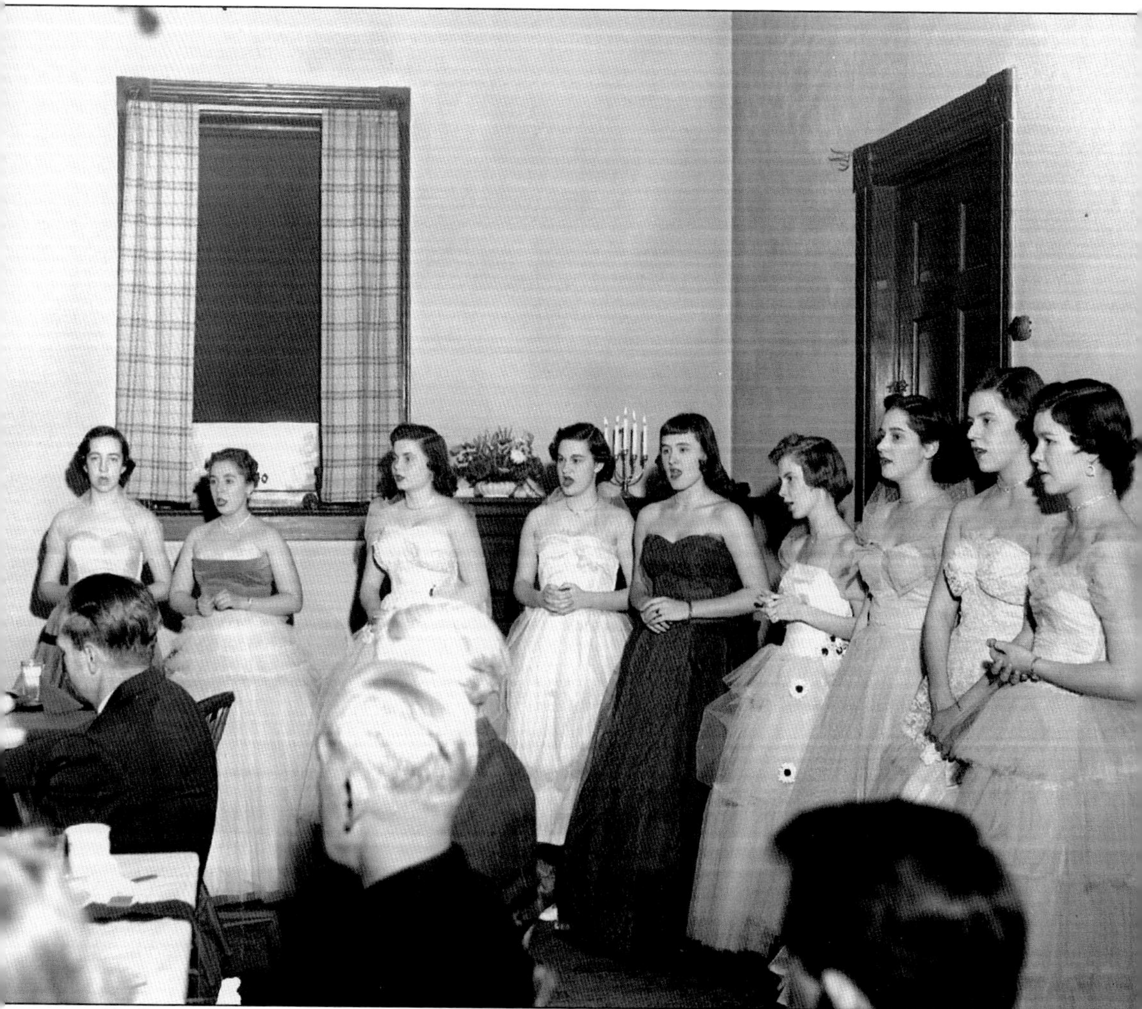

DESOTO HIGH SCHOOL CHORAL GROUP APPEARING AT AWARDS DINNER, FEBRUARY 20, 1954. Pictured, from left to right, are Sharon Jones, Gretchen Roop, Valerie McAlister, Caroline Calahan, Roberta Cole, Patricia McDonough, Ruth Ann Politte, Marian Schrampfer, and Marlene Morris. (Photograph courtesy DeSoto Historical Society.)

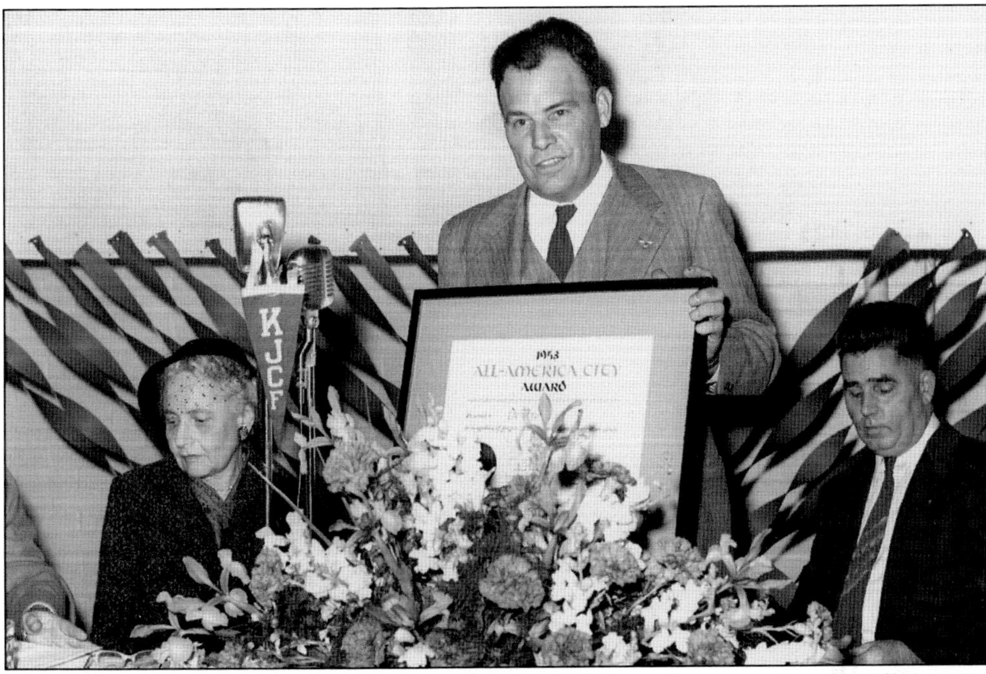

MAYOR VERNON YOUNG. Mayor Young spoke at the dinner after accepting the All America Award for DeSoto. Also pictured are Mrs. Virgil Loeb (director of the National Municipal League), and Walker Ames. (Photograph courtesy DeSoto Historical Society.)

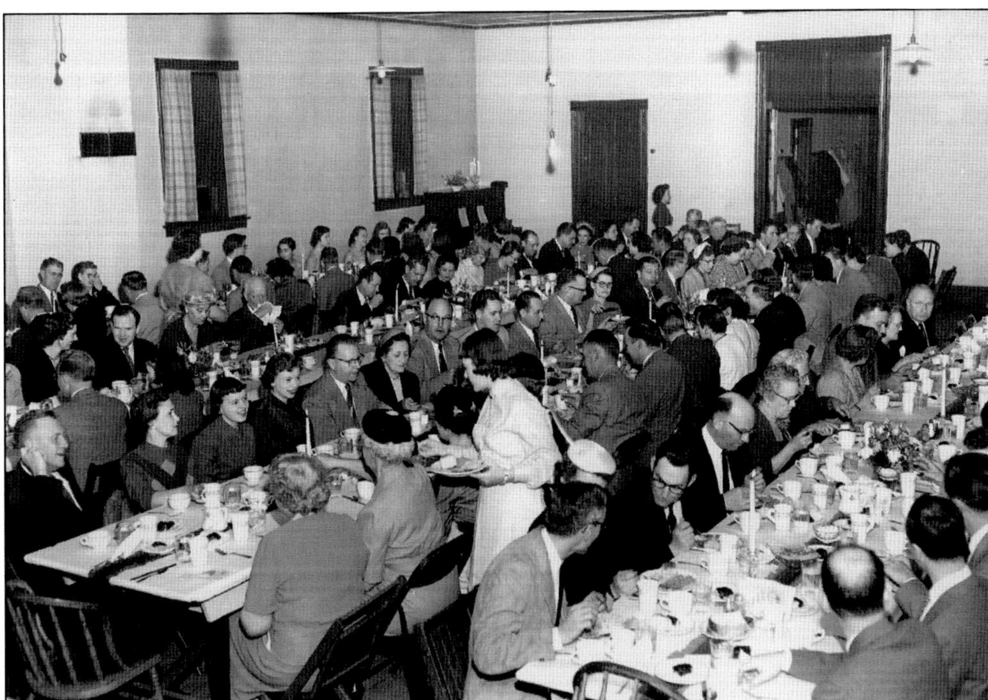

AWARDS BANQUET DINNER. Many prominent DeSotoans and others attended this function on February 20, 1954. (Photograph courtesy DeSoto Historical Society.)

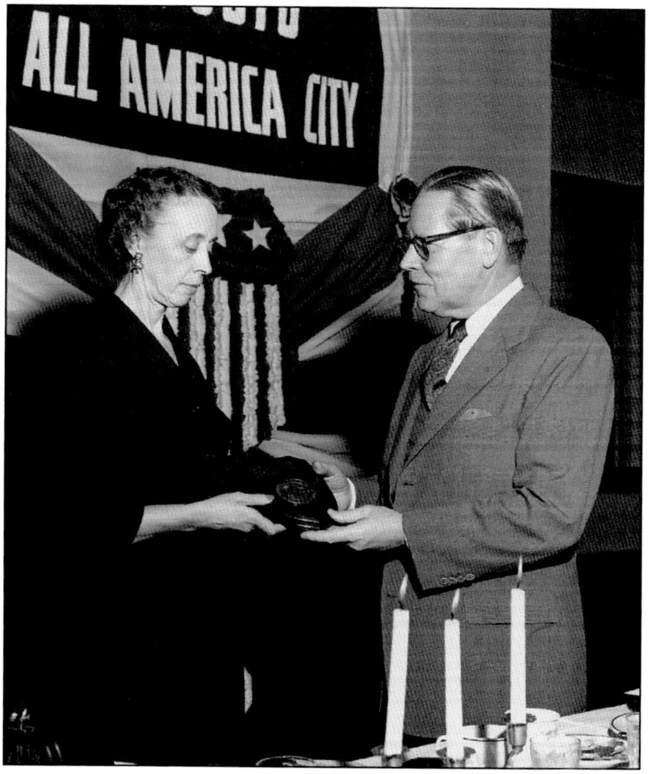

OLIVE FITCH ACCEPTING PLAQUE. Olive Fitch, DHS American government teacher, accepts a plaque from Merrill E. Skinner, vice president of Union Electric which sponsored the Planned Progress Program. (Photograph courtesy DeSoto Historical Society.)

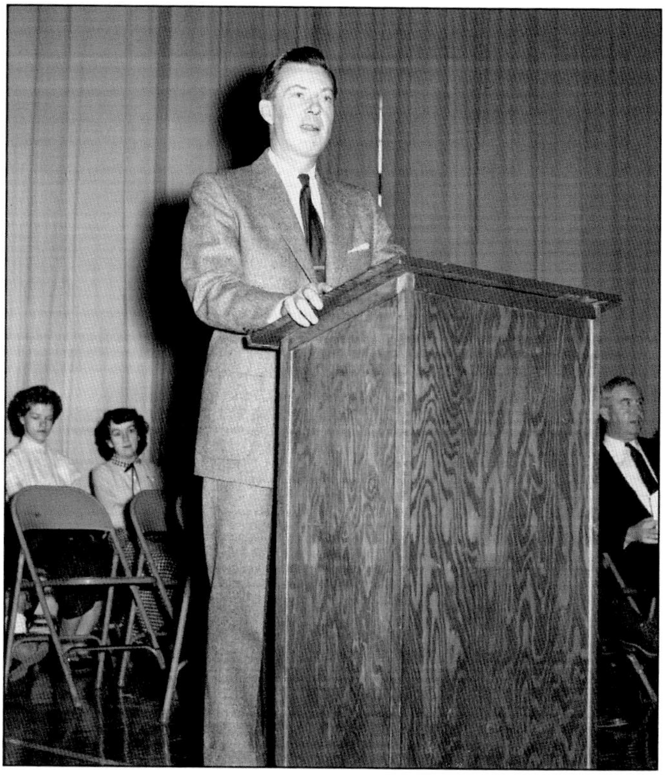

HARRY R. SCOTT, SPEAKER AT ASSEMBLY. Harry R. Scott, regional manager of Union Electric, spoke at the DeSoto High School assembly in January 1955. Scott announced that DeSoto had won second place in the 1954 Planned Progress program. Seated in the background, from left to right, are Jan Ogle, Betty Thebeau, and Thomas "Coke Brickey. (Photograph courtesy DeSoto Historical Society.)

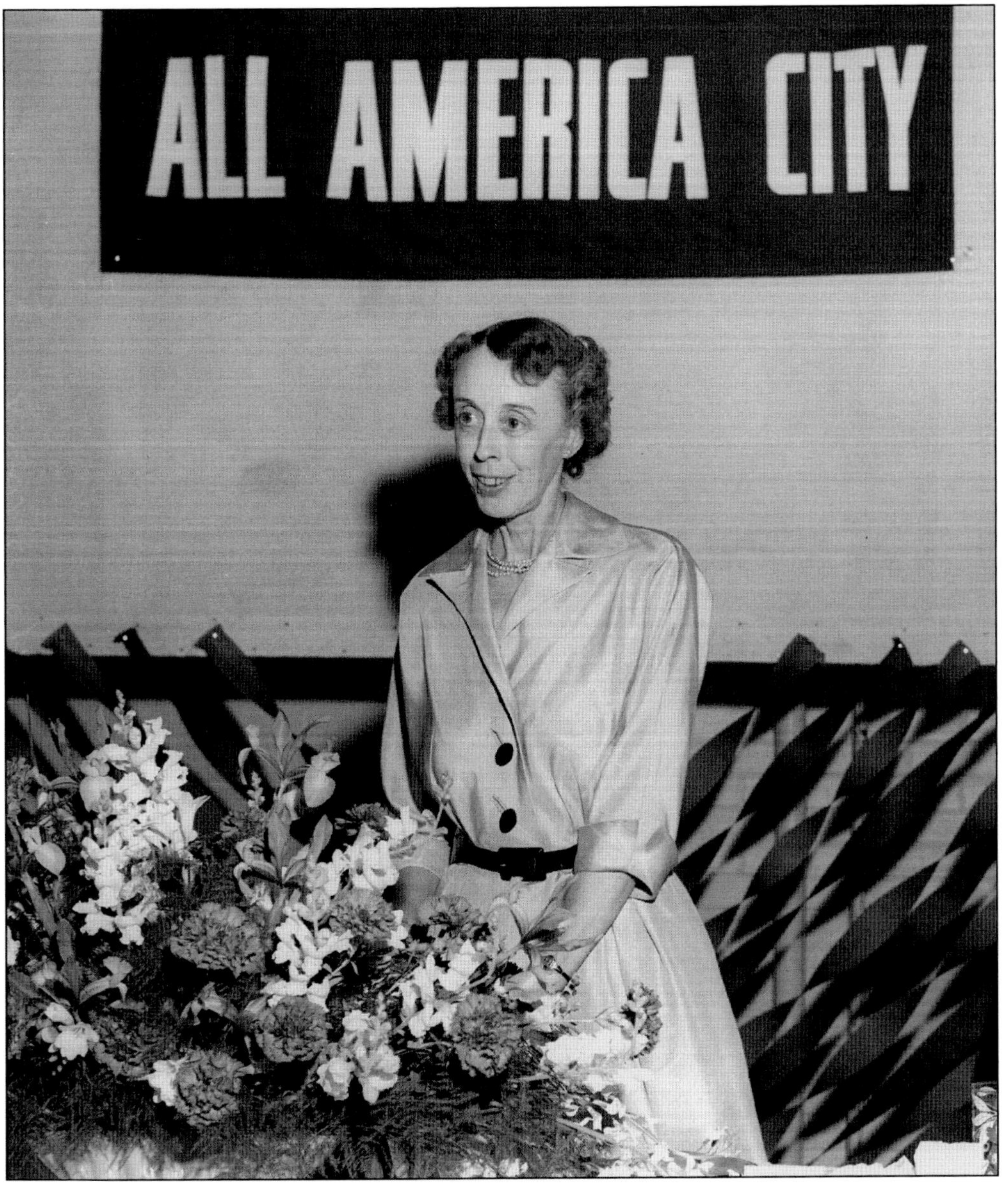

OLIVE FITCH. Olive Fitch was DeSoto High School's faculty sponsor for the All America City Awards Dinner. (Photograph courtesy DeSoto Historical Society.)

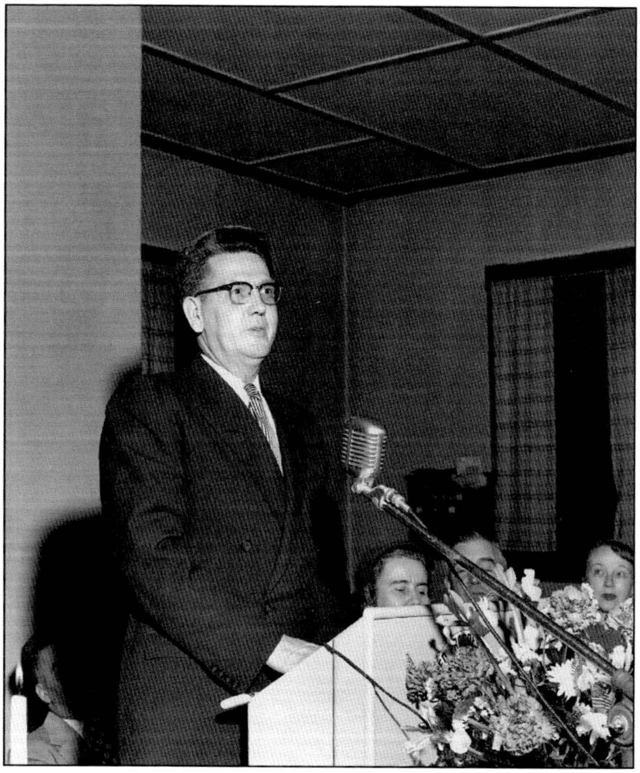

WALTER FINNICAL, CHAIRMAN OF PLANNED PROGRESS OF DESOTO. Walter Finnical spoke at the awards banquet February 24, 1955, at Masonic hall. (Photograph courtesy DeSoto Historical Society.)

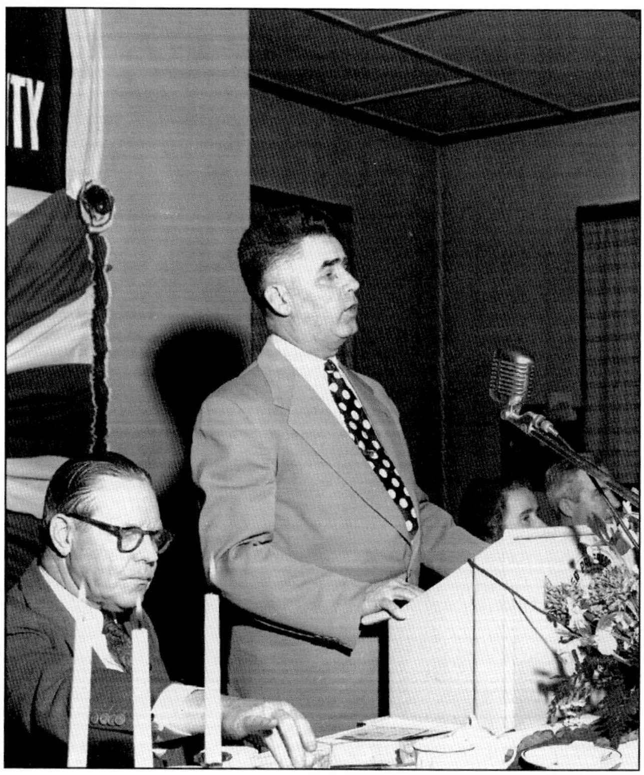

WALKER AMES AT AWARDS BANQUET FEBRUARY 24, 1955. Walker Ames was toastmaster at the Awards Banquet held in the Masonic hall. (Photograph courtesy DeSoto Historical Society.)

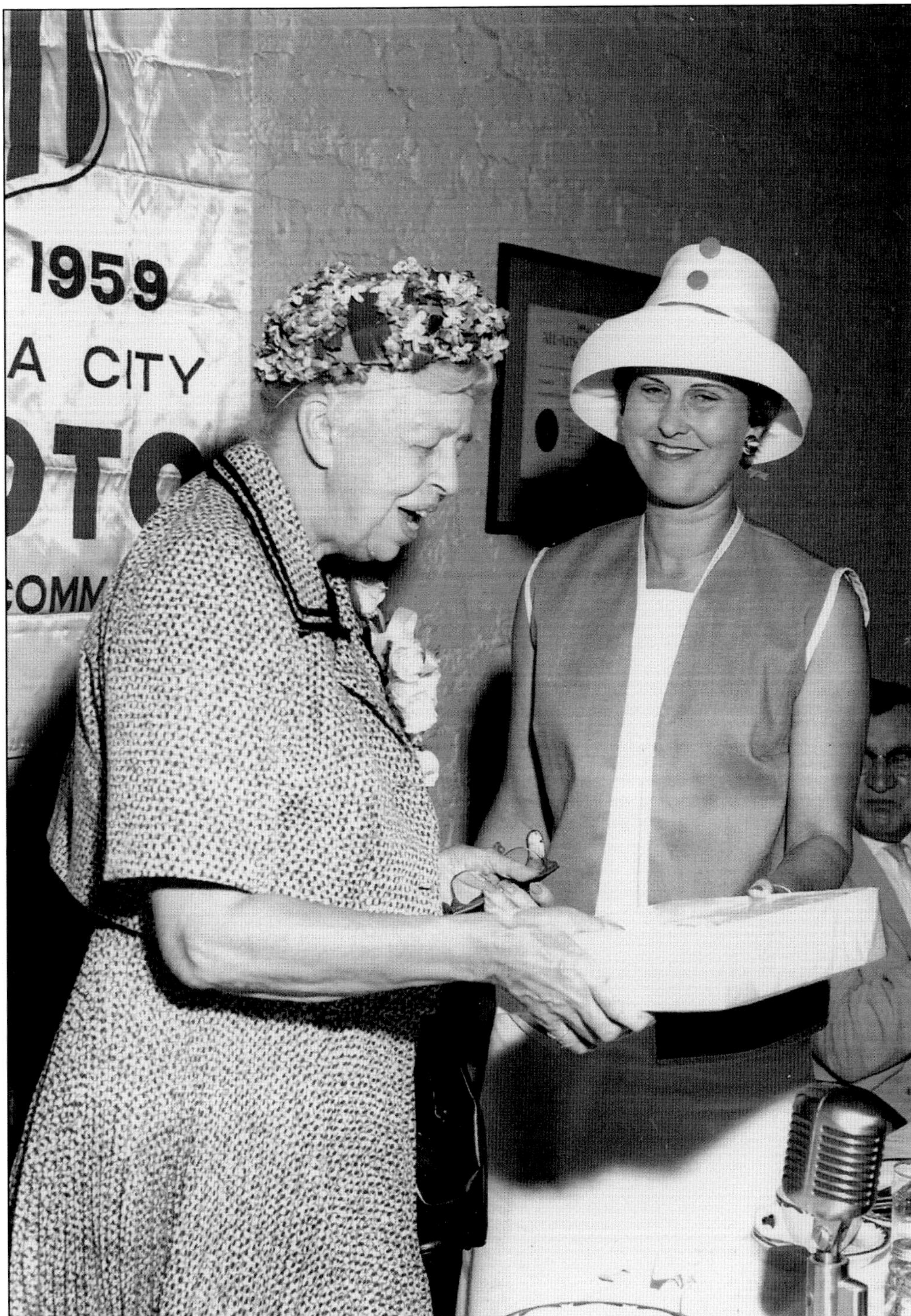

Eleanor Roosevelt and Adelaide Camp. Eleanor Roosevelt was honored at a breakfast in DeSoto at St. Rose of Lima Cafeteria on July 24, 1960. This function was held on behalf of Congressman A. S. J. Carnahan. (Photograph courtesy DeSoto Historical Society and Adelaide Camp.)

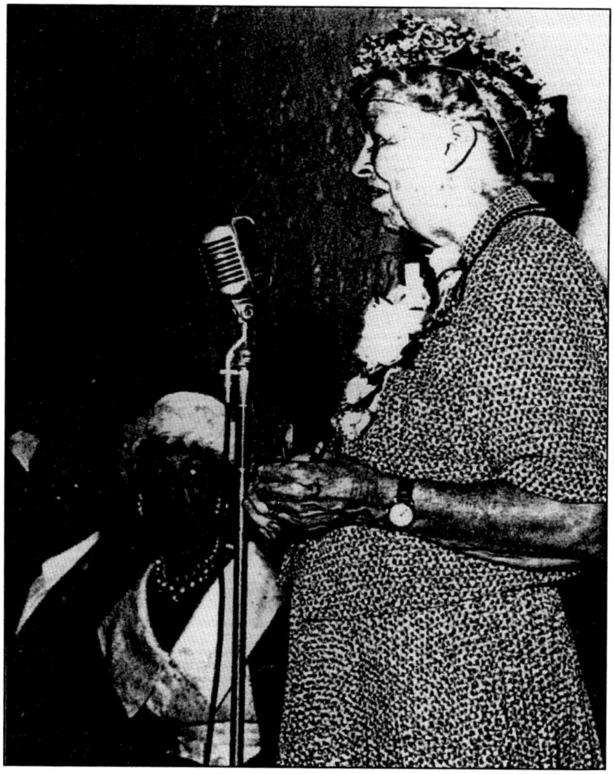

Eleanor Roosevelt at Breakfast. A commemorative plate was presented to Roosevelt at the breakfast given in her honor. (Photograph courtesy DeSoto Historical Society and Adelaide Camp.)

The Note Received from Mrs. Roosevelt:

Mrs. Franklin D. Roosevelt
55 East 74th Street
New York City 21, N.Y.

July 25, 1960

Dear Fellow Democrats,

How kind you were to give me the charming silver plate inscribed in memory of my visit to DeSoto! I am delighted to have this souvenir of an interesting and stimulating visit with you and I want to thank all of you warmly.

With appreciation and my good wishes,

Very sincerely yours,
(Signed) Eleanor Roosevelt

The Note Received from Eleanor Roosevelt. Here, Eleanor Roosevelt thanks the DeSotoans. (Photograph courtesy DeSoto Historical Society and Adelaide Camp.)

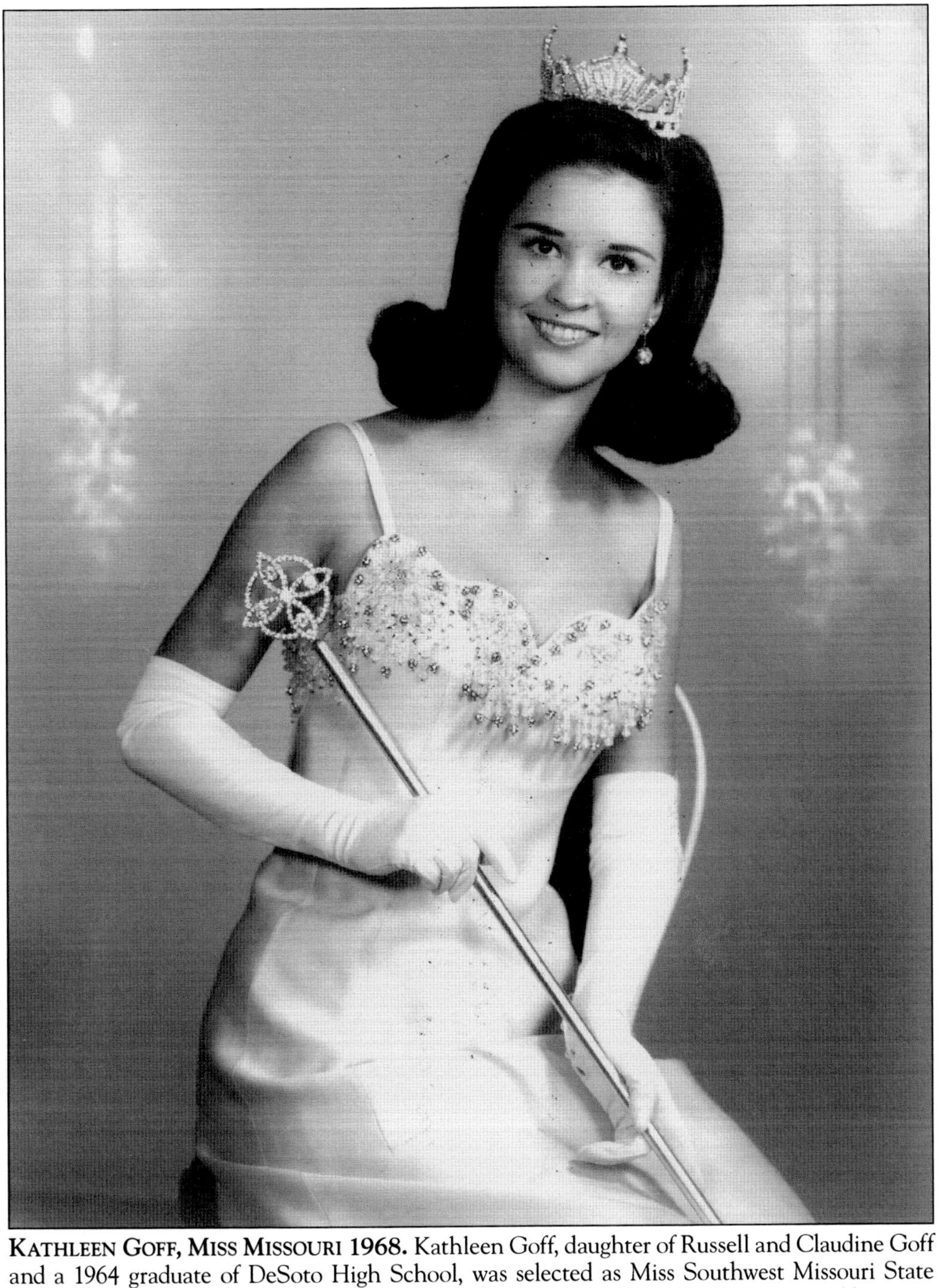

KATHLEEN GOFF, MISS MISSOURI 1968. Kathleen Goff, daughter of Russell and Claudine Goff and a 1964 graduate of DeSoto High School, was selected as Miss Southwest Missouri State College her senior year. She then was crowned Miss Missouri in 1968 and represented her state in the 1969 Miss America Pageant. (Photograph courtesy Kathleen Goff Dietz.)

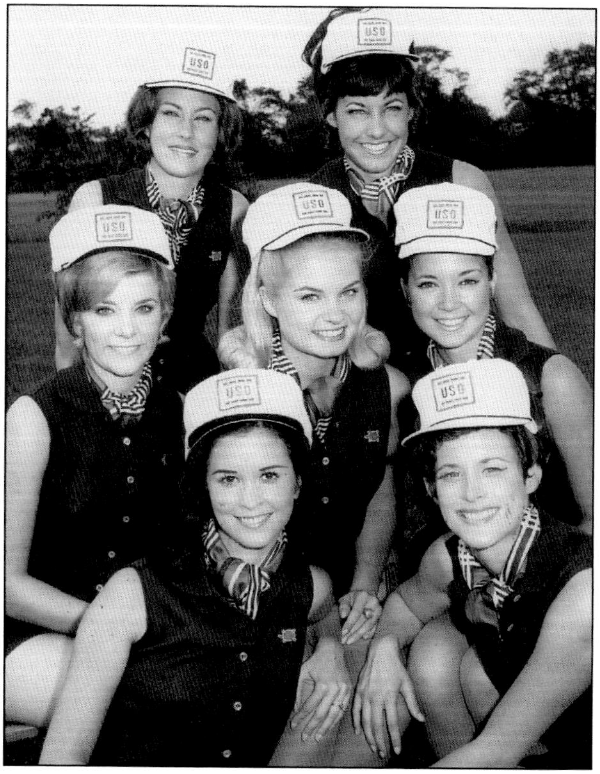

MISS AMERICA USO TOUR TO VIETNAM, 1969. Kathleen Goff, Miss Missouri 1968, was selected to be one of six state queens to perform with Judith Ford, Miss America, in the 1969 Miss America USO tour to Vietnam. Months of preparations preceded the August 9 departure of this group for a 22-day tour of Vietnam military installations. Pictured, clockwise from bottom left, are Miss Missouri Kathleen Goff, Miss Kentucky Janet Hatfield, Miss Arkansas Helen Jennings, Miss Minnesota Charlotte Sims, Miss New Jersey Linda Wilmer, Miss New York Patricia Burmeister, and center is Miss America Judith Ford. (Photograph courtesy Kathleen Goff Dietz.)

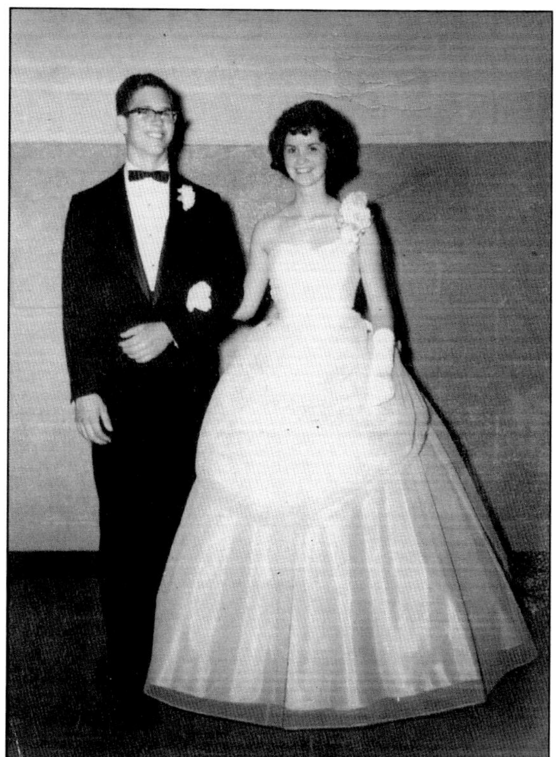

KATHLEEN GOFF AND DOUGLAS DIETZ. Kathleen Goff and Douglas Dietz are photographed at the 1963 DeSoto High School Prom. This couple married 30 years after their first date in 1962, and they reside in Destin, Florida. (Photograph courtesy Kathleen Goff Dietz.)

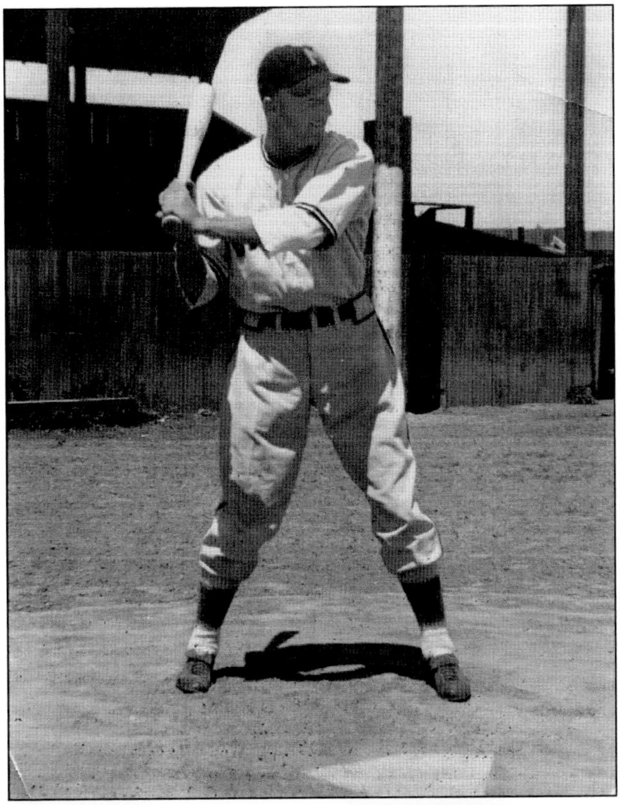

Russ Goff, Athlete. An outstanding DeSoto High athlete (class of 1935), Russ Goff went on to play Minor League Baseball in St. Augustine, Florida, for the St. Louis Browns. The talented catcher often played against Stan Musial who was on the St. Louis Cardinal Minor League team in Daytona Beach. Military service during World War II ended Russell's baseball career. (Photograph courtesy Kathleen Goff Dietz.)

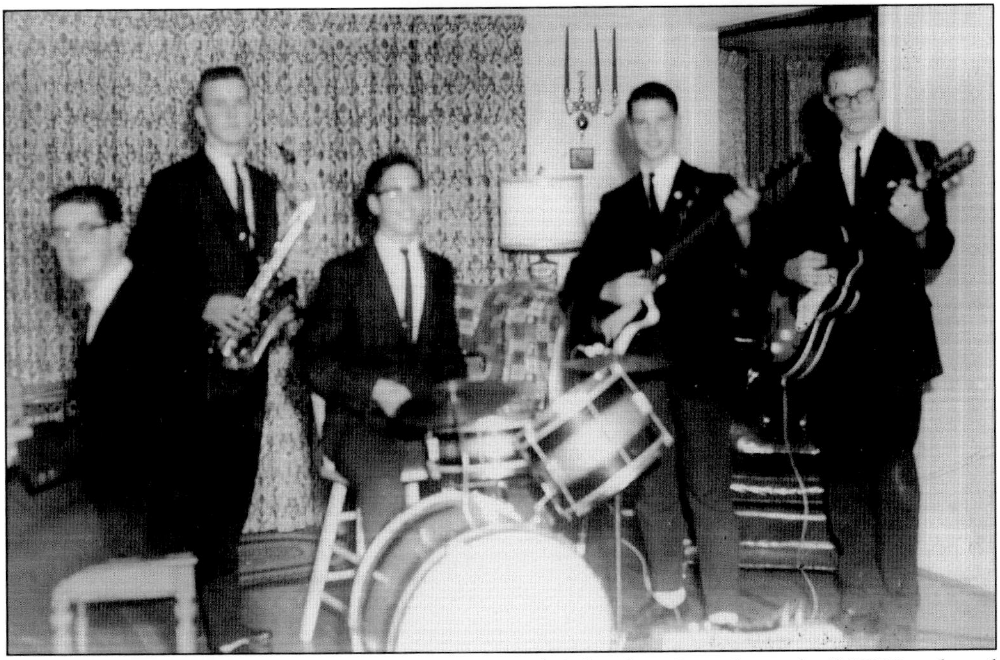

Rock and Roll Band. In 1961, these DeSoto High School students formed a "HOT" rock and roll band. Pictured left to right are Dennis Bay, Gary Fultz, Douglas Dietz, Moroe Mountford, and Ronnie ?. (Photograph courtesy Kathleen Goff Dietz.)

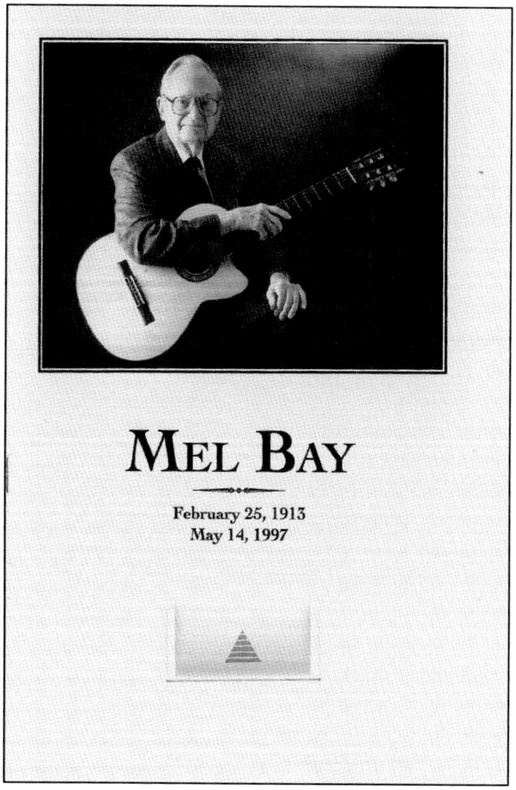

MEL BAY, GUITARIST. Mel Bay, master guitar teacher and former resident of DeSoto, was the publisher of a well-known series of guitar instruction books. He was influential in making the guitar a popular musical instrument. His family operated Bay's Market in DeSoto for many years. (Photograph courtesy DeSoto Historical Society.)

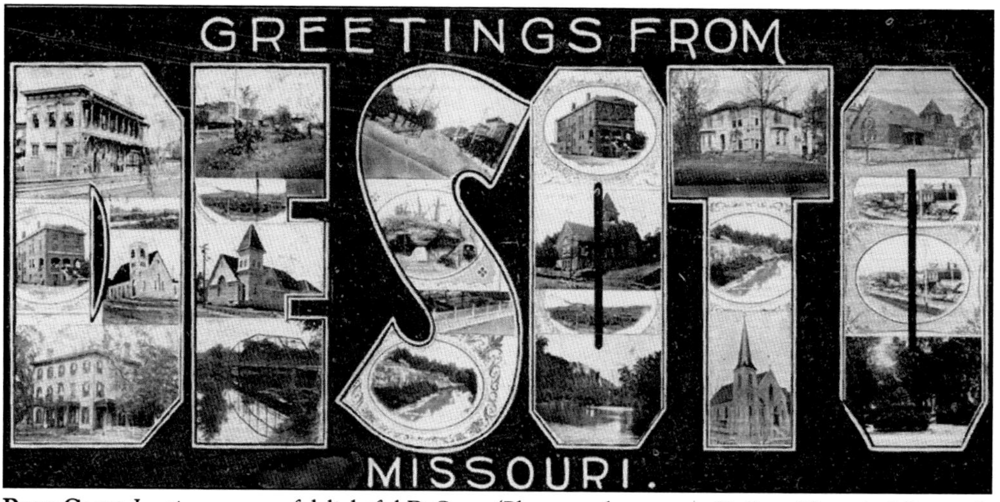

POST CARD. Lasting scenes of delightful DeSoto. (Photograph courtesy DeSoto Historical Society.)